THE VEGETABLE GARDEN DISPLAYED

THE VEGETABLE GARDEN DISPLAYED

written for
The Royal Horticultural Society

by
JOY LARKCOM

*Photography by
Jacqui Hurst*

The Royal Horticultural Society
80 Vincent Square
London SW1P 2PE

Copyright © The Royal Horticultural Society, 1981,
1992
Reprinted 1994

First published 1941

British Library Cataloguing in Publication Data
A catalogue record for
this book is available
from The British Library.

ISBN 0 906603 87 0

Typeset by SX Composing, Rayleigh, Essex, UK.
Typeface 10 on 11pt Ehrhardt linotron
Printed by Tien Wah Press Ltd, Singapore

THE ROYAL HORTICULTURAL SOCIETY

The Royal Horticultural Society is a charitable organization which exists to encourage and improve all forms of horticulture. Founded in London in 1804, the Society is known throughout the world as the foremost of all the great horticultural institutions. Membership of the Society is open to everyone interested in horticulture and gardening, and members enjoy a number of valuable privileges, including:

- free entry to the Society's Gardens at Wisley in Surrey, Rosemoor in Devon and Hyde Hall in Essex

- priority tickets for the Chelsea Show, the world's most famous flower show, the Hampton Court Palace Show and many other regional flower shows including those at Malvern and Harrogate

- a copy of the Society's journal, *The Garden*, every month

- free entry to the Westminster Flower Shows and lectures, held monthly in London from January to November

- advice on gardening problems and plant identification

- free use of the magnificent Lindley Library at the Society's London headquarters

If you would like to receive full details about RHS membership and an application form, please write to:

The Secretary (Membership)
The Royal Horticultural Society
PO Box 313, Vincent Square
London SW1P 2PE.

Contents

Foreword and acknowledgements

The Vegetable Garden Displayed is celebrating its Golden Jubilee. First published in 1941 as part of the World War 2 'Dig for Victory' campaign, it sold over 250,000 copies in its first year. Since then it has been continually in print for the last 50 years and is, perhaps, the best-selling book on vegetable growing in the western world. It has proved both an invaluable practical guide to successive generations of new gardeners, and a useful handbook on the art and science of gardening for more experienced gardeners.

To mark the 50th anniversary of the book's publication, we have indulged in a little nostalgia and looked back to the original forewords contributed by the then Minister of Agriculture and Fisheries, the Rt Hon J. S. Hudson, and the Minister of Food, the Rt Hon Lord Woolton. Lord Woolton, it is interesting to note, urged us to help the war effort by growing our own onions to cut down on the 90 percent imported. There have been similar exhortations in recent years – this time to help the balance of payments. They don't seem to have been very successful: in the last year for which figures are available we imported 86.6 percent of our onions. On the home garden front, however, there *has* been progress. Gardeners can now keep themselves in onions all year round by using specially selected autumn sets and the Japanese overwintering onions.

In the Golden Jubilee edition, for the first time, the bulk of the photography is in colour. We are most grateful to Jacqui Hurst for the energy and enthusiasm with which she tackled the job of re-photographing the complete text. Our thanks also to Reg Perryman and Colin Martin at Wisley Gardens, for their support and help over the photography, and to Bill Masser at Eton College, and Jo Maiden, at Golden Acre Park, Leeds, for allowing us to photograph their enterprises and for helpful comments. Additional photographs were taken by Eric Crichton, Joy Larkcom, Photos Horticultural, Shell Photos and The Harry Smith Horticultural Photographic Collection.

The text for the 1981 edition was completely re-written by Joy Larkcom. It took into account the smaller scale of modern domestic gardening, and incorporated the results of research into commercial vegetable growing relevant to amateur gardeners. The 1981 text has been updated and revised considerably for this Golden Jubilee edition.

Our thanks to Professor J K A Bleasdale, Dr Peter Crisp, Dr Joe Lopez-Real, Tony Burrows of the National Vegetable Society, Dr Majorie Lennartsson of the Henry Doubleday Research Association, for their helpful comments on the text; to John Walker for his help in compiling the planning charts; to Elizabeth Douglass for the line drawings, and to John Fitzmaurice for the design and production. We would also like to thank members of the RHS staff at Wisley, in particular Andrew Halstead, Pippa Greenwood, David Pycraft, Mike Pollock and Peter Barnes.

Introduction

The aim of this publication has been always to provide a straightforward, authoritative guide to vegetable growing for amateur gardeners, particularly for those new to gardening. It is concerned entirely with growing vegetables for home consumption. Those interested in producing giant specimens for showing should consult specialist books on the subject. (See Further reading, p 158.)

When *The Vegetable Garden Displayed* was completely revised in 1981, the trend towards smaller vegetable gardens was becoming marked. So more emphasis was put on intensive, space-saving techniques, such as the adoption of equidistant spacing in a 'bed system'. Much of the science behind these techniques originated in research into commercial vegetable growing, popularized for amateur gardeners in the two volumes of *Know and Grow Vegetables*, (Oxford University Press, 1979 and 1982), written by members of the then National Vegetable Research Station* at Wellesbourne, Warwickshire. These were used extensively in revising *The Vegetable Garden Displayed*.

In the last decade amateur vegetable growers have taken up more ideas from commercial horticulture, such as the use of the perforated and fleecy 'floating films' which can be laid over a growing crop to increase yields, and small walk-in polytunnels. These miniaturized clones of the giant tunnels on commercial holdings have sprouted on many a kitchen garden plot. Although far less elegant than glazed greenhouses, they provide valuable protection at a fraction of the cost, and can be easily moved and erected. On account of their low cost and flexibility, 'floating films' and polytunnels are covered more fully in this edition than hitherto. For vegetable growing in glazed and heated greenhouses, however, consult specialist books.

Today many space-hungry would-be vegetable growers, especially in urban areas, are reduced to growing a few vegetables on patios, balconies or even in window boxes, so for the first time we have included a short section on growing in containers. Again, there are many specialist books on this subject.

Fuelled by the greatly increased range of fruit and vegetables now found in shops and supermarkets, there is a growing interest among gardeners in unusual vegetables. As a result, new entries in this

edition of *The Vegetable Garden Displayed* include sorrel and seakale, omitted from recent editions. An extended section on salad crops (often now grown by space-saving 'cut-and-come-again' techniques), and an extended section on the more easily grown oriental brassicas are included too. The latter are likely to increase in popularity and availability in the near future. In recommending cultivars, (see note p 67) we have included a few recommended by the National Institute of Agricultural Botany as being most suited to organic gardening. These cultivars have qualities such as exceptional vigour (which will overcome a shortage of nitrogen), the ability to form a good root system and rapid leaf canopy over the soil (so they smother weeds more easily), and good pest and disease resistance.

The last 10 years have been notable for a swing back to 'organic' gardening. Recent surveys have indicated that a majority of gardeners today would *prefer* to garden organically, although not all do so, certainly not all the time. However, with increased awareness of the damage caused to our environment by the misuse and overuse of chemicals, and of the risk of high nitrate levels in leafy vegetables, many gardeners are reducing their reliance on chemical products. This edition of *The Vegetable Garden Displayed* breaks new ground (or perhaps simply reverts to the methods of pre-war generations of gardeners), in including organic methods where relevant, that is, in connection with manuring, weed control, and pest and disease control. The term 'organic' implies gardening without the use of chemical fertilizers, weedkillers, insecticides or fungicides, other than those which break down easily into harmless products and are approved by the organic standards authorities in the UK. (For further information, and the address of the principal organic research organization in this country, see p 158.)

Discussion of organic gardening brings us to the 'greenhouse effect'. At the time of writing there is constant debate over the climatic changes our planet is experiencing. Certainly in the last few years weather records have been toppling like ninepins. Some parts of the British Isles have recorded the driest conditions for many years; others the wettest or mildest. Whether these changes are simply 'blips' in the long-term pattern, or significant indicators of serious long-term changes, nobody knows for sure, although most scientists now accept that the planet is warming appreciably, at an ever-accelerating rate. How this will affect different areas is very uncertain.

Gardening is intricately bound up with the weather, and in the present state of uncertainty, we need to develop a flexible response. If we find ourselves with a longer and warmer growing season, it

---

* Now Horticulture Research International.

will become easier to grow tender vegetables such as aubergines, peppers and tomatoes outside, and we may find ourselves growing semi-tropical vegetables – sweet potatoes and soya beans – in unheated greenhouses. We will find ordinary vegetables continuing to grow in winter – and flourishing in unheated polytunnels – where previously they merely remained alive. The other side of the coin will be an increase in pests, insect pests in particular being a much more serious problem at higher temperatures.

If on the other hand our climate turns colder, we will need to make increased use of protective cropping, and to develop and grow hardier cultivars. We may find ourselves benefiting from the hardiness of some of the oriental brassicas, notably various types of mustard.

If conditions become drier, water conservation will be of great importance. We should consider planting further apart, as is done in desert conditions, so that plants can utilize what moisture there is. On the other hand, if it becomes wetter, drainage will have to be improved – or again – we may turn to increased use of protective cropping and the opportunity it affords to control the elements. If stormier weather becomes more frequent, as it appears to have done of late, more attention will have to be paid to shelter. It is certainly a challenging situation.

On a more humdrum level, there has always been considerable variation in climate within the British Isles, and no recommendations for the timing of sowing, planting or other operations apply throughout the British Isles. Those given in *The Vegetable Garden Displayed* are generally appropriate for average conditions in the south of England. As a rule, spring operations are carried out *later* in the north and cold parts of the east, on exposed sites, and on wet heavy soils, and *earlier* in mild coastal areas, sheltered gardens, and on exceptionally light soils. Conversely, autumn operations are carried out earlier in less favoured regions and sites. However, garden operations should never be carried out by the calendar: *primary* guides are the state of the soil and prevailing weather conditions.

Lastly, it is advisable to keep brief records of operations in your kitchen garden. In the long run, these personal records will provide the most reliable guidance on what to do, when, and in what quantities, to meet your requirements and circumstances. It is unwise to rely on memory. It can play more tricks than the weather!

Tools

There is no substitute for good tools, the best are made of stainless steel with ash or fibreglass handles. Unfortunately, there are many poor quality and gimmicky tools on the market today. The former are short-lived; the latter, in the main, useless.

It is difficult to lay down the law on precisely which tool, or type of tool, to use for each purpose. Everyone has personal favourites. What is important is to select tools which 'feel right' for you; in other words, those that are the correct weight, length and balance, allowing use without strain. Where bending is difficult, special tools with very long handles are recommended.

The working life of tools is extended if they are well cared for. After use, scrape off the soil and wipe tools clean with an oily rag. The blades of spades and hoes occasionally need to be sharpened with a file or carborundum stone.

The *minimum* requirements for a small garden are a garden fork and spade, a rake, a hoe and a trowel. For larger gardens, the more of the following tools available the better.

Spade This is the traditional digging tool; it is also used for shovelling soil and compost. The border spade is a smaller, lighter form.

Garden fork The standard garden fork has four or five rounded prongs or tines, and is used both for turning over the soil to make it workable, and for digging – for example, on stony soils – where using a spade is difficult. The flat-pronged 'potato fork' is used for lifting potatoes. The 'ladies' fork' is a lighter garden fork with shorter tines.

Rake The metal-pronged garden rake with a cast head is the most popular today. It is used mainly for raking the soil surface to create a fine tilth for a seedbed. Wooden-pronged rakes are used for levelling ground, raking up grass and garden rubbish.

Cultivator This is a multi-pronged tool, with three or five prongs but sometimes more, which is used to break up rough soil clods in the first stage of preparing a seedbed.

Hoes There are many types of hoe. Hoes are used primarily for weeding, but also for earthing up, thinning and drawing drills. Among long-handled hoes the Dutch or push hoe is used in a to and fro motion, the flat blade slicing off weeds at ground level. It needs to be sharp to perform this function. The draw hoe's blade is set at a right angle to the handle and a chopping action is used to weed. It is also used for

earthing up. With push hoes, which are more suitable for light soils, the operator walks backwards
without treading on uprooted weeds or hoed soil.
With draw hoes the operator walks forwards, treading over the hoed area. There are types of hoe with
serrated blades which improve their slicing action,
and triangular hoes, which are convenient for drawing drills. The short-handled, swan-neck onion hoe
is an extremely useful, light tool, enabling you to
weed very close to plants.

Hand trowel This small tool is used for planting. As
it needs to be very strong, concave steel-bladed
trowels with a curved shank are considered best.

Hand fork A small version of the garden fork,
normally three-pronged, this is used for weeding
and working the soil surface Short- and long-
handled forms are available.

Dibber This short, single-pronged, pointed tool of
wood or steel is traditionally used to make planting
holes. However, care should be taken in using it, for
if the hole is too smooth or deep the plant may be left

suspended in a pocket of air. It is used for planting
brassicas and leeks, and for sowing large seeds, such
as runner beans.

Measuring tools A garden line of strong nylon cord
on a reel facilitates sowing or planting in a straight
line. A measuring rod marked out in commonly used
distances saves time when planting.

Watering can A strong watering can with detachable
fine and coarse roses is necessary. The long-necked
'Haws' type is very convenient to handle. A separate
can should be ear-marked for the application of
weedkillers or other chemicals, so that there is no
risk of damage to cropping plants. (For automatic
watering equipment see p 42.)

Sprayers For applying small amounts of pesticide a
hand syringe or hand sprayer of 0.5–1 litre (about
1–2 pt) capacity is adequate. For larger quantities a
hand pressurized sprayer is recommended. Capacity
ranges from 1–8 litres (about 2–16 pt). The larger
models are free-standing and operated with a lance.
The knapsack type is hung over the shoulder or
worn on the back.

Mechanical cultivators As their purchase is only jus-
tified in large gardens, mechanical cultivators are
outside the scope of this book. For small gardens it is
more economic to hire a cultivator for the few hours
work required each year.

Plant raising equipment A collection of seed trays,
modules, pots, soil firmer and miniature dibber and
a soil sieve is required for plant raising. (For details
see pp 35-36.)

Essential tools for the larger garden: **1** *cultivator;* **2** *draw hoe;*
3 *garden line;* **4** *spade;* **5** *hand fork;* **6** *hand trowel;* **7** *garden
fork;* **8** *rake;* **9** *onion hoe;* **10** *dibber;* **11** *Dutch hoe;* **12**
watering can; **13** *wheelbarrow.*

Soil fertility

Soil fertility is indisputably the key to successful vegetable growing, and consciously or unconsciously, the efforts of good gardeners are always directed towards improving the fertility of their soil. There is no precise definition of fertile soil, but the following are desirable characteristics: it has a good crumb structure, is rich in humus and nutrients (plant foods), is well drained but retains a reasonable amount of moisture, and is slightly acid or neutral.

One of the soil's most important functions is its role as a reservoir of the mineral nutrients a plant needs. These are taken in by the roots, dissolved in water. Some, such as nitrogen, phosphorus, potassium, calcium, magnesium and sulphur, known as the major elements, are required in relatively large quantities; while others, the minor or trace elements, are needed only in very small quantities. These include iron, manganese, boron, zinc, copper, and molybdenum.

All these elements are released naturally by the weathering of the mineral particles in the soil and by the breakdown or decay of organic matter and humus. Nitrogen is also obtained from the air in the soil, converted into forms suitable for plant use by bacteria, including the nitrogen-fixing bacteria on the root nodules of leguminous plants. Other micro-organisms are responsible for breaking down the organic matter and humus in the soil so that nutrients can be released from it. However, these micro-organisms can only operate when they have adequate supplies of oxygen and water – and adequate supplies are largely dependent on the soil having a good structure.

Soil structure
Structure is determined by the soil 'crumbs', the small lumps of soil which cannot be broken down by hand. They consist of mineral and organic particles joined together. In a good soil the crumbs vary in size, and between them and around them a network of spaces and pores is built up which forms the soil structure. The channels made by these spaces and pores act as the aeration and drainage system of the soil: excess water drains off through the large pores preventing waterlogging, but is held in the smallest pores, which act as a reservoir. The larger pores then fill with air, supplying the oxygen which is essential both for the plant roots and for the living organisms in the soil.

The crucial difference between the various types of soil encountered in gardens is their ability to form crumbs. At one extreme are the clays, made up of tiny particles which stick together to form impenetrable clods. At the other are sandy soils, composed of large particles reluctant to join together to form crumbs. Silty soils have intermediate sized particles, and some of the characteristics of clays and sands. Clay soils, although slow to warm up in spring, are apt to become waterlogged and airless, but have the potential of a good structure; sandy soils are well drained, airy, and quick to warm up in spring but it is often difficult to improve their structure. The ideal garden soil is a balanced mixture of clay, sand and silt. Chalk soils also are naturally well structured.

In most cases the main agent for improving structure is humus. Not only is it a source of nutrients but it is able both to coat particles of sand and silt so that they adhere together to form crumbs, and to help in the breakdown of large clay clods into smaller clods, which in turn break down into crumbs. Besides these qualities, it has a great capacity for increasing the amount of water held in the soil. Humus is obtained by the breakdown of organic matter, and the regular incorporation of organic matter into all types of soils will help to improve their structure and water-holding ability. Chalk soils are less responsive to the addition of organic matter because of their good structure. The main sources of organic matter are bulky animal manures, garden compost, seaweed and various waste products. (See Bulky organic manures, p 12.)

In a soil rich in organic matter with a good structure, vegetable plants should be able to obtain all the necessary nutrients from the soil. In practice, optimum yields often are achieved only with supplementary feeding, using either fast acting, concentrated artificial fertilizers or, for the organic gardener, the much slower acting organic fertilizers or ground minerals. (See Fertilizers, p 17.)

Preserving the soil structure
Improving soil fertility is bound to be a gradual process, but care must be taken not to undo the good work by destroying soil structure. Never cultivate the soil when it is very wet or very dry, and avoid treading on cultivated ground: these are all processes which tend to destroy the soil structure.

Heavy rain beating on bare soil has the same effect. For this reason most soils benefit from being covered in winter – poorly structured sand or silty soils with a green manure (see Green manuring, p 15), or even weeds, provided they are dug in before they seed, and heavy soils with a mulch or manure.

Note that with clay soils any mulch or manure is best applied to roughly dug soil, to allow winter weathering and frost penetration, which improves the structure.

Drainage

Poor drainage is a common cause of infertility; waterlogged soils are airless and cold. Signs of poor drainage are often obvious, such as water lying on the surface several days after rain, or lying permanently within, say 30 cm (12 in) of the surface. Poor vegetation, no earthworms, small shallow roots rather than deep roots, and greyish, bluish or mottled rather than brown soil are other signs of bad drainage.

The problem may be caused by the poor nature of the topsoil – a good example is clay soil with little humus. Sometimes it is caused by an underlying layer of impervious subsoil or rock, or even a compacted layer in the soil, known as a 'hard pan'. This must be broken up with a spade or pickaxe before any further action is taken.

Forking in plenty of bulky organic manure, which will absorb a great deal of water and encourage worm activity, goes a long way towards improving a drainage problem. Where the problem is more persistent, simple trench drains can be dug in a garden, either across the lower end of a slope, or on either side of a level site. A trench about 30 cm (12 in) wide and 60–90 cm (2–3 ft) deep is taken out, and the bottom half filled with rubble such as stones, clinkers and broken bricks, before replacing the soil. Such a trench will, in most cases, absorb surplus water and render the soil more workable.

Where waterlogging is very serious it may be necessary to lay a permanent system of herringbone drains throughout the garden, with clay or plastic pipes in the drains. The whole system needs to be designed to drain away either to a natural outlet such as a ditch, or to an artificial soakaway. This is a specialized and expensive undertaking. Where it is impractical, do not attempt to grow vegetables.

Soil acidity

Soil infertility is often due to a soil being too acid or too alkaline. Soil acidity/alkalinity is measured on the pH scale which, broadly speaking, reflects the amount of calcium in the soil. The neutral point on the scale is 7, soils with a pH below 7 becoming progressively more acid, and those above 7 progressively more alkaline.

Most soils have a pH in the range of 4.5 to 7.5. The pH level can be measured reasonably accurately with a soil testing kit. It is well known that certain plants prefer certain pH levels – rhododendrons, for example, only do well on acidic soils. Most vegetables prefer a slightly acid soil (around pH 6.5) although on organic (i.e. peaty) soils, they will tolerate a lower pH than on normal 'mineral' soils.

Soils in the British Isles tend to become acid, as rainwater is continually washing calcium out of the soil. This is accentuated in industrial areas, due to the acids in the atmosphere, and on light sandy soils. Heavy, clay soils may have enough calcium reserves to replenish the calcium leached out.

Correcting acidity

Acidity is corrected by applying lime, but there has been a tendency in the past to apply lime whether or not the soil needs it, resulting in over-liming. This has harmful effects on plant growth as it suppresses the availability of minor nutrients. Where crops are growing well it is safe to assume there is no need to lime: but where crop growth is poor, where the soil has a somewhat sour look with moss growing on the surface, where vegetation is not decaying or where weeds such as sorrel and docks predominate, lime is probably needed. This can be confirmed with a soil test.

The pH of an acid soil can be raised only gradually. The aim should be to raise it to a level of 6.5 with several annual dressings of lime. Lime is best applied to the surface in the autumn, before digging, ideally on ground which will subsequently be planted with a lime-loving crop such as brassicas. The rate of the dressing depends on the nature of the soil and its present pH. The modern recommendation is to apply ground limestone at the following rates:
Sandy soil: 270 g/sq m (½ lb/sq yd)
Loamy soil: 550 g/sq m (1 lb/sq yd)
Clay or humus-rich soil: 800 g/sq m (1½ lb/sq yd). These rates are for soils with moderate acidity (pH 6). More acid soils need larger quantities of lime.

For organic gardeners the use of dolomite, which contains calcium and magnesium carbonate, is recommended. It is slower, but gentler in action. It is applied annually in the autumn at 270 g/sq m (½ lb / sq yd), until the soil pH has risen to the required level.

Certain plant diseases are accentuated by pH level; clubroot in brassicas is more serious in acidic soils, and potato scab in alkaline soils. When applying lime to the soil do not incorporate it at the same time as manure or fertilizers containing ammonia. The reaction between the two will cause the escape of ammonia as a gas without benefiting the crop.

Correcting over-alkalinity

The problem of over-alkaline soil is rare, but nevertheless does occur in some chalky soils, and is difficult to correct. Powdered sulphur or ferrous sulphate can be applied at the rate of 130 g/sq m (4 oz/ sq yd): ammonium nitrate will also reduce the pH level. In a very alkaline garden, avoid using fertilizers such as nitro-chalk, which contain calcium. It may be necessary to avoid growing crops, such as potatoes and rhubarb, which require acidic conditions. Problems of excess acidity or alkalinity are less likely to arise in soils to which organic matter is regularly applied.

Making a start on poor soil

When starting to cultivate very poor soil it is advisable to concentrate available organic matter into relatively small areas, for the first sowings or plantings. For example, fertile 'pockets' can be created by making small trenches up to 15 cm (6 in) deep, filled with well-rotted garden compost, and covered with 2.5 cm (1 in) of a soil and compost mixture. Here spring onions, radishes, carrots, dwarf beans or lettuces could be sown.

Potatoes and Jerusalem artichokes are also useful crops to plant on poor, roughly cultivated ground: they help to break up the soil and so start to improve soil structure. Indeed, soil structure tends to improve simply as a result of the ground being cultivated and cropped, not least because the plant roots help to build up the organic matter.

Bulky organic manures

The term 'manure' implies any organic material, of animal or vegetable origin, which is added to the soil in reasonable quantities primarily to improve soil fertility. (See Soil fertility, p 10.) Most manures are relatively low in available nutrients. However, through complex biological and chemical processes they enable nutrients already in the soil to be released in forms available to plants; nutrients are also released when the manures rot down and are converted into humus.

The bulky manures, particularly those of animal origin, also play an important role in encouraging the worm population. Worms in their turn improve soil fertility in many ways. Worms 'eat' their way through the soil, and soil and organic matter are intimately mixed in the process of passing through their bodies: this is the first important stage in the conversion of organic matter into humus. Their tunnelling breaks up clods of soil, so improving soil aeration and drainage, and making it easier for roots to penetrate the soil. The casts worms deposit in the soil help in the formation of soil crumbs, and moreover are very rich in minerals, micro-organisms and plant nutrients. Finally worm bodies are rich in protein, and contribute considerable quantities of nitrogen to the soil when in turn they die and decompose.

How much organic manure should be put on the garden? In practice the answer is as much as possible, the limitations today being availability and cost. The poorer the soil, the more it will benefit from heavy applications of organic manure. Organic matter tends to break down and disappear fairly fast, so if possible, work in some every year. As a rough guide, aim for at least 2.75–5.5 kg / sq m (5–10 lb/ sq yd) every year, the higher figure being essential on poor soils.

Organic manures can be either worked into the soil when digging in autumn or spring, or spread on the surface. Horticulture Research International (Wellesbourne) generally recommend the former course and advocate mixing the manure throughout the soil, rather than the traditional practice of placing it in a layer at the bottom of a trench. It should also be worked into the soil as *deeply* as is feasible. Vegetable roots can penetrate several feet deep in favourable conditions, so drawing nutrients and moisture from lower soil levels. Deep rooting should be encouraged as the best insurance against the effects of drought.

Alternatively, organic manures can be spread on

the surface of the soil in a layer 8–10 cm (3¼–4 in) deep. If this is done in autumn or during the winter, worms will usually work most of it into the top layers of the soil by spring. Any residue can be easily dug in in spring. This method does not distribute the manure so thoroughly in the rooting area, but on the other hand, light soils in particular benefit from being covering during the winter, when rains are likely to wash nutrients out of bare soil. One school of thought advocates putting relatively fresh organic matter on the surface, and digging in well-rotted organic matter.

Well-rotted bulky manures can also be applied as mulches to growing crops. (See Mulching, p 44.)

The following are some of the bulky organic manures used in gardens.

Animal manure Farmyard and other animal manure is generally best when mixed with plenty of straw and litter (but not sawdust or wood shavings). Fresh manure (due to the release of ammonia) is liable to scorch plants, can cause forking in root crops, and may contain pests and weed seed. So if the manure is not well rotted it should be composted for about six months before use. To minimize the loss of nutrients, stack it on a concrete base and cover it to protect it from rainfall.

Where there is no alternative to manure mixed with sawdust or wood shavings, store it for at least 18 months before use.

Poultry, pigeon and rabbit manure is very concentrated, and is best worked into compost heaps in small quantities.

Spent mushroom compost This is usually sterilized, so it is free of weed seed. The chalk fragments in the compost help to break down heavy clay soils. However, on account of its high chalk content it is inadvisable to use spent mushroom compost on alkaline soils.

Treated sewage sludge, recycled municipal waste These are potentially useful products, but *should only be used if they are guaranteed free of heavy metals.*

Straw This is excellent for improving soil. It must, however, be well rotted or nitrogen is robbed from the soil during the breakdown process. Fresh straw should be stacked for about six months in layers about 15 cm (6 in) thick, each layer being watered thoroughly. Thin layers of poultry manure, lawn mowings or an activator (see Compost) can be spread between the straw layers to enrich the heap and hasten decomposition.

Seaweed Seaweed is an excellent form of manure. It can be used fresh, dried or composted.

Garden and household compost (See Compost.)

Compost

Compost made by processing organic wastes is a valuable source of organic matter, and all gardeners should make their own. True composting is an 'aerobic' process, in which a heap of aerated vegetable and animal wastes generates heat and is worked on by a range of micro-organisms, until it is converted ultimately into humus.

Aerobic compost should be made with fairly large quantities of waste in well-insulated bins with access to air. When compost is made well, the end product is blackish brown, moist, crumbly and uniform in texture. There is also an anaerobic process, in which material is allowed to decompose *without* air. This takes place in sealed containers or covered piles, where air is excluded.

The advantages of aerobic composting are that almost any organic material can be included; that weed seeds, roots of most perennial weeds and disease organisms are killed; that no odours are produced or flies or vermin encouraged, and that it produces homogeneous compost at an acceptable degree of acidity, so it does not require liming. The compost is normally ready for use in two to six months, depending on the season.

Its disadvantages are that it requires fairly careful preparation and attention, and some kind of box or container; that the material must occupy a minimum volume of about 1 cubic m (over 1 cubic yd) or the heat generated is wasted, that it may require turning, and that the carbon/nitrogen ratio should be roughly correct. Autumn and winter heaps are therefore likely to need an activator.

The anaerobic process, on the other hand, requires little preparation or attention, no turning, and the heap can be of any size. The carbon/nitrogen ratio is not important so no activator is required. Its drawbacks are that weed seeds, perennial weeds and diseases will not be killed, that tough material will not be broken down, and that it may produce odours and attract flies unless carefully covered. The compost may be cold, heavy and rather acid, so requiring liming. It takes about a year to produce good compost in this way, and it may not be completely decomposed. This doesn't matter in fact, as unrotted compost is still food for worms; large pieces of undecomposed material can be removed or sieved out before use.

It must be stressed that gardeners should *aim* to make aerobic compost, which gives the best and most rapid returns. If this is difficult, perhaps because only small quantities of waste are available, it is still worth making anaerobic compost, even though the process takes longer and is less efficient. The point is that valuable organic matter is being returned to the soil.

Making aerobic compost

The site Bins should be erected in a permanent position, preferably on a soil foundation so that worms can move into the compost in the final stages. Shady corners can be utilized.

Bins Where possible, construct two bins side by side – or one bin with two, or even three, compartments, so that while one is being built up the other(s) can be maturing. Minimum dimensions for a bin are 1 m sq (3½ ft sq) square, and 1m (3½ ft) high, but the larger it is (provided you have enough material to fill it), the better.

The structure must be strong. At least three walls should be made of materials with good heat insulation properties, such as breeze blocks, bricks, straw bales or timber. Timber for side panels should be 1.5–3 cm (½–1¼ in) thick, with corner posts of 5 x 10 cm (2 x 4 in) timber.

It is useful if the front wall is made up either of loose boards, which can be slid in behind uprights, or with removable panels of timber. This makes access to the heap easier, both when it is being made and when the compost is being used. In areas of high rainfall the heap should be protected with a roof – corrugated iron is sufficient – to prevent it becoming saturated. Leave a gap for ventilation.

Building the heap Start by forking the base soil lightly. The next step, to ensure drainage and aeration from underneath, is to lay a 7.5 cm (3 in) thick layer of brushwood or prunings on the ground. Alternatives are several rows of land drain pipes, or double rows of bricks with 5 cm (2in) gaps between the pairs of rows. This foundation can be covered with a strong wire screen of about 2.5 cm (1in) mesh to support the compost.

The heap is best built in layers 15–23 cm (6–9 in) thick. Try to accumulate enough material to make a complete layer at once, rather than adding small quantities to the heap daily. Kitchen wastes can be collected in closed plastic bags until required. Ideally the whole heap should be built in one operation.

In each layer mix the material together as thoroughly as possible before putting it in the box. Never make a thick layer of any one material; this applies most to grass cuttings which become a slimy mass if packed densely. Either allow them to dry out for several days first, or mix them well with other material before incorporating them into the heap. Suitable garden wastes include weeds, vegetable re-

mains, leaves from herbaceous plants, bonfire ash, thin prunings. Nettles, comfrey and green bracken make particularly good compost. All can be mixed with kitchen waste. Paper can be used but never more than 10% by weight, and well soaked beforehand. Cut or shred thick material such as cabbage stalks and prunings into small pieces, 5–7.5 cm (2–3 in) long. Bonfire ash is a valuable source of minerals and can be mixed into the heap.

Perennial weeds should be killed first by being dried in the sun. All non-rotting material, for example bones, plastics, metals, china, man-made fibres, should be excluded. The pre-mixed wastes should be watered, if necessary, until just damp but not sodden.

Autumn leaves rot very slowly, and are best gathered into a heap enclosed by wire netting at least 60–90 cm (2–3ft) high. They take about a year to rot into beautiful leafmould, which can be used as a mulch or in potting compost. Alternatively, store them in black plastic bags: they will take up to two years to rot.

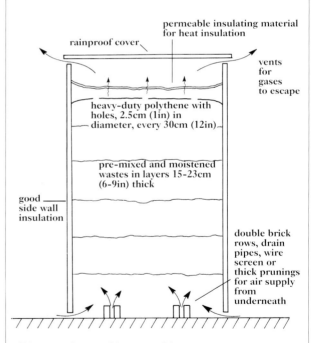

Diagram of an aerobic compost bin

Use of activators For optimum microbial activity the carbon/nitrogen ratio of the heap needs to be roughly 30:1. Carbon is found mainly in stems (such as straw), roots; nitrogen in green leaves and manures. In the summer months there is naturally enough leafy material in composting materials for the balance to be about right, but in autumn and winter additional nitrogen needs to be added to each layer of the heap. This can be in the form of:

- concentrated organic fertilizers such as dried blood, fish and bone at 270 g / sq m (8oz / sq yd)
- poultry or other animal manures, about 1 bucket per sq m or sq yd.
- concentrated seaweed extracts or proprietary activators as instructed by the manufacturers.

The activators should be well mixed in with the wastes before putting them into the heap.

Completing the heap The heap is built up in layers until the top of the bin is reached, or it is 1–1.5 m (3½–5 ft) high. To retain the heat of composting, cover the top layer with a piece of plastic sheet punctured with 2.5 cm (1 in) holes, about 30 cm (12 in) apart. Finally, cover with some permeable insulating material such as hessian sacks, matting, old carpets or old straw.

Turning the heap Reasonably high temperatures in a compost heap are necessary to encourage decomposition, and to destroy disease pathogens and weed seed. A temperature over 50 C (122 F), for 72 hours kills most diseases, and over 70 C (158 F) for 30 minutes kills most weed seeds. Temperature can be tested with compost thermometers.

The temperature in a well-made heap should rise to about 60–70 C (140–158 F) within a week and then start to fall. To reactivate it, the heap should then be turned, which means rebuilding it 'sides to middle', the cooler outer layer being placed in the middle of the heap. In a compost bin with several compartments the heap is transferred to an empty compartment. Turning is a laborious task, but there is no doubt that the more the heap is turned, the better it is aerated and the faster compost is made. It can be turned once a week in fact! This is counsel of perfection: but turn it at least once if you can, especially if the bin is not very well insulated. After turning, cover the top again with the plastic sheet and insulating material.

The anaerobic process

The simplest form of anaerobic heap is made by piling up wastes on the ground as they accumulate, to a height of 1.5 m (5 ft). To get the best end product possible, mix different types of material in the heap. Cover it with polythene sheeting. The heap will take about a year to decompose.

If you have only very small quantities of waste material, simply keep household and garden rubbish in tied black plastic bags until it has decomposed.

Green manuring

Green manuring is a technique of growing a crop which is dug into the soil to improve fertility. Depending on the crop used, a green manure benefits the soil by increasing the organic matter, by adding nutrients, and where overwintered, by protecting the soil surface and taking up nutrients which would otherwise be washed out of the soil during the winter. These nutrients are returned to the soil when the green manure rots down or is dug in in spring. Green manures grow densely and help keep down weeds on uncultivated ground. They can also be grown for cutting as a source of compost material. Spare or unused ground in a vegetable garden can be sown with a suitable long-term green manure, left for up to a year or more, to improve its fertility while out of use.

Green manures cannot be used as the sole source of manure in a garden. Indeed, like any crop, they will not perform well on poor soils. But they are a useful way of supplementing manures and fertilizers being used, and of improving soil fertility generally. They are especially useful on poorly structured sandy and silty soils. It is worth experimenting with the use of one or two, choosing those that suit your soil and requirements.

Green manures must be sown in the correct season, and, to get the maximum benefit, dug in at the optimum time. In most cases this is just before flowering, and always while the plants are lush and before the stems become woody. If a green manure has grown very bulky, it may be necessary to cut it down first, and compost the leafy parts, before digging in the roots. Green manures are usually broadcast or sown in closely spaced rows.

There are three main types of green manures.

Fast growing leafy crops These are normally in the ground for a couple of months, and are mainly grown to give a quick release of nitrogen when the leaves decay after being dug in. Examples are mustard, rape, and *Phacelia tanacetifolia*.

Leguminous crops These are crops whose root nodules 'fix' the atmospheric nitrogen in the soil; the nitrogen becomes available to subsequent crops when the leguminous crop is dug in. Examples are various species of clover, winter field beans, winter tares and bitter lupin. They can be in the ground for a few to many months; the hardy species can be overwintered.

Fibrous-rooted crops These are grown primarily to increase the organic matter content of the soil. The best example is grazing rye.

Some green manures used in gardens

Winter field beans (Vicia faba) Winter hardy, nitrogen-fixing beans. Sow from September to November, spacing seeds 13 cm (5 in) apart, and dig in before flowering the following spring. Winter field beans do best on heavy land and do not tolerate drought.

Mustard is a fast growing green manure which is best dug in before it flowers.

Grazing rye is a winter hardy green manure recommended for improving soil structure.

Alsike clover (Trifolium hybridum) Winter hardy, nitrogen-fixing clover. Sow from April to August at the rate of 2–3 g / sq m (or sq yd). Either dig in after a few months or leave the clover for a year or more, in which case it should be cut down when flowering to encourage new growth. It stands wet, acid soils.

Essex red clover (Trifolium pratense) Winter hardy, deep rooting, nitrogen-fixing clover. Sow from April to August at a rate of 2–3 g / sq m (or sq yd). Unsuitable for poor or acid soils. Dig in as Alsike clover above.

Bitter lupin (Lupinus angustifolius) Nitrogen-fixing, slightly hardy plant. Sow seeds from March to June approximately 13 cm (5 in) apart and 3.5–4 cm (1¼–1½ in) deep. Dig in the crop two to three months later before the flowers open. Bitter lupins are recommended for light, and slightly acid soils.

Mustard (Sinapis alba) and rape (Brassica napa var. napus) Fast growing, moderately hardy plants primarily used as a quick source of nitrogen. Sow from March to early September at a rate of 3–5 g / sq m (or sq yd). Dig in three to eight weeks later, before flowering. These plants are susceptible to clubroot, so should not be grown where clubroot is a problem.

Phacelia tanacetifolia A fairly hardy, fast growing, attractive, weed-suppressing plant. Sow from the end of March to early September, at a rate of 2–3 g / sq m (or sq yd). Dig in the crop before flowering, after four to eight weeks in summer, or if overwintered, in spring.

Grazing rye (Secale cereale) A winter hardy, fast growing type of rye, recommended for improving soil structure. Sow this annual from mid August to early November at the rate of 30 g / sq m (1 oz / sq yd) protecting it from birds. Dig in the crop the following spring when the flower heads can be felt developing within the stalks.

Winter tares or common vetch (Vicia sativa) A hardy, nitrogen-fixing, leguminous plant. Sow from March to May for summer use, or from July to early September to overwinter, at 20 g / sq m (¾oz / sq yd). The seed should be sown 4 cm (1½ in) deep. Dig in any time before flowering, after two to three months in summer, or in spring after overwintering. This plant does best on heavy soils, and does not do well on light or acid soils.

Many other crops can be grown as green manures. (See Further reading, p 158.)

Fertilizers

Although adequate vegetable crops are obtained from gardens where extensive use is made of compost and manure, in most cases higher yields can be obtained by the use of supplementary artificial fertilizers. These are supplied both as straight fertilizers supplying one, or two, nutrients or as compounds supplying several nutrients. (Organic gardeners use concentrated organic fertilizers, see below.)

Supplying plant nutrients

The three major plant nutrients derived from the soil are nitrogen, phosphorus and potassium, and artificial fertilizers are used to supplement the soil's supply. The plant can only take up the chemicals in certain forms, so the content of available nutrients is quoted on the fertilizer bag or label as % N for nitrogen, % P_2O_5 for phosphate, and % K_2O for potash. Contents vary considerably, so it is important to know how much of each nutrient is being supplied by any particular product.

In theory, the amount of each nutrient required depends on the crop to be grown and the amounts already present in the soil. Unfortunately, it is not easy for amateurs to get a nutrient analysis of their soils, though some organizations offer a soil analysis service. Amateur soil testing kits give only limited information.

Nitrogen

Nitrogen is the plant nutrient most likely to be in short supply. It is easily washed or leached out of the soil by heavy rain, particularly when the soil is bare during the winter months. So nitrogen needs to be applied annually to obtain good growth and maximum yields.

The most common 'straight' fertilizers supplying nitrogen are nitrate of potash (12% N plus 60% K_2O), calcium nitrate (15.5% N plus calcium), nitrate of soda (15.5% N), sulphate of ammonia (21% N), and Nitro-chalk (21% N plus calcium).

Vegetables differ considerably in their nitrogen requirements, and can be grouped accordingly. For example, peas, which have nitrogen fixing nodules on their roots, require no extra nitrogen; carrots and radishes have low nitrogen requirements; broad beans, parsnips, lettuces, onions, calabrese, French beans and turnips have moderate requirements; potatoes, beetroot, spinach, cauliflower, Brussels sprouts and cabbages have high nitrogen requirements.

The amount of nitrogen fertilizer applied annually per square metre or square yard depends on the crop and the nitrogen content of the fertilizer, quoted as % N on the bag. The table on p 18 gives a guide to the total annual requirements of a range of vegetables, assuming an average garden soil to which crop residues are regularly returned in the form of compost. The table is based on the use of sulphate of ammonia or Nitro-chalk fertilizers with 21% N. So a plant requiring 12 g / sq m (⅓ oz / sq yd) of Nitro-chalk would need three times as much of a compound fertilizer such as National Growmore, which contains 7% N.

As nitrogen fertilizers are rapidly washed out of the soil they are applied both as a base dressing shortly before sowing or transplanting, and as a top dressing when the plant is established and growing vigorously. They should never be added to bare ground in the autumn, as they will be leached out, so contributing to the nitrate pollution problem.

Nitrogen fertilizers have to be used carefully, as high concentrations of the dissolved chemicals in the soil can damage young plant roots. The base dressing can be worked into the soil surface, preferably a month before sowing. It *can* be mixed in just before sowing, but only if the soil is moist. As a general rule, no more than one third of the crop's total requirement should be applied before sowing. Higher concentrations than this at an early stage of growth are likely to depress seedling growth and emergence. The remainder of the nitrogen needed can be applied as a top dressing during growth once the crop is established.

Overwintered crops, such as spring cabbages and autumn sown onions, need most of their nitrogen in spring, when it is applied as a top dressing. When leafy crops with high nitrogen requirements, such as cabbages, cauliflower, calabrese, kale, leeks, spinach, spinach beet (chard) and beetroot are sown directly in the ground, they need about one third of their total nitrogen requirement when sown, and the remaining two thirds during growth.

Phosphorus and potassium

While nitrogen is very mobile in the soil, and is easily washed out during the winter, phosphate and potash are relatively immobile and residues of one year's application will remain in the root area for more than one season. It has been calculated that just under 15g / sq m (½oz / sq yd) of phosphate and potash are needed each year to maintain adequate levels in the soil for vegetables. This amount can be satisfactorily supplied by an annual application of farmyard manure at the rate of about 5.5 kg / sq m (10 lb / sq yd) or of good garden compost at 2.75 – 5.5 kg / sq m (5 – 10 lb / sq yd).

Phosphate and potash requirements can also be supplied with artificial fertilizers, but if they are used, additional organic matter must be worked into the soil to maintain and improve the soil structure.

Phosphate can be supplied by the annual application of superphosphate (20% P_2O_5), at the rate of 65 g / sq m (2 oz / sq yd), or triple superphosphate (44% P_2O_5) at half that rate.

Potash is supplied by the annual application of sulphate of potash (49% K_2O) at the rate of 35g / sq m (1 oz / sq yd), or of nitrate of potash (36% K_2O), which also contains some nitrogen, at a slightly higher rate.

The nutrients from these fertilizers are released into the soil much more slowly than nitrogen, so the fertilizers need to be applied well before the growing season. The exact timing is not critical, but autumn is usual.

Wherever possible, it is advisable to have the soil analysed every five years or so to check that levels of available phosphate and potash are adequate.

Trace elements

Although plants require trace (minor) elements, of which there are many, in only minute quantities, the deficiency of any one can result in poor growth. Some crops are particularly vulnerable to certain deficiencies – cauliflower is vulnerable to molybedom deficiency, for example.

Identifying deficiencies is a specialist task, but once identified, they can be corrected with fertilizers containing the necessary elements, usually applied as a foliar feed for quick action. In practice, trace element deficiencies are unlikely to occur on soils which have been well manured, though they may be induced by over-liming. Indeed, high pH caused by over-liming is one of the commonest causes of trace element deficiencies.

Rates of application of nitrogen fertilizer for different groups of vegetables*

(These are total requirements.)

No nitrogen
Peas

---

*This assumes the use of Nitro-chalk or sulphate of ammonia, fertilizers with 21% N. To find the rate of application for other nitrogenous fertilizers, multiply by the figures indicated: nitrate of potash (12% N): × 1.8; calcium nitrate and nitrate of soda (15% N): × 1.4; National Growmore (7% N): × 3.

Very low nitrogen – 12 g / sq m ($\frac{1}{3}$ oz / sq yd)
Carrots
Radishes

Low nitrogen – 25 – 35g / sq m ($\frac{2}{3}$ – 1oz / sq yd)
Artichokes, globe
Asparagus
Aubergines
Beans: broad, French, runner
Celeriac
Chicory
Cucumber
Endive
Florence fennel
Kohl rabi
Marrows
Onions
Parsnips
Salsify, scorzonera
Seakale
Swedes
Sweet peppers
Tomatoes (outdoor)
Turnips

Medium nitrogen 45 – 55g / sq m ($1\frac{1}{3}$ – $1\frac{2}{3}$ oz / sq yd)
Artichokes, Jerusalem
Broccoli, purple sprouting
Cabbage, winter storage
Calabrese
Cauliflower
Kale
Lettuces
Potatoes (early)
Rhubarb (young)
Spinach
Sweet corn
Texsel greens

High nitrogen – 65 – 100g / sq m (2 – 3oz / sq yd)
Beetroot
Celery
Leeks
Potatoes (maincrop)
Spinach beet

Very high nitrogen – 110g / sq m ($3\frac{1}{3}$ oz sq yd)
Brussels sprouts
Cabbage, Chinese
Cabbage, spring
Cabbage, summer
Cabbage, winter
Rhubarb (cutting years)

Compound artificial fertilizers

A limited range of general purpose compound fertilizers is available to amateur gardeners. These are mixtures of chemical compounds supplying varying proportions of N, P_2O_5, and K_2O–quoted for example as 20:10:10 in the case of a fertilizer with 20%N, and 10% each of P_2O_5 and K_2O.) They are easy to apply, and convenient when all three nutrients are required. For general garden purposes, compound mixtures with a relatively high level of nitrogen, and lower levels of phosphorus and potash, are most appropriate.

Organic fertilizers

Under organic systems the emphasis is on feeding the *soil*, and not the plants, with reliance on manure and garden compost to create a highly fertile soil. Organic gardeners avoid the use of artificial fertilizers on the grounds that the rapidly released chemicals can be damaging to the soil life, and encourage rapid, sappy plant growth which is prone to pest and disease attacks. Where supplementary feeding is necessary to bridge the nutrient gap (fertile soils can't be built up overnight), and obtain optimum yields, organic gardeners use organic fertilizers and organic liquid feeds.

Organic fertilizers differ from chemical fertilizers in several ways. Their composition and quality is variable, depending on the source. In almost all cases the plant foods are not immediately available and have to be broken down by soil micro-organisms: so the fertilizers are 'slow release' rather than rapid in action. This is a disadvantage where plants require a quick boost of nitrogen in spring. The micro-organisms responsible for the breakdown of organic fertilizers to release nitrogen do not function until the soil has warmed up to a certain level. But organic fertilizers supply nutrients over a longer period than artificial fertilizers.

Organic fertilizers are less soluble than artificial fertilizers so less likely to be leached out of the soil. The rates of application are less critical, but they are relatively more expensive. They may supply minor elements, trace elements and growth-promoting substances as well as major elements or nutrients, which is not the case with artificial fertilizers.

Commonly used organic fertilizers

(All analyses are very approximate.)

Dried blood (12–14% N, 2.5% P_2O_5, 1% K_2O)
Exceptional in being soluble and releasing nitrogen rapidly. Used for early spring to midsummer to stimulate growth in leafy vegetables, preferably as a liquid suspension, diluted at the rate of 50g in 1 litre (2oz in 2 pints) for application on a sq m (sq yd). The powered form can be scattered around plants.

Fish, blood and bone meal (3.5% N, 8% P_2O_5)
Used as a general fertilizer at rates of 65–200 g / sq m (2–6 oz / sq yd), applied either two weeks before sowing or planting or as a top dressing during growth.

Bone meal and bone flour (new bone meal 6% N, 15% P_2O_5; bone flour 3.5% N, 22% P_2O_5)
Used mainly when planting fruits and shrubs when phosphorus is low, and for vegetables on light land. It is applied at 100–135g/sq m (3–4oz/sq yd).

Hoof and horn (14% N, 2.5% P_2O_5)
Used primarily as a slow release source of nitrogen, applied to leafy crops in spring and summer at roughly 135g/sq m (4oz/sq yd).

Seaweed meal (2% N, 2.7% K_2O plus trace elements)
This appears to contain various compounds which encourage bacterial activity and plant growth, so acts as a soil conditioner and is beneficial on poor soils. It is generally hoed in in the autumn at the rate of 135–200g/sq m (4–6oz/sq yd).

Rock phosphate (26% P_2O_5)
This is pure ground rock, which is used for the long-term improvement of soils deficient in phosphorus, applied at rates of 200–270g/sq m (6–8oz/sq yd). It is not always very effective.

Compound organic fertilizers

Various concentrated organic mixtures are available, of varying analyses, made from animal and vegetable waste products. They release nutrients slowly, and are used as general purpose fertilizers, applied at rates of 135–410g/sq m (4–12oz/sq yd), depending on the product and the condition of the soil.

Organic liquid fertilizers

There are a number of approved* organic products available only in liquid form (see below). Some are seaweed extracts, some are made from cow slurry and farmyard manure. They are widely used to stimulate plant growth and supply some nutrients. Liquid feeds can also be made from comfrey (*Symphytum officinale*, which has a high potash content and is therefore a useful tomato fertilizer), stinging nettles and manure. In the main, these products are diluted and either watered on the ground or applied to plants as a foliar feed. (See Further reading, p 158.)

* UKROFS (United Kingdom Register of Organic Food Standards)

Worm casts

Worm casts are rich in nutrients and appear to be very beneficial to plant growth. Casts from worms fed largely on seaweed are available. They are sprinkled along the drill before sowing, or on the soil between seedlings and young plants, or applied when transplanting, at a rate of 100g/sq m (3oz/sq yd).

It should be stressed that, as with artificial fertilizers, none of the above organic products are bulky manures, so they contribute little to the improvement of soil structure. They should be used only in addition to regular applications of manure, compost or other forms of bulky organic matter.

Applying fertilizers

Fertilizers are sold in solid forms – dusts, granules or pellets – or as concentrated liquid solutions. They must be prepared and used according to the manufacturer's instructions. Excessive use is counterproductive and can be damaging.

Dry forms of fertilizer are sprinkled on the soil surface as evenly as possible and raked or hoed in. If the ground is dry the fertilizer must be watered in to dissolve and wash it down to plant roots. Some forms of pelleted fertilizer are placed in the soil near the roots.

Liquid fertilizers are diluted and watered on the soil. Plants take them up faster than they take up solid fertilizers.

Foliar feeds are sprayed or watered on to the plants, as plants can take in limited amounts of nutrients through their leaves. Foliar feeding is useful where it is necessary to correct a nutrient deficiency, either of a major element such as magnesium or a trace element such as manganese. Proprietary liquid fertilizers are sometimes recommended for use as a foliar feed.

Siting and shelter

Today most vegetable growers have little option about where to site their vegetable garden. The ideal site is an open but not exposed position, free from the damaging drips of overhanging trees, or of shade cast by tall buildings or trees. Frost pockets should be avoided, though it is sometimes possible to cut a gap in a hedge on the lower side of a frost pocket, so that the cold air can drain away. In exposed sites windbreaks should be planted or erected. (See below). Sites with poor drainage should also be avoided. (See Soil fertility, p 10.)

If there is a choice rows should run north to south, to make maximum use of sunlight. This is especially important with tall-growing crops such as runner beans, to prevent them casting shade on neighbouring crops. However, on a steep slope it is advisable to cultivate *across* the slope, whatever the direction, to minimize erosion.

Shelter

Research has shown that with almost all vegetables shelter from even light winds can increase yields by up to 20 to 30%. Protection from strong winds will give even greater increases. Shelter is particularly valuable in winter when temperatures are low, for it is the combination of low temperature and strong wind which does serious damage to plants. In coastal areas windbreaks provide valuable protection against salt spray.

The best windbreak is about 50% permeable, so that the wind is filtered through it. When wind encounters a solid barrier it is forced over it, creating a very destructive area of turbulence on the far side. A windbreak is most effective for a distance of from six to ten times its height and provides less and less shelter as the distance from it is increased. So for maximum effect, erect barriers about 1 m (3 ft 6 in) high, 6 m (20 ft) apart.

Windbreaks fall into two categories: living and artificial. One of the most effective artificial fences is a lath screen, constructed by nailing horizontal lath strips 2.5 cm (1 in) wide and 2.5 cm (1 in) apart, on to a lath framework.

There are many manufactured net and web materials on the market for use as windbreaks. These are attached to stakes with battens. In strong wind fences and nets must take tremendous strain so need to be very securely erected. Stakes used should be sturdy (at least 5–7.5 cm / 2–3 in diameter), and rot proof. They should be erected about 1.8 m (6 ft) apart for netting; and 3 m (10 ft) apart for wooden lath fences.

Around the circumference of a garden artificial windbreaks normally need to be at least 1.8 m (6 ft) high, which represents a fairly expensive investment. Where this is impossible, smaller windbreaks, rather on the style of tennis nets, can be erected between rows of plants to give very valuable protection. These need be no more than 45 cm (18 in) high. Home-made windbreaks of this type can be made from material such as hessian. Even 13 mm (½ in) mesh wire netting has some effect as a windbreak, breaking the force of severe winds and mitigating hail damage.

Trees and hedges offer the most permanent windbreaks, but take several years to become effective, require maintenance, compete for water and nutrients, and may create shade. On a smaller scale, tall growing crops such as sweet corn, Jerusalem artichokes and sunflowers can serve as temporary living windbreaks.

Severe wind damage can be caused by draughts and wind funnels, often created by gaps between buildings. It is worth erecting windbreaks across such gaps, to stretch a couple of feet beyond the gap on either side. Where shrubs are planted in gaps as windbreaks, artificial protection may be necessary until they are established.

In some circumstances walls provide excellent shelter: in spring early crops can be raised at the foot of south-facing walls, and in summer they may provide the necessary warmth for sun-loving crops such as tomatoes and peppers. But the soil at the foot of walls is very prone to drying out, and walled-in gardens sometimes suffer from the turbulence mentioned above.

Cloches, frames, low and walk-in polytunnels and greenhouses all provide shelter. (See Protected cropping, p 46.)

Although shelter is invaluable, if plants are grown in totally sheltered, still conditions, there is the risk of a rapid build-up of pests and disease.

An artificial windbreak using netting and wooden stakes.

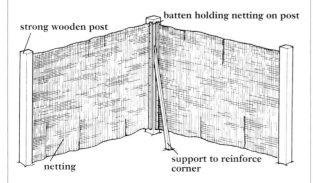

strong wooden post

batten holding netting on post

netting

support to reinforce corner

The bed system

The typical, traditional vegetable garden consists of an extensive plot or series of plots in which the vegetables are grown in widely spaced rows and spaced within the rows. The whole plot is dug over and manured, and much of the ground is trodden in the process of working the soil, tending the plants and collecting the harvest.

In the bed system the vegetable garden is divided into a number of narrow beds, generally separated by permanent paths. Most of the plants are grown at equidistant spacing across the bed, rather than in widely spaced rows. (See also Planting, p 37.) For the reasons outlined below this system is more efficient, and is now being widely adopted by amateur vegetable growers.

Interestingly, the bed, or 'strip' system was the principal method of vegetable growing before the invention in the 18th century of the seed drill which enables vegetables to be sown in rows on a large scale, and the subsequent introduction of the horse-drawn hoe, to weed down the rows between them. These developments led to farmers abandoning beds for widely spaced rows and gardeners followed suit – although the new system's merits did not apply on a small scale. Curiously, modern commercial practice is reverting to the old system, with vegetables in tractor-width beds cultivated by tractors which straddle the beds.

Advantages of the bed system

- All the work can be done from the paths. This virtually eliminates the need to tread on the soil, which damages the soil structure. (See Soil fertility, p 10.)

- Bulky manure and compost is concentrated on the ground where the vegetables are being grown, rather than wasted on ground between rows, or ground which in practice functions as a path.

- The gardener's energy is saved by digging only those areas where vegetables will grow.

- The beds tend to become more fertile than ordinary garden beds due to the concentration of manure and the preservation of the soil structure.

- As a result of the fertility, plant roots penetrate more deeply, so enabling plants to withstand drought better and to be grown closer together. This leads to higher overall yields.

■ When equidistant spacing is used, competition between plants for nutrients, light and water is minimized, resulting in even and balanced growth. Moreover, when mature the leaves of the crops will, in most cases, form a canopy over the soil. This largely prevents the germination of weed seeds and their subsequent growth. Exceptions to this are narrow leaved plants, such as onions, which will not form a canopy.

■ Over the course of time, the beds tend to become slightly raised due to working in organic matter and not treading on the soil. This improves drainage, and makes the beds warm up faster in spring. (See also Raised bed.)

■ It is easier to practise rotation with the flexibility of several narrow beds rather than one large plot. (See also Rotation, and Planning, pp 23–26.)

■ Narrow beds are easily covered with long, low polytunnels for protection. (See also Protected cropping, p 46.)

■ The paths tend to become beaten hard by use, so there is less splash-up onto plants, keeping them cleaner and healthier.

Types of bed

Standard narrow bed   This can be any convenient width, but is usually 90–150 cm (3–5 ft) wide. The narrower the bed, the easier it is to reach the centre, but the higher the overall ratio of path to bed within the garden. If you intend to use low polytunnels, it is convenient to have beds the same width as the tunnel hoops. (See Protective cropping, p 46.) Of course beds can be any length, although if too long, inevitably short cuts are taken across them. Although usually they are straight, they can be curved to blend in with the design of a garden. The soil is prepared and cultivated in the same way as a garden plot. (See Soil preparation, p 26.)

Raised bed   In raised beds the soil is up to 30 cm (12 in) above ground level. A typical raised bed is about 1.2 m (4 ft) at the base and 90 cm (3 ft) across the top. The sides of the bed are usually sloped, but the top can be level or rounded. The benefits of raised beds

Equidistant spacing on the bed system makes good use of ground.

Bricked raised beds make it possible to garden without bending.

Raised beds made of wooden railway sleepers.

The grassed paths at Eton College garden fit a 60cm (24in) mower.

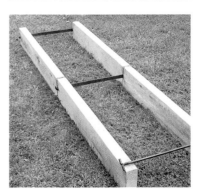

Rigid metal 'straps' keep the concrete edging slabs in place.

A good stand of leeks in the Eton College garden bed system.

are improved drainage, faster soil warming, and if the beds are rounded, increased surface area. Moreoever, in northern latitudes the south facing side of *rounded* beds attracts increased sunlight and radiation: a five-degree angle to the slope gives the same benefit as moving 30 miles south. The extra height of a raised bed is normally obtained with soil excavated from the path area between beds and by working in large quantities of organic matter. Raised beds are sometimes edged with timber. At the Golden Acre Park in Leeds, raised beds are edged with one railway sleeper on one side but two at the back, so the beds can be converted into frames in winter.

Intensive and deep beds These are highly fertile beds, prepared by double digging and working in a great deal of organic matter. They are sometimes raised and sometimes at ground level. (See Further reading, p 158.)

Raised beds for disabled gardeners These beds are built on a brick or concrete foundation, so they are of a height (normally about 60 cm / 24 in high) easily worked from wheelchairs or without bending. (See Organisations, p 158.) However to be really useful the beds should be tailored to the individual needs of the disabled person and their ability to use special tools.

Paths

The minimum width for paths between beds is about 30 cm (12 in), though it is convenient to have some wider paths to take cumbersome wheelbarrow loads. The paths can be of bare earth, concrete, gravel, stone, weatherproof brick, or other material. In organic gardens, old carpet is sometimes laid on paths to prevent weed growth. Mown grassed paths can set off vegetable beds beautifully. The illustration shows the grass paths between the narrow beds in the Eton College garden. In this case the 60 cm (24 in) paths (the width of the lawnmower) were edged with concrete edging slabs 90 cm (3 ft) long, 5 cm (2 in) wide and 10 cm (4 in) deep. As the slabs have a tendency to 'creep' into the beds, they are held rigidly in position with 2.5 cm (1 in) wide metal 'straps' between the blocks, notched at the ends and bent outwards to embrace adjoining blocks.

The potager concept

The word 'potager' has come to imply a vegetable garden laid out in a pattern of designed beds, so that it is decorative as well as functional. In a potager, trained fruit, herbs, and flowers are often grown beside or among the vegetables to enhance its decorative qualities. This intermingling of crops may help to keep down pests, so the concept is favoured by organic gardeners. (See Further reading, p 158.)

Rotation

Rotation is the practice of growing closely related vegetables on a different piece of land each year, in a regular sequence, usually over a three- to four-year cycle.

There are several reasons for rotation. When the same crop is grown in the same place for several years, yields often start to fall – this phenomenon is known as 'soil sickness'. In most cases soil sickness seems to be caused by the gradual build-up of soil pests such as eelworm, or of soil-borne diseases, such as onion neck rot. As the soil pests and diseases in question only attack a range of closely related plants, growing a different type of crop prevents them building up to damaging numbers. Rotation also helps to prevent them becoming established in the first place.

Rotation has other benefits. When related to a manuring programme it is a means of maintaining soil fertility. Leguminous crops, such as peas and most beans, add nitrogen to the soil. Hence the traditional practice of following legumes with nitrogen-hungry brassicas. On the other hand, one crop may exhaust the soil of certain nutrients it requires: changing the crop allows the soil reserves to be replenished.

Rotation can also be a tool in weed control. Potatoes, for example, are a good crop for 'cleaning' the ground, partly because their dense foliage prevents weed germination, partly because earthing up in itself destroys weeds and exposes weed seed to birds. This makes them a useful crop to precede onions and carrots, which are difficult to grow in weedy ground.

In the most basic rotation plan a garden is divided into three plots; the main vegetable groups grown in succession are legumes, brassicas, and potatoes and other root crops. Onions and other miscellaneous crops are usually grouped with the legumes.

A SIMPLE THREE-YEAR ROTATION PLAN

	Plot A	Plot B	Plot C
Year 1	Legumes	Brassicas	Potatoes
Year 2	Brassicas	Potatoes	Legumes
Year 3	Potatoes	Legumes	Brassicas

In the typical small, modern garden this type of rotation is often impractical and too inflexible. You may not want to devote a third of your garden to any one type of crop. Moreover, in small gardens crops will, in practice, be moved only a few yards in one direction or another each year, which is insufficient to prevent the build-up of soil pests and diseases. Another factor is that some serious pests and diseases can survive much longer than three years: potato cyst eelworm can survive up to six years, clubroot and onion white rot up to 20 – making a mockery of an important reason for rotation. (See 'The case for *not* rotating' below.) Despite this disadvantage, it is sound garden practice to try and rotate: the order in which crops are grown is not very important.

■ As far as possible, plan your vegetable garden so that closely related vegetables (see the main groups below), are grown in a different piece of ground or bed in successive years, returning to the original spot ideally one year in four or five. This, incidentally, is much easier to organize where the vegetable garden is divided into a number of narrow beds rather than into a few large plots.

■ At the very minimum, avoid following a crop with another from the same group for at least two years.

Main groups for rotation purposes

Brassicas Brussels sprouts, broccoli, cabbage, calabrese, cauliflower, oriental greens, such as Chinese cabbage, pak choi and komatsuna, kale, kohl rabi, mustard, radish, salad rape, swedes, Texsel greens, turnips.

Legumes Beans, peas, green manures, such as clovers, tares, field beans.

Onion family Onions, leeks, garlic, shallots.

Solanaceous family Potatoes, tomatoes, peppers, aubergine.

Umbelliferous family Carrots, celery, parsley, parsnips.

The case for not rotating

In view of the long-term persistence of some pests and diseases in the soil, especially in small gardens, a case can be made for concentrating a crop in one area *until* a problem arises. For example, onions can be grown on one site until there is a problem with onion white rot. At that point, they can be moved to another part of the garden which is unaffected. Similarly, to prevent clubroot or limit its spread, brassicas can be restricted to one area of the garden, where the soil is limed more frequently and kept at a higher pH than the rest of the garden, which helps to combat clubroot.

In much the same way the soil in one area can be brought into a state where it is ideally suited to one crop: highly fertile and moisture retentive for runner beans; well-drained, light, and rich in organic matter for carrots. At any sign of serious soil-borne pest or disease problems, however, the crop must be moved to another site.

SITING VEGETABLES

Within the overall requirements of the rotation plan, it is convenient to group together plants which are likely to be harvested at roughly the same time. This makes it easier to clear a reasonably sized piece of ground for sowing or planting.

Perennial vegetables Perennial vegetables such as asparagus, rhubarb, sorrel, seakale and globe artichokes are best excluded from a rotation plan. It is often convenient to group them together at one end of a garden.

Herbs For practical purposes, herbs should be as near the kitchen as possible, or grown along the edges of paths or beds.

Warm sites Any particularly warm sites, for example, the south side of a wall, should be used for early crops such as salads and peas in spring, for late salads in autumn, and for tender crops such as tomatoes, aubergines and peppers in summer.

Two main groups in crop rotations: solanaceous – tomatoes (foreground) – and legumes – French, runner and broad beans.

Planning for continuity

Most people growing vegetables want a constant supply for the household – preferably fresh. Some vegetables, such as asparagus and sweet corn, are only available fresh at certain times of year. Others, such as cabbage, cauliflower, and lettuce, are available at almost any season provided a succession of appropriate cultivars is sown at the correct time. In other cases, examples are onions and potatoes, a continuous supply depends on growing some for storage. Vegetables can also be grown specifically for freezing. All these factors have to be borne in mind when planning.

Within the overall rotation plan, it is useful to draw up a rough plan for each garden bed. Given the vagaries of the weather and crop growth, it should be considered very flexible. The vegetable planning chart on pp 68-69 provides useful basic information.

Steps in planning

- Decide on the major vegetables you want to grow.

- Indicate on the bed plan how long they are likely to be in the ground.

- Where possible, follow or precede them with another major crop. For example, early potatoes lifted in June or July can be followed by marrows; mid-season potatoes lifted in August by overwintered onions; overwintered broad beans cleared in June by Brussels sprouts.

- Where this is impossible, fit short-term and minor vegetables in before or after the main crops, or grow a short-term green manure. (See Green manuring, p 15.)

Vegetables maturing in under eight weeks Radishes, seedling salad plants, Texsel greens, turnips harvested young.

Vegetables maturing in under 12 weeks Asparagus pea, beetroot (harvested young), carrots (early), Chinese cabbage, Chinese pak choi, komatsuna greens, claytonia, fennel, iceplant, kohl rabi, summer lettuces, spring sown spring onions, spring sown early peas.

Avoiding gluts and gaps

In practice, even the best-planned gardens suffer from gaps and gluts. The unpredictability of the British weather and variability in growing conditions must take much of the blame, but steps can be taken to minimize the problem.

The 'hungry gap'

The notorious so-called 'hungry gap' between February and May, when few vegetables are maturing, can be bridged with planning. In fact, there is quite a range of vegetables which can be harvested in this period, and any plan should aim to include a few of them. Examples are: asparagus, stored beet, purple sprouting broccoli, Brussels sprouts, Savoy and spring cabbage, winter cauliflower, celeriac, hardy varieties of Italian chicory, corn salad, kale, land cress, leeks, overwintered lettuces, rhubarb, spinach, Swiss chard, turnip tops, salad seedling crops and various oriental vegetables.

Successional sowing

Gluts commonly occur with relatively fast growing vegetables which tend to 'bolt' or run to seed, or rapidly become tough, soon after maturing. The most common examples are lettuces, radishes, turnips, and spinach. Here the answer is to sow 'little and often' instead of making one main sowing. It is not always easy to gauge the right interval between each sowing, as crops tend to grow faster at some times of year. Lettuces, for example, mature much faster in summer than in spring. A useful rule of thumb is to make the *next* sowing when the previous sowing has appeared through the ground.

Intercropping

To save both time and space a fast-growing crop is sometimes sown or planted between rows of, or alongside, a slower growing crop. The fast-growing crop is cleared before the slower one requires the entire space for its later stages of growth. Or young plants can be planted alongside a maturing crop, ready to utilize the whole area when the maturing crop is uprooted. The space between rows of slow-growing vegetables can sometimes be used as a

Early potatoes will be lifted and followed by other crops. Beetroot, carrots and parsnips continue to mature.

seedbed for vegetables which will later be transplanted into permanent positions elsewhere.

Undercropping, where a low crop is grown beneath a tall one, is a form of intercropping. Sweet corn is the ideal subject for undercropping. (See also Intersowing in a drill, Sowing outdoors, p 31.) Intercropping will only succeed where neither crop will deprive the other of moisture, nutrients, light and space. It may be necessary to plant a little further apart than usual to achieve this.

Vegetables such as radishes, cut-and-come-again seedlings, (see Sowing outdoors, p 30), small lettuces such as 'Tom Thumb' and 'Little Gem', fast-growing turnips, kohl rabi, Texsel greens, corn salad, land cress, salad rocket, can be grown between rows of shallots or winter brassicas, or beneath sweet corn. These same vegetables can be used as catch crops. (See below.)

Winter brassicas, lettuce, turnips, carrots, spinach and leaf beet can be planted or sown alongside, or between rows, of early peas or dwarf beans.

Catch crops

A catch crop is a quick-maturing crop which is grown on a piece of ground before the main crop is planted. The later crop could be a tender one such as tomatoes, sweetcorn or courgettes, which cannot be planted until all risk of frost is over, or winter brassicas, which are not transplanted until summer. Any of the fast-growing vegetables suggested above for intercropping can be used. Fast-growing green manures can also be grown as catch crops. (See Green manuring, p 15.)

Pot-raised plants

Often plants can be raised in pots or modules (see p 35), enabling them to grow to a fairly advanced stage. They can be kept 'waiting in the wings' for planting the moment a piece of ground is cleared of an earlier crop, so saving growing time and space. Brassicas, lettuces, leeks, and onions are among the many plants which can be grown this way.

Extending the season

The natural season for a vegetable can be extended by the use of protected cropping. Plants can be made to mature sooner by being raised under cover, then transplanted outside earlier than would otherwise be possible; they can also be grown entirely under cover. The cropping season can be extended by covering plants in late summer or autumn. (See Protected cropping, p 46.)

Soil preparation

The purpose of digging, forking, raking and most other forms of cultivation is to get the soil into the best possible state for sowing seeds or planting. Of all these operations, digging has the most fundamental effect, in that it disturbs the soil, breaks down clods, lets in air, and provides a practical means of removing weeds and incorporating organic matter into the soil. This also helps to improve drainage.

Digging

Digging is best carried out in the autumn or early winter on heavy soils, so that frost can break down or weather the clods over the winter. Light sandy or silty soils which do not need weathering, and may indeed lose their structure during heavy winter rains, are best left to the spring. It is practical to incorporate manure or some form of organic matter into the soil when digging.

Various traditional systems practised are:

Single digging, in which a single spit (spade's depth) is worked. The process starts with making a narrow trench, filling it with soil from the next trench.

Double digging, in which a much wider trench is cut initially, and the soil in the bottom forked over thoroughly before turning in soil from the next trench.

Trenching is a big operation in which a depth of two spits is dug.

Although the modern tendency is to dig less thoroughly, experiments at Horticulture Research International (Wellesbourne) have indicated that even apparently good soil becomes compacted in the lower levels. When this compaction is broken up by deeper digging, roots penetrate more readily and extract more water from lower levels, so conserving water in the upper layers. As plant nutrients are mainly in the upper layers, and can only be taken up by plants when the soil is *moist*, this benefits plant growth. Deeper digging is not necessary every year; its effects should last for three years.

For modern gardeners, a practical compromise between the old labour intensive forms of double digging and trenching, and the recognized need to work the soil as deeply as possible, is a halfway house between single and double digging.

The procedure is as follows:
1. Mark out the plot to be dug. If it is very large, divide the area into two or three sections and tackle each in turn.

2. Spread manure over the area to be dug to ensure even distribution. Alternatively, keep it in a wheelbarrow for use as required.

3. Take out a trench about 40 cm (16 in) wide and about 25 cm (10 in) deep across the plot.

4. Wheel this soil to the far end of the plot, or if it is divided into two then it can be laid alongside the first trench, ready for filling in the last trench.

5. Fork over the soil at the bottom of the trench.

6. Put a layer of manure in the trench.

7. Fork the soil and manure together, so that the manure is thoroughly spread throughout the soil.

8. Fill the trench with soil from the adjacent strip.

9. Fork over the bottom of the second trench, incorporate manure and soil from the third strip, mix them together and so on.

10. The last trench will be filled with the soil deposited at the end of the plot.

Pile soil from the first trench (right) alongside the end of the second section where digging finishes (left).

Fork over soil in bottom of first trench.

Spread manure over the forked soil.

Fork manure and soil together to mix.

Turn the next strip of soil into the first trench.

Digging in grass Lawns and grassland are sometimes converted into vegetable gardens. They are best dug in the autumn. Slice the turf off the top, and either chop it up and bury it in the bottom of the trench, or build up the turves into a separate heap, grass-side down. After a year the turves will have rotted into very useful potting soil.

Digging technique

Don't tackle too much initially as digging is strenuous exercise for those unaccustomed to it.

Never dig when the ground is very wet or there is heavy frost. Not only is this difficult to do, but it will destroy the crumb structure.

Start by making slits in the soil at right angles to the trench: this makes it easier to remove the soil cleanly.

Always put the blade of the spade into the soil vertically, rather than at an angle, to work the ground to the maximum spade depth.

A slightly twisting motion is used so that the soil is inverted as it is put into the preceding trench.

Do not bring subsoil up to the surface as this contains very little organic matter and nutrients.

Do not break up the soil finely. It is sufficient to turn it over roughly, as frost action will break up the clods during the winter.

Remove roots of perennial weeds such as dock, ground elder, bindweed, dandelion, couch grass and thistles as completely as possible with a fork, either before starting to dig or during the digging process. Remove weeds which have gone to seed and burn them; smaller weeds can be dug in.

Forking

Forking breaks up the top layer of soil by a digging action using a garden fork. In spring it may be all that is necessary to bring the autumn-dug soil into a workable condition.

During the growing season, ground often becomes compacted and dry where a crop is grown; it may be necessary to fork over the ground between clearing one crop and sowing or planting the next.

Seeds

Most vegetables are grown from seeds, and it always pays to use the best quality seeds available. Vegetable seeds sold in this country legally have to conform to minimum standards of viability (ability to germinate), cleanliness and purity, and normally can be relied upon to give good results. However, seeds are grown all over the world, and inevitably the seed harvest is better in some years than others and this is reflected in the quality. Seeds are also liable to deteriorate rapidly unless kept in cool dry conditions (see below): poor germination is often a result of bad storage conditions at home.

Seed merchants are only allowed to sell vegetable varieties which are on the approved National and EEC lists, which has meant the disappearance of a number of older cultivars. In a few cases they are still available under another name.

Choice of cultivar

The term 'cultivar' (abbreviated as cv), which has now replaced the term 'variety', denotes a plant raised and maintained in cultivation. The work of plant breeders all over the world has given the modern gardener a wide choice of cultivars. Many have outstanding characteristics, such as high yields, resistance to particular diseases and pests, early maturity, resistance to bolting, and compactness.

For the vegetable grower, one of the most satisfactory ways of buying seeds is through the mail-order seed catalogues, which frequently offer a wider choice than is normally available in shops, together with valuable information on cultivation.

The following are factors to consider in choosing a cultivar.

F_1 hybrids These are obtained by crossing two parent lines, each of which has been inbred for several generations. Because of this the progeny has exceptional vigour and uniformity. F_1 seed is more expensive than ordinary 'open pollinated' seed, but in many cases (especially in those of Brussels sprouts and cabbages) is worth the extra cost. It is not worth saving seeds from F_1 hybrids, as they will not produce the same characteristics in the next generation. (Open pollinated seed is seed produced from random pollination. Unlike F_1 hybrids, the resulting plants may be very varied.)

Disease resistance An increasing number of vegetable cultivars are being bred with varying degrees of resistance or tolerance to common diseases. Examples include lettuce (downy mildew), tomato (mosaic virus, leaf mould), parsnip (canker).

These cultivars are not always readily available to amateurs but it is worth looking in catalogues and considering any which are listed. The diseases themselves may eventually develop strains which overcome the resistance, so plant breeders have to be constantly producing new resistant cultivars.

Several vegetable diseases are seed borne, and seed is sometimes tested and sold as guaranteed free, or with only a very low percentage, of infected seed. For example lettuce seeds tested for lettuce mosaic virus can be declared as having less than one infected seed in 30,000, i.e. less than 0.003% infected.

Pest resistance At the moment there are few vegetable cultivars with resistance to pests apart from eelworm-resistant potatoes, but more are likely to be bred in future. The lettuce cultivars 'Avoncrisp' and 'Avondefiance' have considerable resistance to lettuce root aphid.

Seed treatments for disease control Seeds can be treated or dressed with a fungicide before packaging. In some cases seeds are treated against specific seed-borne diseases (for example, celery or celeriac seeds treated against celery leaf spot). In other cases seeds are treated with a fungicide for protection against general damping-off diseases, which affect seeds during slow germination in cold soils.

Chemically treated seeds should be always handled carefully, and hands should be washed after sowing. They should be used the year they are bought, as viability may be affected by the treatments. Organic gardeners can usually buy untreated seeds from specialist seed suppliers.

Seeds dressed with fungicide are recognized by their colour. Here treated (bottom) and untreated broad beans are shown.

Outstanding cultivar awards

The Royal Horticultural Society carries out trials of new and established cultivars and makes the Award of Garden Merit to those judged outstanding. In the USA the All America Awards Scheme awards Gold, Silver and Bronze medals. These awards are often noted in seed catalogues, enabling selection of good cultivars.

Types of seed

The most usual way of buying seeds is in a packet which contains single 'naked' seeds. In the case of beetroot the seed is, botanically, a fruit containing several seeds; these have to be thinned on germination. Seeds are also available in other forms.

Pelleted seeds Each seed is coated with a protective substance which disintegrates in the soil. Pelleted seeds look like tiny balls, and are easier to handle and to place precisely where required than ordinary seeds, so the need for thinning is reduced or even eliminated. However, germination problems are sometimes encountered. Pellets should be sown shallowly at a depth of about twice their diameter, in soil that is neither too wet nor too dry. The soil must remain moist until the seeds germinate. Gently firming the ground after sowing helps to retain soil moisture. Once these seeds have been exposed to the air they are likely to deteriorate quickly, as the material used for coating absorbs moisture from the air.

Seed tapes and 'sheets' Individual seeds are incorporated, usually several centimetres (a couple of inches) apart, into soluble tapes or sheets of Kleenex-like paper.

These are simply laid on the seedbed or in the seed tray, and watered and covered with soil as if sowing normal seeds. The seedlings, being already spaced out, do not need thinning.

Chitted seeds These are seeds which have started to germinate and are posted to customers in tiny sachets to prevent moisture loss. The technique is used mainly for seeds which are difficult for amateurs to germinate, perhaps because they are exceptionally small, or require high temperatures to germinate, such as cucumbers. The seeds are pricked out normally on arrival.

Primed seed Before being put into seed packets, this seed has been brought to the point of germination, and then dried. When sown it germinates exceptionally fast. The seeds must normally be used within a couple of months of purchase. The technique is currently being applied to seeds such as carrots and onions, where germination can be slow.

Seed quantities

Seed catalogues and packets often indicate the quantity of seeds in a packet, and the length of row, or number of plants, which can be raised from them.

Seed storage

Seeds deteriorate with age, progressively losing viability and vigour, so that germination falls off and poorer crops are obtained. Deterioration is fastest when seeds are kept in moist, warm conditions. (In general seed storage life is halved with each rise of 5 C (9 F) above 0 C (32 F) and with each increase in seed moisture content of 1% between 5% and 14%.) Seeds should always be stored in as cool and as dry a place as possible – never in the kitchen or a damp garden shed. It is best to store unopened seed packets in an airtight jar or tin, in which there is an open dish or bag of cobalt-chloride-treated silica gel (obtainable from chemists and used at 1 teaspoon per 30 g (1 oz) of seed) to absorb the moisture. The gel is blue when dry, turning pink when moist. It can be dried in an oven when moist and returned to the jar or tin for further use. Most seeds stored thus will continue to germinate well for three to four years. An exception is parsnip seed, which cannot be relied upon for more than two seasons.

Seeds packed in vacuum-sealed foil packs retain their viability for three to four years, until the packet is opened, when normal deterioration begins. They too can be stored in airtight conditions with the silica gel as described above.

Testing viability

Test seeds bought in a previous year before sowing outdoors, by putting a few seeds on moist blotting paper or paper towelling in a warm place in the dark. Provided they are kept moist and reasonably warm they should germinate within two to three weeks, the first sign being the emergence of the seedling root. It should be noted that peas and beans, as well as smaller seeds, swell when moistened, but this is a mechanical reaction and not necessarily an indication that they are viable.

Sowing

Depending on the crop, the season and the circumstances, garden vegetable seeds are sown in one of three ways.

Sowing systems
- *Direct or in situ sowing*: in the ground where they will be grown to maturity.

- *In a seedbed outdoors*: in relatively close rows, from which young plants will be lifted and transferred into their permanent positions.

- *Under protection (indoors)*: in a seed tray or other container, in a protected environment such as a cloche, cold frame, greenhouse, propagator, or on an indoor windowsill.

Direct sowing This is used where transplanting is unnecessary, for example with peas and beans, and where it is unlikely to succeed, as in the case of root crops such as beetroot, carrots, parsnips, turnips, radishes and lettuces in midsummer.

Seedbeds These are used as a means of saving space, mainly for vegetables with a long growing season. Brassicas (which includes cauliflowers, cabbages and Brussels sprouts) are commonly raised in seedbeds. The ground they will eventually occupy can be used for another crop until they are ready for transplanting. A close watch can be kept on seedlings in a seedbed.

Protected sowing This is a means of avoiding adverse weather conditions early in the year. It is used for half-hardy vegetables such as tomatoes, cucumbers, sweet peppers and French and runner beans, which cannot be planted out until risk of frost is past; for plants which benefit from a longer growing season, such as onions, leeks, celery and celeriac; and for other vegetables where earlier crops can be obtained by sowing indoors, such as lettuces.

Seed germination
Seed packets contain a known percentage of seeds which are capable of germination, but when they are sown not all will emerge as young plants. Several factors act on the seed or emerging embryo and affect its emergence.

First is the condition of the soil at sowing. The technique of preparing a seedbed is described in the next section, but it is important that the soil is damp enough for the seeds to take up moisture and start the germination process.

It is also important that the soil is within the right range of temperatures for germination of the particular crop. Germination and emergence are usually poorer at low temperatures. This generally means that it is a waste of seed to sow in spring when the soil is still cold.

Several vegetables, for example, cabbages, peas and broad beans, will germinate at soil temperatures of 5 C (41 F) or above, others such as leeks and onions need 7 C (44 F), but crops which originated in warmer climates, such as runner and French beans and cucumbers, need 13 C (55 F) as a minimum. There are also upper limits for some crops; butterhead lettuces, for example, will not germinate, or will germinate only slowly, when soil temperatures are above 25 C (77 F).

Depth of sowing also affects emergence. For the first few days after germination the seedlings are dependent on their own resources for food. If these are exhausted before the seedling reaches the light and can manufacture a new food supply, then the young plant will die. Small seeds, therefore, are sown nearer the soil surface than larger seeds.

Finally, as discussed earlier, the germination and emergence of seedlings can be damaged by applying too much nitrogenous fertilizer to the seedbed. (See Fertilizers, p 17).

SOWING OUTDOORS

Preparing the seedbed The term 'seedbed', rather confusingly, is used both for any piece of ground on which seeds will be sown *in situ*, and for an area set aside for raising plants for transplanting.

Before sowing seeds in the open, the soil needs to be firmed but not consolidated, and the surface to be broken down and raked into what is called a 'tilth', ie free of stones and lumps, with a crumbly texture. The degree to which the crumbs are broken down depends on the size of the seeds to be sown. The smaller the seeds, the finer the clods should be broken down, so that the seeds will be in close contact with the soil and moisture, so encouraging germination. For larger seeds, such as peas and beans, the soil can be left rather rougher; this will discourage the germination of weed seeds.

Breaking down a rough surface into a good tilth is not always easy. A soil that has been dug over roughly in the autumn may require only a little forking in spring, followed by raking to remove stones. But this varies with the nature of the soil. Much depends on knowing the soil and recognizing the precise moment to start working it. Soils with plenty of organic matter in them, that is, those with a good structure, are generally easiest to work.

Soil must never be cultivated when very wet or very dry. If soil sticks to the shoes when walking on it, it is too wet. Leave it a few days to dry out. Cloches or clear plastic can be put on the soil to help dry it out. It cannot be over-emphasized that little is gained by sowing in cold or wet soil.

If the soil is dry and dusty it will need watering before working. It is always better to water before rather than after sowing, as this helps to avoid 'capping'. This phenomenon of the surface crust drying and setting occurs on some types of silty soils, and may prevent seedlings pushing their way through.

Some soils dry out very rapidly in spring, before it is time to sow. A light mulch of straw or similar material laid on the soil after preparing the seedbed conserves the moisture and creates a surface which can be easily raked into a good tilth just before sowing. The mulch is first raked to one side.

The traditional recommendation to tread the seedbed before the final raking is no longer generally recommended, as it tends to compact the soil. However it may be necessary on the lightest of soils, on very loose soils or if the soil surface has become very uneven. *Never* tread wet soil.

For a 'stale seedbed', see Pests and Diseases, p 56.

Seedbed for raising plants

A seedbed from which plants will be transplanted must be in an open position, not in an out-of-the-way and perhaps shaded corner where seedlings may become drawn. Clean the ground as thoroughly as possible of annual and perennial weeds. The rows in a seedbed can be relatively close together, say 20 cm (8 in) apart for brassicas, but sowing *in* the rows must be as thin as when sowing direct in drills, so seedlings are at least 4 cm (1½ in) apart, otherwise plant roots become overcrowded and entangled, and are damaged when lifted.

Sowing in a drill

This is the commonest method of sowing outdoors. Prepare the seedbed as above, then mark the position of the row with a line, making a drill along the line, using the point of a trowel or the corner of a draw hoe. Pressing the narrow edge of a plank into the ground is a good way to make an even drill. A drill can also be drawn along the edge of a plank. The depth of the drill depends on the size of the seed, but it is important to keep the depth uniform, otherwise germination will be uneven, with seeds sown more deeply emerging more slowly.

Very large seeds like beans need to be 4–5 cm (1½–2 in) deep, peas and sweet corn 2.5–4 cm (1–1½ in) deep, brassicas 2–2.5 cm (¾–1 in) deep, and small seeds like carrots, leeks, lettuces and

Make a seed drill using a draw hoe.

Space seed using a measuring stick.

onions 13–20 mm (½–¾ in) deep. If the soil is dry, water the drill before sowing.

Seeds are sown along the drill *as thinly as possible*, to reduce the need for thinning. If sown too thickly, the overcrowded seedlings will be poor specimens, with little chance of producing a quality crop. With practice, small seeds from a pinch held between thumb and forefinger can be dropped singly into the drill. Otherwise tap them from the packet or use a patented seed dispenser. Small seeds can be sown more evenly if they are mixed with sand. Pelleted seeds (see p 29) can be easily sown by hand at the spacing required.

Seeds can be either spaced evenly along the row or 'station sown' in groups of three to four seeds at intervals a few centimetres (a couple of inches) apart. For example, where seeds will eventually be thinned to 25 cm (10 in) apart, they can be sown initially in groups 12 cm (4¾ in) apart.

Finally, press the seed gently into the soil with the index finger or the palm of the hand before covering it with soil, with a rake, hand trowel or by hand. If birds are a problem, put one or two strands of strong black cotton, attached to sticks, along the length of the drills, about 5 cm (2 in) above soil level. This will protect the emerging seedlings from birds.

Intersowing in a drill

To make good use of space, two different crops can be sown in one drill, for example slow growing parsnips between 'station sown' fast growing radishes or small cultivars of lettuce. The radishes or lettuces will emerge earlier, indicating where the rows are (which makes early hoeing easier); they will mature long before their space is needed by the parsnips.

Wide drills

A wide drill is flat-bottomed, rather than V-shaped, and anything from about 8–15 cm (3¼–6 in) wide. It is usually made with a draw hoe or onion hoe. Wide drills are used either for sowing single large seeds, such as peas, well spaced apart, or for closely spaced, virtually 'broadcast' seed of vegetables suitable for cut-and-come-again seedling crops (see below). In this case, parallel drills are made as close together as possible. The advantage over broadcast sowing is that weeding is easier, and in dry weather, it is easier to water the individual drills before sowing.

Sowing large seeds

Very large seeds such as pumpkins, marrows, sweet corn, and beans can be sown by making a small hole with a dibber. Place the seed carefully in the hole, making sure it has reached the bottom, and cover with soil. Jam jars can be put over the seed to keep the soil moist and so encourage germination. Sow a few 'spares' for transplanting into any gaps caused by germination failures, or sow several seeds per station, thinning to one per site after germination.

Broadcasting

Seed is scattered on the surface of a moist, well-prepared seedbed as thinly and evenly as possible. The seed is raked into the soil first in one direction, then at right angles to the first raking, or is covered by riddling soil over the seed.

Broadcasting makes good use of the cropping area, but because of the uneven distribution of the plants broadcast patches are difficult to weed. Make sure the ground is clean before sowing; if there is time, prepare the seedbed, allow the first flush of weeds to germinate and hoe them off before sowing.

Broadcasting is used for growing patches of crops such as early carrots, mustard and cress, radish, turnip tops, and green manures. It is also recommended for cut-and-come-again seedling crops.

Covering seeds after sowing

One of the most common causes of seeds failing to germinate is soil drying out. This can be prevented by covering the seedbed or drills with newspaper, plastic film or even light straw until the seed has germinated. The plastic can be anchored by burying the edge in the soil. Any covering, except perforated plastic or spun fibre films, (see Protected cropping, p 49), *must* be removed as soon as any seedlings are visible, or they become drawn. As mentioned earlier, watering the soil after sowing is a bad practice as the fine top layer may 'cap', making it difficult for seedlings to emerge.

Sowing in adverse conditions

Sowing in cold and wet conditions is inadvisable, but where it is unavoidable, work from a wooden board placed on the ground, to avoid compacting the soil. A drill can be opened up and covered with cloches for a few days, to warm and dry out the soil; alternatively, a little sowing or potting compost, or material such as Perlite, can be put in the bottom of the drill before sowing. This will absorb moisture from the soil and help the seed to germinate.

Sowing in dry conditions

This situation is most likely to occur with late spring or summer sowings. Take out the drill and water the bottom of the drill *only*, not the surrounding soil, with a small-spouted can. Then sow the seed and cover it with *dry* soil. The dry soil acts as a mulch, so preventing evaporation, and enabling the seed to germinate.

Pre-germinated seed

Large seeds such as French or runner beans and peas can be pre-germinated before sowing to increase the chances of success in adverse soil or weather conditions. Use the method suggested for testing seed viability (see p 29), sowing seeds carefully when the emerging root is no more than 6 mm (¼ in) long.

Fluid sowing

Seeds of several vegetables (for example, beetroot, carrots and parsnips) need a higher temperature for germination than for the subsequent growth of seedlings. In a cold spring the soil will be slow to warm up and seeds sown into a cold soil will not germinate. A technique called fluid sowing overcomes this. Seeds are germinated indoors in favourable conditions, and the very small seedlings, which can

Fluid sowing

1   Wash the germinating seeds off the paper into a sieve.

2   Mix seeds carefully with the carrier gel.

3   Cut off the corner of the bag before sowing.

4   Squeeze the seed/gel mixture along the drill.

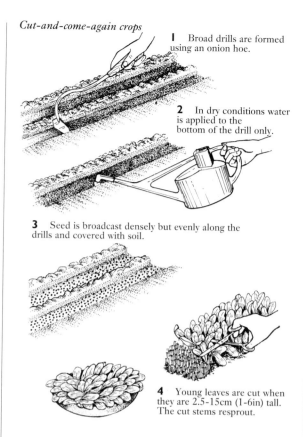

Cut-and-come-again crops

1 Broad drills are formed using an onion hoe.

2 In dry conditions water is applied to the bottom of the drill only.

3 Seed is broadcast densely but evenly along the drills and covered with soil.

4 Young leaves are cut when they are 2.5-15cm (1-6in) tall. The cut stems resprout.

develop in slightly cooler soil conditions than the seeds, are then sown outside.

Seeds are germinated a few days before sowing outdoors, the interval depending on the crop. Lettuces, for instance, will germinate in a day at room temperature, but celery may take 10 days to reach 50% germination. The seeds are sown on damp absorbent paper and kept at about 21 C (70 F). The seedlings are ready for sowing when the young roots are no longer than 5 mm ($\frac{3}{16}$ in). These young plants are mixed with a gel which acts as a carrier. The gel with the seedlings is put into a flexible container, such as a plastic bag or bottle, and expelled along the seed drill. The drill and the seedlings are covered in as with conventional sowing.

As well as improving the emergence of seedlings, fluid sowing makes it easier to spread out the seeds in the drills, especially when sowing small seeds. With practice there is no need for thinning later. For detailed information see Further reading, p 158.

Gel kits
Some proprietary kits are available, in which seeds are germinated in a gel. The seeds germinate rapidly, and can be then transplanted directly into the soil.

The cut-and-come-again technique
This is a highly productive method of growing mainly salad crops, utilizing the fact that many young leafy plants will resprout several times, if cut *above* the tiny seed leaves, leaving about 2.5 cm (1 in) of stem. Cut-and-come-again crops are grown fairly densely (sown at a rate of approximately 12 g / sq m (½ oz / sq yd), and are usually left unthinned; leaves are cut with scissors or a knife at any stage between a height of about 2.5 and 15 cm (1-6 in), depending on the plant. The seedlings and young leaves are highly nutritious, very tasty and ready for use within a few weeks of sowing. Spinach, cress, endive, oriental greens, leaf chicory, and some types of lettuce are among many vegetables which can be grown this way. (See also Oriental greens, p 93 and Salad plants, p 150.)

Thinning
Thinning is the process of removing superfluous seedlings, so that plants can develop to their optimum size without competition. The final distance to which plants are thinned depends on the crop, and the size at which it is being harvested. Thinning disturbs the roots of neighbouring plants and can attract pests, so it should be minimized by sowing thinly or station sowing.

Thinning can be carried out as soon as the seedlings are large enough to handle; it should always be done before they show signs of becoming lanky. Thin in stages, leaving enough space for each seedling to stand just clear of its neighbour. To minimize root disturbance, thin when the ground is moist, watering the soil beforehand. A good method of thinning is to nip off the surplus seedlings just above ground level, leaving the roots intact. This can be done even when the soil is dry. Firm the soil around remaining plants and bury any thinnings in the compost heap.

SOWING INDOORS

As mentioned above, sowing 'indoors' implies sowing in some kind of container which is placed anywhere under cover, from an indoor windowsill to a garden frame, for the seeds to germinate and develop.

By sowing in protected conditions higher rates of germination can be achieved than by outdoor sowings. Moreover, plants can be given a head start by indoor sowing when conditions outside are still unsuitable for sowing.

There are basically two methods of sowing indoors: sowing into one container and subsequently 'pricking out' into another, or sowing directly in modules.

For both these methods germination can be accelerated by sowing in a heated propagator. Plants will also need to be hardened off before planting outdoors.

Sowing and potting composts

Sowing and potting composts are the growing media used for plant raising. This is another case of confusing gardening terms, as the term 'compost' is also used for the rotting end product of a garden compost heap. This however, is too rich to be used in concentrated form in plant raising.

Proprietary sowing and potting composts are widely used today. One of their great merits is that they are sterile, so largely eliminating the risk of seedlings being infected with damping off diseases. (See Pests and diseases chart, p 63.)

Hitherto the proprietary composts have been based on either peat or soil. The peat-based composts have the advantage of being lighter in weight, but the drawback of being much more liable to dry out, and difficult to re-wet once dry. With the current concern about exhausting the world's supply of natural peat, alternative products are being developed, and these should be used where possible. Alternatively, use the soil-based composts, though most of these are made up according to the established John Innes formula and do contain some peat. In practice, many of the proprietary composts on the market are formulated so as to be dual-purpose, and can be used for both sowing and potting.

The standard potting composts all contain artificial fertilizers and are therefore unsuitable for organic gardening. A few products are available for organic gardeners: among the best are the worm composts.

Gardeners can make up their own composts, though results are rarely as consistent or as good as those obtained with proprietary composts. For a general purpose compost suitable *only for the early stages* of plant growth, mix two parts of sand with one part of sieved leafmould and one part of sieved loam. If the seedlings do not appear to be growing healthily, they can be fed with dilute general purpose fertilizer or dilute liquid seaweed until planted out.

The composts used for making soil blocks (see Sowing in modules, below) incorporate an additive which makes them adhesive and easier to mould into a compact shape. Currently, a blocking compost made from worm compost is available which is suitable for organic gardeners.

Propagators

The majority of vegetable seeds germinate fastest at temperatures of 13–16 C (55–60 F), the temperature of the soil being more important than air temperature. To obtain this requisite 'bottom heat', early indoor sowings are often made in small, electrically heated propagators. Many types are available, the cheapest being plug-in units in which a light bulb or electric cables supply heat beneath the seed tray. They are often covered with a dome to create a moist atmosphere. Once seeds have germinated, they can be moved from the propagator to a lower temperature to continue growing.

Sowing and pricking out method

This is the traditional method of raising plants. Seeds are sown into a small seed tray, pot or pan, in a light porous sowing compost, and after germination are pricked out or transplanted into a larger container in a coarser, richer potting compost, containing plant nutrients in some form. They are normally grown in this until ready for planting outdoors, though in some cases they may need to be potted on individually into a larger pot.

Sowing Fill the seed tray or pot loosely with well moistened compost, levelling off the loose compost with a small piece of wood. Then firm and level the

Sowing indoors

I   Level moist compost in the tray with a piece of wood.

2   Use a presser board to firm the surface.

3   Sow seeds thinly and evenly over the compost surface.

4   Cover seeds with a thin layer of compost by sieving.

remaining compost by pressing it with a small board or any even surface, to give a 13 mm (½ in) space at the top of the container. Sow seeds thinly on the surface, and cover by sieving a little dry compost over them. Finally press the surface level again.

If the compost was well watered initially, no further watering will be necessary. However, if the surface remains dry, stand the container in a basin of water so that it will soak up moisture, taking care not to flood the seed tray or pot and dislodge the seeds. Where bottom heat is required, put the container into a propagator. The propagator does not need to be in bright light at this stage.

To maintain a moist atmosphere and encourage germination, cover the container with a sheet of glass or plastic film. Some seed trays and propagators have a plastic dome incorporated which serves the same purpose. Remove the cover for about half an hour every day for ventilation, wiping away any condensation, and remove it altogether as soon as the seeds have germinated.

Once seeds have germinated they must be moved into a good light, though they will need to be shaded from very bright sunlight in the early stages. Do not allow the compost to dry out at any stage. Standing seed trays on spongy capillary matting is an excellent way of ensuring moisture retention.

Pricking out As soon as the seedlings become crowded in their original container they must be pricked out individually into a bigger container, such as a standard 35 × 21 × 5cm (14 × 8½ × 2 in) tray, to allow each seedling space to develop.

Fill the larger container with moist potting com-

Pricking out

1 Lift each seedling carefully by its leaves to avoid damaging the root hairs.

2 Seedlings are spaced out equidistantly in the seed tray, 2.5-5cm (1-2in) apart.

post. Water the seedlings, then using a small dibber, a kitchen fork, a miniature trowel, or even a strong plant label, lift small groups of seedlings and separate them carefully holding them by their leaves so that the delicate root hairs are not damaged. Make a small hole in the compost just large enough for the roots, and press the seedling gently but firmly into the hole so that the lowest leaves are just above soil level. Spacing varies according to the seedlings, but is normally between 2.5–5 cm (1–2 in) apart.

In most cases the seedlings remain in these containers until they are planted out.

To bypass the pricking out stage, seeds can be sown direct into potting compost in a large container, spaced several centimetres (an inch or so) apart. The disadvantage is that this takes up far more space at the earliest stage where a propagator is being used.

Sowing in modules

In this more modern method of plant raising, adapted from commercial horticultural practice, seeds are sown directly into some kind of cell or small pot, in which they develop until planted out. This not only eliminates the need to prick out, but means that each seedling, from the start, grows without any competition, so developing into a high quality plant with a vigorous, compact root system. There is virtually no root disturbance when it is planted out, so the plants 'get away' very rapidly. Another advantage is that plants will not suffer unduly if planting out has to be delayed.

The use of modules is especially recommended where amateur gardeners require only a limited number of plants. The main drawback is that modules generally use more compost and take up a lot of space in a heated propagator. For this reason, seed is sometimes sown in a seed tray and pricked out into a module after germination.

There are many types of module.
Any small flower pot Whether of clay, plastic, fibre, or polythene, a pot can be filled with potting compost and used as a 'module'. Depending on what is being grown, it does not need to be more than about 4 cm (1½ in) diameter and the same depth.

Standard seed trays Seed trays can be converted into modules with the insertion of interlocking plastic dividers.

Moulded plastic and polystyrene cellular trays These are popular types of module. These are preformed units with holes or cells which are filled with compost. They usually stand on some kind of base tray. When ready the young plants are pushed out from below for planting.

Sowing modules

Cellular polystyrene tray

Moulded plastic tray

Range of small pots and containers

Standard seed tray with interlocking dividers

Multi-celled professional growers' plastic tray

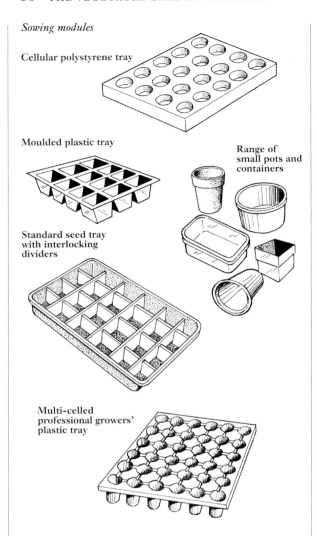

Soil blocks These are made by compressing special blocking compost into small cubes with a blocking tool. The tool makes a small indentation in the top of the block into which the seed is sown. Block sizes vary from tiny 'miniblocks' about 13 mm (½ in) square, to blocks 5 cm (2 in) diameter. Provided good compost is used, excellent seedlings can be raised even in the tiny blocks. The blocks can be packed closely in a standard seed tray to germinate. The young plants are generally ready for planting when roots have penetrated the block. The blocks must be kept moist at all stages and should be watered well when planted out.

Sowing In most cases (but see multi-sowing below), the whole point of a module is to have one plant growing in each cell or unit. To achieve this, either sow one seed per module, or if you are uncertain of the germination, sow several seeds, nipping out the surplus seedlings to leave the strongest once they have germinated.

Seeds too small to be handled easily can be pushed carefully off a piece of board, paper, or glass, or lifted individually on the point of a small damp watercolour paint brush. A seed will adhere to the brush, but drops off on contact with the soil. Cover the seed with a little soil or compost pushed over it from the edges of the block.

Multi-sowing This again is a technique borrowed from commercial horticulture. Instead of one seed, several seeds are sown in each cell, which is eventually planted out as one unit at about twice the normal spacing. Once planted, each plant develops normally, in spite of its crowded start. The technique saves compost, and planting and handling time. It is only suitable for certain vegetables, such as *round* types of early carrot (about four seeds per cell), spring onions or chives (about 10 seeds per cell), and beetroot, bulb onions and leeks (four to five seeds per cell).

Hardening off

Whatever system is used for raising plants indoors, before planting out they must be 'hardened off' or acclimatized, over a 10 to 14 day period. If the plants are in frames or under cloches, ventilate or remove the frames or cloches for increasingly longer periods each day. If in a greenhouse, move plants into frames or cloches as an intermediate stage, or move them outdoors, first for a few hours a day, then for longer periods.

A novel method of hardening off, which avoids moving seedlings outside before planting, has been developed by the Japanese. Seedlings are brushed for up to a minute a day, or in some cases twice a day in each direction, over the normal hardening off period. The brushing is done either with a piece of paper or cardboard, or with a special brush.

When planting, hold the plant in place with one hand while soil is filled in around the roots.

Planting

When to plant is determined by soil and weather conditions, and the state of the plant itself. Planting represents a check to the plant, and everything should be done to minimize the check so that the plants become established rapidly. For this reason, planting in wet and/or cold soil and in adverse weather conditions is never advisable. Half-hardy plants cannot be planted outside until the risk of hard frost is over, which varies from early May in the south of England to early or mid June in cold parts of the British Isles.

Within reason, the younger a plant is transplanted the better. Lettuces can be planted at the four to six leaf stage; brassicas when they are about 10 cm (4 in) high. Transplanting root crops is not very satisfactory except when they are very small. This does not apply to plants raised in modules which, provided they have not become starved, can be planted successfully at almost any stage.

Planting

The ground is prepared in advance by forking (except when planting brassicas), removing weeds, and raking over the surface. A fine tilth is unnecessary and undesirable as it encourages weed-seed germination, but a relatively level surface makes planting easier. Ideally the soil should be moist. It is best to plant in the evening or when conditions are overcast, so that the plant is not put immediately into conditions that may lead to wilting.

Whether the plants are in a seedbed, pots, boxes or modules, they must be watered well several hours before planting. This has been shown to be far more important than watering after they are planted – although in very dry conditions both may be necessary.

Where transplanting from a seedbed, lift individual plants carefully using a trowel, holding them by the leaves or stems rather than the roots, as the root hairs are easily damaged. Plants raised in cells are pushed out, and plants in pots are loosened by knocking the pot rim against a hard suface. Using a trowel, make a hole in the soil large enough to accommodate the roots easily. Hold the plant in place with one hand, and fill the soil in around the roots. Finally firm the soil around the stem, tugging a leaf to make sure the plant is not loose. Block-raised plants are planted whole with no root disturbance.

Where the ground is dry, water around the base of the plant after planting. Mulching (see p 44) at the same time will help to conserve moisture. In very hot weather shade the plants from strong sun for the first few days until they become established, using cones of newspaper.

For plants that will require staking eventually, such as runner beans, it is best to put in the stake just before planting or sowing.

Heeling in

When plants have been bought in, but weather conditions make immediate planting impossible, you can heel them in for up to a week as an emergency measure to prevent the roots from drying out. Make a small V-shaped slit a number of centimetres (a few inches) deep in the soil. Disentangle the plants and lay them singly but close together in the slit, the roots at the bottom, and the stems against one side of the V. The roots and lower parts of the stem are then covered with moist soil, so that all the roots are in contact with the soil.

Occasionally it is necessary to lift the last of a crop, of parsnips or leeks, for example, at the end of their season in March or April when the ground is needed for the next crop. The plants can be heeled in similarly until required for use. They will keep in a reasonable condition for several weeks.

Spacing

As discussed in The bed system (p 21), the traditional method of growing vegetables in rows with relatively wide spaces between the rows is now being challenged by the concept of growing plants at equidistant spacing in narrow beds.

The argument against rows is that *within* each row individual plants compete for nutrients, water and light, while *between* rows, the weeds, having no competition, flourish. In practice, plants take their requirements for food and water from only a relatively small circular area around them. So the most productive means of using ground is to space plants an equal distance apart, so that when mature the leaves just touch, the circles of ground allotted to each just overlapping. To convert conventional row spacing to equidistant spacing, simply take an average of the inter-plant and inter-row spacing: for example, plants spaced 15 cm (6 in) apart in rows 45 cm (18 in) apart, can be grown at an equidistant spacing of 30 cm (12 in) apart.

Where planting in rows is still practised, closer plantings than previously are being adopted. Whatever system is used, it is important to allow each individual plant enough space in each direction to grow to its optimum size. Planting in adjacent rows should always be staggered.

Research has also been done on the relationship between spacing and vegetable size, so that in many cases spacing can now be used as a tool to determine the size of the vegetable you want. To take an example: onions can be sown 13 mm (½ in) apart in 30 cm (12 in) rows to get pickling onions, 2.5 × 10 cm (1 × 4 in) apart for spring onions, and 4 cm (1½in) apart in 30 cm (12 in) rows to obtain large cooking onions. With summer cabbage the highest yields of small heads are obtained by planting at 35 × 35 cm (14 × 14 in); larger cabbages are produced by planting at 45 × 45 cm (18 × 18 in). So where a family requires only moderate-sized summer cabbages the former spacing is advisable, but where extra large cabbages are required, a more generous spacing can be adopted. With cabbages this would give slightly earlier yields – though earliness and sparser planting do not necessarily go hand in hand. Further examples will be mentioned where appropriate.

Intercropping

Just as two crops can sometimes be sown within a row to save space, different crops can be intercropped, that is, one crop can be sown or planted between rows of another. (See Planning for continuity, p 25.)

Wherever intercropping is practised, care must be taken to allow enough space, light and moisture for each crop to develop. It is important to remember that competition from weeds or another crop can affect yields. There must also be enough room for access for cultivation and picking. For these reasons it may be advisable to have rows a little further apart than usual where intercropping is planned. It is best to avoid intercropping naturally sprawling vegetables such as potatoes, which tend to engulf smaller plants in their vicinity. But marrows and dwarf beans, for example, can be grown successfully beneath sweet corn.

Intercropping lettuce with brassicas – the lettuce will be harvested leaving brassicas to mature.

Containers

Where space is restricted to balconies, patios or very small gardens, people are often keen to grow a few vegetables in containers, though on the whole it is more difficult to grow vegetables than flowers in containers. Container growing is also one of the options for tomatoes. Greenhouse soil can become 'tomato sick' after growing tomatoes for many years, so if you grow tomatoes in a container instead you can avoid replacing or sterlizing the greenhouse soil.

All sorts of things can be used as containers, from large plant pots and window-boxes to wooden tubs and compost-filled polythene sacks or 'growing bags'. Whatever is used must be as large as possible, must have some means of drainage, be strong enough to withstand the weight of the soil and the crop, and be stable. A tall crop can make a container very top heavy and liable to topple over. If containers are mounted on castors they can be moved around easily.

Where vegetables are concerned, the volume of the container is very important: the more soil it holds the better. This is primarily to minimize the risk of the soil drying out, but also to allow room for the roots to develop. The minimum size varies with the crop being grown. Undemanding Mediterranean herbs like thyme and marjoram can be grown in pots 10–13 cm (4–5 in) in width and depth. Small vegetables, such as lettuces and radishes can be grown in containers 15 cm (6 in) wide and deep. Larger vegetables need containers at least 20–25 cm (8–10 in) wide and deep. The standard growing bag is about 90 cm (3 ft) long, 15 cm (6 in) deep, and 30 cm (12 in) wide.

Soil in containers

Most ordinary garden soil is unsuitable for containers, as it is liable to become very compacted with frequent watering. It is common practice to use some kind of potting compost instead. (See Sowing indoors, p 33.) Composts based on peat or peat substitutes have the merit of being light in weight (a factor to consider in roof and balcony gardens), and well draining. However, nutrients are rapidly leached out so supplementary feeding is soon necessary. (See Fertilizers, p 17.)

The soil-based composts are heavier, hold moisture and therefore nutrients better, but are less well drained so the soil may become stagnant.

Container soil is always improved by working a little *well rotted* organic matter into it – such as manure, garden compost, seaweed or spent mushroom compost. It will also benefit from the presence

A crop of broad beans grown in large plastic pots with plenty of room allowed for root development.

of earthworms, so try and introduce them, though if the soil becomes too hot the worms will move out to cooler quarters. Where possible, the soil should be renewed every year.

Vegetables in containers need supplementary feeding, preferably using dilute liquid feeds once or twice a week (for details see under individual crop). Concentrated and strong feeds should be avoided. To help maintain soil fertility the soil can be top dressed with a few centimetres (an inch or so) of well rotted manure or compost once or twice during the growing season.

Watering and drainage

In practice, one of the problems in growing vegetables in containers is striking a happy medium between good drainage and adequate water supply. Roots soon die in a waterlogged container. For this reason, one or more drainage holes should be made in the bottom of the container. They should be at least 13 mm (½ in) diameter and in large containers, 7.5 cm (3 in) apart. Cover the drainage holes with a layer of broken crocks. Drainage is less of a problem with moisture absorbing peat-based composts and most peat substitutes. This is why drainage holes are unnecessary in most proprietary growing bags.

All containers dry out rapidly, and at the height of summer may need watering twice a day. The following are some measures which can be taken to cut down on water loss.

Site the containers carefully, avoiding windy situations which will desiccate the soil. Don't put them too close to walls, which shield containers from natural rainfall. Line them with heavy duty polythene, with a few drainage holes cut in the bottom, to help conserve moisture. The surface can be mulched with up to 5 cm (2 in) of gravel or stones to cut down evaporation. Where possible, stand containers in shallow trays filled with gravel or moisture absorbing granules. Where growing bags are used, just cut small squares in the film for planting, rather than exposing the whole surface. This lessens evaporation.

Utilizing containers

As container space is limited, exploit it to the full. Almost any vegetable *can* be grown in a container if the right conditions are created, but on the whole it is best to avoid large and deep rooted vegetables and those with long growing seasons. Pumpkins, rhubarb, the slower growing brassicas such as Brussels sprouts, purple sprouting broccoli and cauliflower are not really suited to container growing. Most of the warmth-loving crops such as French beans, tomatoes, aubergines, peppers and courgettes do well in containers, as do fast maturing vegetables such as spinach, Swiss chard, spring onions, radishes, beetroot, carrots, turnips, mizuna greens, lettuces and other salad plants. The highest returns are probably obtained by growing cut-and-come-again seedling crops of salad or oriental brassicas. (See Salads, p 150 and Oriental greens, p 93.)

Herbs are particularly suited to containers as many have decorative as well as culinary properties. The mints, parsley, ordinary and Chinese chives need reasonably fertile conditions to grow well, but the following are among the less fussy herbs: thyme, coriander, dill, basil, marjoram, summer and winter savory, rosemary, and sage. On the whole, they tolerate dry conditions and poor soil and need little attention.

To maximise the cropping potential of a container, it pays to raise the main crop plants in modules. Not only will they be good quality, but the container can be used for a quick crop of direct sown radishes or salad seedlings, for example, until the plants are large enough to plant out.

(For more information on container growing see Further reading, p 158.)

Water and watering

Vegetables grow well only when they have a sufficient supply of water, which is taken in through their roots and evaporated from their leaves. This constant uptake of water keeps the stomata on the leaves open and the plant turgid, enabling respiration, photosynthesis, and the absorption and use of nutrients to take place at maximum efficiency. Growth is reduced if for any reason there is a shortage of water.

The soil is the plant's reservoir of water. When, after free drainage has taken place, the soil is holding as much water as it can, it is said to be at *field capacity*. When there is so little water in the soil that roots can no longer extract it and plants wilt, it is at *permanent wilting point*. Between these extremes water in the soil is *available* to plants.

Soils vary tremendously in the amount of available water they can hold, depending on their texture and structure. The better the structure, the more water it can hold and the longer it can sustain plants without recourse being made to supplementary watering. Soils with the largest particles – the coarse-textured soils such as light sandy soils – have the poorest water holding capacity; those with a good proportion of all particle sizes – the medium-textured soils, such as silty loams – are the best for retaining available water.

Water is mainly lost from the upper layers of the soil, through evaporation from both the soil surface and plant leaves. Sunshine, temperature, wind, relative humidity and the amount of moisture in the soil surface all affect the rate of evaporation. Evaporation is greatest from a moist surface in dry sunny windy weather. Once the top 3 cm or so (1 in or so) of soil have dried out evaporation is very much reduced – a fact which has important implications for water conservation in the soil.

Another fundamental fact is that the soil becomes wet layer by layer. Until the top layer is saturated, the soil beneath remains dry. Water will only reach a point say 15 cm (6in) down when all the soil above is saturated. So watering lightly on the surface is quite ineffective; watering has to be thorough if water is to reach the lower parts of the root zone.

Measures for reducing watering

It is a waste of time and resources to over water. By taking the various measures below to conserve the water in the soil, the need to water can be minimized.

Improving the soil structure Working well-rotted bulky organic matter such as farmyard manure or compost into the soil regularly, mixed thoroughly over the whole depth of rooting, increases the water-holding capacity of most soils.

Mulching This prevents evaporation from the soil. It is best done after watering or after rain. (See Mulching, p 44.)

Deep digging This encourages roots to grow to greater depths, so drawing water from deeper reserves.

Shallow cultivation In dry weather cultivation should be restricted to surface hoeing, carried out *only* when necessary to remove weeds. Deeper cultivation brings moist soil to the surface, from which water is lost by evaporation.

Weeding Established weeds compete for water and contribute to water loss from the soil through transpiration. Aim to remove them as seedlings.

Sparse planting Wider spacing enables each plant to draw water from a larger volume of soil: it can be adopted where space is unlimited – especially on light soils.

Shelter Windbreaks help to cut down water losses from evaporation in windy conditions. Living windbreaks such as hedges, however, compete for water in the soil.

When to water

In a normal year, winter rains bring the soil to field capacity at the start of the vegetable sowing season. Water is lost throughout the summer by evaporation, unless natural rainfall replenishes the supply. In most summers *adequate* yields can be obtained without extra watering. However, for *optimum* yields the plants need ample water (and nutrients) applied at the right time, so supplementary watering is necessary.

In general, watering encourages leaf growth; so it is most directly beneficial for plants with edible foliage such as brassicas, lettuces and spinach.

Too much water may in some cases be counterproductive. It can increase plant growth without increasing the edible part; with root crops, for example, excess water may encourage lush leaf growth without a corresponding response from the roots. Excess water also discourages roots from penetrating the soil, making plants more susceptible to drought; it may leach nitrogenous fertilizers away from the root zone; and it may reduce flavour. Tomatoes and carrots grown with copious supplies of water seem to have less flavour than those grown on a more frugal water regime.

With root crops, such as carrots and parsnips, watering after a dry spell can cause the roots to swell so rapidly that they split. Watering bulb onions in the later stages of growth can delay ripening.

However, if the soil becomes dry and root growth is restricted, watering is beneficial and necessary. But it is important to understand the effect of watering at different stages of development on different parts of the plant.

Many plants go through moisture-sensitive periods in their development when the supply of water is critical. Examples are peas when flowers and pods are forming, and maincrop potatoes when tubers are at the marble size. Watering at these sensitive stages increases yields; when water is scarce, confine watering to these critical periods.

The art of watering effectively, especially where water, or time to water, is scarce, is embodied in three principles: limiting amounts, limiting frequency, and concentrating on moisture-sensitive and other critical periods.

Limiting amounts and frequency A few heavy waterings give the best returns on time and effort. In hot weather it is generally not worth giving less than 11 litres / sq m (2 gal / sq yd) at any one time. Directing water at the base of the plant, and leaving the surrounding area dry, is the most economical way of watering. Where this 'point watering' is adopted, however, watering needs to be more frequent than when the whole area is watered. Frequency and quantity need to be varied according to the soil. Light soils need to be watered more frequently than heavy, moisture-retentive soils, but with smaller quantities of water at each watering.

Although heavy watering is recommended, big *droplets*, applied overhead, can damage the soil surface and seedlings. The gentler the watering, and the smaller the drops of water, the better.

Critical periods

Establishing seeds and seedlings Seeds will not germinate nor will seedlings become established if there is insufficient water in the soil. Where the ground is very dry in spring, water the seedbed a couple of days in advance of sowing. This gives time for the surface to dry out sufficiently to be raked to a tilth before sowing. An alternative is to water individual drills at the rate of about 1 litre to 1.3 m (1 gal to 20 ft). Where seedlings must be watered, use a light rose with the spray directed upwards, so that a shower of small droplets is produced.

Transplanting If the soil is not moist at planting, water each transplant, confining the water to a circle about 15 cm (6 in) diameter around the plant stem. As roots tend to be damaged by transplanting, this is one case where watering little but often is the rule until the plants become established. In dry weather daily watering with 140 ml (¼ pt) to each plant is recommended.

Leafy crops For most leafy crops (brassicas, lettuces, spinach, celery), frequent watering results in heavy yields and succulent crops. In the dry months of summer they will benefit from 11–16 litres / sq m (2–3 gal / sq yd) per week. Where this is impossible, confine watering to a heavy application of about 22 litres / sq m (4 gal / sq yd) from 10 to 20 days before maturity. Brussels sprouts are an exception: they are generally so widely spaced that no extra watering is normally required.

'Fruiting' vegetables The critical periods with vegetables where the seeds and fruits are eaten – tomatoes, cucumbers, marrows, sweet corn, peas and beans – are at flowering time and when fruits are setting and swelling. Water generously at these stages, giving up to 22 litres / sq m (4 gal / sq yd) per week. Watering in the period after establishment and

Perforated plastic tubing laid out between crops.

Oscillating-type sprinkler in use on brick raised beds.

Rotary sprinklers can give uneven distribution of water.

before flowering is only necessary if the plants show signs of wilting. Excess watering during this period induces too much leaf growth.

Root crops With most root crops such as carrots, beetroot, radishes, parsnips, the aim is to apply enough water to maintain steady growth without encouraging lush foliage. In the early stages 5 litres / m (1 gal / yd) of row is sufficient in dry weather; but when the storage roots are actively growing, 16–22 litres / sq m (3–4 gal / sq yd) every fortnight may be necessary. At no stage should the soil be allowed to dry out. (For potato watering, see p 135.)

Watering equipment

For watering in small gardens a watering can is quite adequate, with a fine rose for watering small plants.

For larger gardens there are various types of automatic sprinklers on the market, which can be connected to the mains supply with a garden hose. These wet fairly large areas of ground but need to be moved frequently. Distribution of water is sometimes uneven, particularly with rotary sprinklers which water a circular area, resulting in overlapping and unwatered areas. Regulating meters can be attached to the tap, so the water supply is automatically cut off when sufficient water has been applied.

There are various automatic watering systems in which types of perforated plastic tubing or permeable rubberized hose are laid on the ground between or among plants. When connected to a tap or hose pipe, water trickles or seeps through the tiny holes or the walls of permeable hose, gently watering the plants, usually in a strip about 30 cm (12 in) wide. The great advantage of these systems is their flexibility: they are easily moved from one row or bed of plants to another. Within small areas they can be run at very low pressure from a water supply in a large volume tank. However there are operating limitations which can only be determined by experiment.

Some makes of permeable hoses can be buried several centimetres (a few inches) deep in the soil to minimize water loss and supply water direct to the plant roots.

Weeds

Weeds in vegetable gardens compete with the crop for water, nutrients and light. Moreover, many common weeds are closely related botanically to many common vegetables, and may harbour serious pests and diseases, sometimes providing a host for these during the winter.

There are two classes of weeds. *Perennials*, generally characterized by invasive spreading stems or roots or very deep tap roots, persist in the soil from one year to the next. Ground elder, field bindweed, dock, dandelion, couch grass, creeping thistle and horsetail are some of the worst. *Annuals* germinate, flower and die in one season, and may even complete several cycles in a year; chickweed, groundsel, annual meadow grass are typical of these.

Annuals

There are thousands of viable seeds of annual weeds in the top centimetres (few inches) of soil. Some (groundsel, chickweed) are relatively short-lived; others (fat hen, fool's parsley) can remain dormant in the soil for decades. When soil is regularly cultivated about 50% of these seeds are lost each year through germinating on the surface, germinating under the soil and failing to emerge, or through exposure to birds, climate, weathering and so on. It takes the proverbial seven years ('one year's seeding is seven years' weeding') to reduce the seed reserves in cultivated soil to about 1% of the original level. Regular cultivation, therefore, helps to keep down weeds. It is particularly important to prevent weeds going to seed: a single plant of fat hen has produced as many as 70,000 seeds.

In uncultivated ground far fewer seeds are lost annually. So when such ground *is* cultivated there is a huge flush of weeds. The best way to deal with this is to cultivate the ground, allow the first flush to germinate, and then hoe off these weeds before sowing or planting. Shallow cultivation is advisable in the early stages to prevent more seeds being brought up from lower levels.

Research has shown that the weeds which offer the most serious competition to growing vegetables are those *between* rather than within the rows. So weeding between the rows is always beneficial, even if there is not time to weed in the rows. In general, competition from weeds begins to become serious about three weeks after a vegetable crop has germinated, so efforts should be concentrated on removing weeds by this time. Start weeding as soon as the crop row can be seen.

Crops with broad and spreading leaves such as

Shallow hoeing minimizes the damage to roots. Small weeds can be left on the surface in dry weather.

beet, brassicas and carrots, naturally smother much of the weed growth by forming a canopy over the soil. This canopy is established fastest and is most effective where equidistant spacing is adopted. However, when plants are still small, before the soil surface is completely covered, it may be necessary to hand weed between the plants. Alternatively, mulch carefully between the young plants to prevent weed seeds germinating. (See Mulching, p 44.)

Crops with narrow leaves such as onions have no smothering capacity. If they cannot be hand weeded, it is best to grow them in rows, which are more easily hoed, or to keep them mulched. Hoeing, hand weeding and the use of plastic film and organic mulches (see Mulching, p 44) are the most practical means of keeping an established garden free of annual weeds. Always hoe as shallowly as possible to minimize damage to the plant roots, to prevent more weed seed being brought to the surface, and to minimize evaporation from the soil. Preferably hoe when the weeds are small, and in dry weather. They can then be left on the soil surface to die. If large weeds are left on the surface in wet conditions they may re-root. Weeds are rich in nutrients and minerals and should be composted unless they have gone to seed, in which case they should be burnt.

Perennials

Perennials must be recognized and uprooted, which is usually easiest when the soil is being dug over in winter. Take care to remove even small pieces of tap root, creeping roots and rhizomes. Many will re-sprout if left in the soil, or if the top is knocked off leaving the root intact. An exception is dock, which will not regenerate once the top 10 cm (4 in) of the root has been removed. Perennial weeds should not be put on the compost heap unless they have been killed by exposure to the sun; otherwise they should be burnt.

Chemical weed control

The use of chemical weedkillers (herbicides) in an established vegetable garden is not generally recommended because of the risk of damaging plants and of residual effects in the soil. Where herbicides are used they are generally applied with a watering can with a dribble bar attached. If possible keep one can for this purpose alone.

Dalapon is mainly translocated in action but is also taken up by roots. Its principle use is in the control of couch grass in uncropped areas. Its only approved uses in the vegetable garden are with the perennial crops asparagus and rhubarb where couch grass has become established.

Clearing new ground

Chemical herbicides are sometimes used to clear rough, weed-ridden ground to make a vegetable garden. In this situation double-digging to remove all weeds by hand can prove too daunting a task; and while rotovating may destroy the surface annual weeds, it can exacerbate the perennial weed problem by cutting the roots into numerous pieces which will regenerate.

Glyphosate is very effective against both annual and perennial weeds, including couch grass, and will usually check strongly even the most troublesome perennials, such as bindweed and horsetail. It is best applied when weed growth is vigorous, between early July and mid-September. Glyphosate acts slowly over three to four weeks. It is translocated from foliage to roots but leaves no harmful residues in the soil and as soon as the weeds are dead the site can be cultivated, sown and planted.

If a crop of seedling annual weeds is encountered on a previously cleared site, apply a proprietary contact-acting herbicide, such as paraquat with diquat mixture. This acts on contact and leaves no harmful residues in the soil. Paraquat with diquat will only kill the topgrowth of perennial weeds leaving underground parts unharmed to regrow, and therefore, is of little value in site clearance. Where there is a serious problem with annual and perennial weeds a lightproof mulch of carpeting or heavy black polythene film should be left in place for up to a year. If this is impracticable mulch the ground in summer and leave it until the following spring. The mulch kills off the surface weeds and weakens the roots systems of the perennials, making digging much easier when the mulch is lifted. It seems to have the beneficial side effect of encouraging earthworm activity.

WARNING NOTE Before using weedkillers read the product label. Then mix and apply strictly according to the manufacturer's recommendations.

Mulching

Mulching is the practice of covering the soil around plants with a layer of protective material. Traditionally, mulches were organic materials such as straw or compost which rotted into the soil. In today's gardens plastic film mulches are also used for a variety of purposes.

The value of any particular mulch depends on its characteristics. The following are some of the benefits offered by mulching:

- Mulches suppress weeds and prevent weed seeds from germinating, so lessening the need to cultivate. Any weeds which push their way through a mulch are easily pulled out.

- Mulches conserve soil moisture by slowing down evaporation. If the upper layers of the soil remain moist roots can continue to extract nutrients, which they are unable to do from dry soil.

- Organic mulches improve soil fertility and conserve the soil structure by protecting the soil from heavy rain, by mitigating the effects of treading on the soil, by encouraging earthworm activity and by the addition of organic matter and nutrients to the soil.

- Organic mulches can be used to insulate the soil, keeping it cooler in summer and warmer in winter. They can be packed around overwintering plants to lessen frost penetration into the soil, and make lifting easier in winter. Dried bracken and straw are good materials for this purpose. Plastic mulches can be used to warm up the soil, especially in spring.

- Mulches help to keep trailing crops, such as bush tomatoes, marrows or cucumbers clean by preventing soil from splashing up onto ripening fruit. This also helps to prevent disease.

- White plastic mulches can hasten growth and ripening by reflecting light up on to the leaves and fruit.

- Chequered and shiny plastic film mulches can deter insect pests such as aphids. (See Pests and diseases, p 53.)

- Black plastic mulches can be used instead of earthing up to prevent greening in growing potatoes. (See Potatoes, p 135.)

Organic mulches

A wide range of materials can be used for mulching, including all the bulky manures mentioned previously (see p 12). If used for mulching they should be well-rotted, or nitrogen will be taken from the soil in the early stages of decomposition. This applies especially to mulches derived from wood, such as sawdust, wood shavings, shredded and pulverized bark, and to pine needles. On the whole these are unsuitable for the vegetable garden unless they have been left outside to break down for a couple of years. In general, avoid materials which would form an impenetrable layer, preventing rain from seeping through, or anything which is unpleasant to handle.

The following organic mulches all contribute to soil fertility, as well as keeping down weeds and conserving moisture: well rotted animal manures, garden and mushroom compost, leafmould, lawn mowings from grass that has not been treated with weedkiller; seaweed (sprinkle it with soil if it is attracting flies); hay and straw (especially short straw); some proprietary recycled products.

The following organic substances are used primarily to conserve moisture and prevent weed growth, but make little contribution to soil fertility: wood derivatives, layers of newspaper or cardboard, old carpeting. Mulches of unsightly material are best used for weed control in out of the way corners; or sprinkle them with lawnmowings or sawdust to disguise them.

Applying organic mulches

The key fact about mulching is that it maintains the *status quo* of the soil. So avoid mulching when the soil is cold, dry or very wet. Ideally mulch when the soil is warm and moist. In many cases the best time to mulch is when planting. When seeds have been direct sown, mulching should be delayed until the seedlings are a reasonable size. Otherwise birds are likely to scatter the mulch over the young seedlings and smother them. It makes sense to hoe off any weeds before mulching. Vegetables such as peas, carrots and onions, which are not easy to weed, can be mulched once well established. So can vegetables which like plenty of moisture, such as celery and celeriac, and the various types of bean. Celeriac, parsnips, overwintering radishes and leeks are among winter vegetables which are easier to lift if mulched before winter sets in.

As a general rule, the thicker the mulch the better. A good garden mulch would be from 4 – 10 cm (1½ – 4 in) deep, but much depends on the material used and the stage of growth of the crop. At the end of the season organic mulches can be either dug into the ground, or simply left on the surface for the earthworms to work in.

Plastic film mulches

There are now several types of plastic film available to gardeners, and the range may increase in future. Film thickness is measured in 'gauge' or 'microns', 60 gauge (15 microns) being a very lightweight, thin film, 600 gauge (150 microns) a heavy film of the type used for walk-in polythene tunnels. Thin plastics normally last for one season, but with care, thicker plastics can last for two or three seasons. Store plastic film out of the light when not in use. Plastic films give off toxic substances when burnt, so should be buried where feasible, or disposed of carefully when their useful life is over. Biodegradable horticultural films may soon become a practical proposition.

Black unperforated films These are fairly lightweight films used primarily to exclude light and suppress weeds, and also to conserve moisture in the soil.

Runner beans are mulched with well-rotted compost to help retain moisture.

They do little to warm up the soil, and do not let water through. They are used mainly to mulch growing crops, but are also used to cover potatoes to avoid earthing up. (See Potatoes, p 135.)

Black perforated film and fabrics The perforations allow rain to penetrate and make watering easy; the dark colour discourages weed germination. These materials are useful for mulching perennial crops, but can also be used for annual vegetables. The original films were very lightweight plastic, which did not allow for easy penetration of water; but they were good for weed control and reasonably durable.

Recently introduced are some much softer, almost fleecy, very permeable but less durable films. They are very useful for indoor crops. Much heavier, coarser fabrics, widely used commercially for paths and ground cover, can also be used very satisfactorily for mulching. They are excellent for perennial crops and fairly large vegetables, as well as for weed control on paths.

Clear films Films of varying weight are used to warm up the soil before sowing or planting and to mulch growing crops, to encourage faster growth. Clear films do not prevent weed seed germinating, but to some extent prevent weeds pushing through. They can be used for mulching seedbeds, but must be removed as soon as the seeds are through. Clear films are also used over low tunnels. (For low tunnels, and perforated clear films, see Protected cropping, p 46.)

Opaque white films These thicker films suppress weeds to some extent because of their thickness, but are used primarily on crops such as melons, tomatoes, peppers and aubergines to reflect light up on to the plant and encourage growth and fruit ripening.

Black and white films In these films the upper surface is white and reflects light upwards, but the lower surface is black and suppresses weeds. They are useful for mulching the fruiting vegetable crops listed above.

Applying plastic films

Plastic films are usually anchored by burying the edges in shallow slits made in the soil with a trowel or spade. They can also be anchored simply by weighting the edges with stone, lumps of soil or pieces of wood, but the former method is more satisfactory.

Large seeds, such as beans or sweet corn, can be sown directly through holes made in the plastic with either a dibber or knife. Watch out for the seedlings as they germinate to make sure they emerge through the hole and do not get caught beneath the plastic.

More commonly, plastic is laid at the planting stage. One method is to anchor the plastic in position on the ground, then cut cross-shaped slits in it, through which the plant roots can be slipped for planting.

The alternative method is to unroll the plastic over a row of established plants, cutting holes above them and easing the leafy parts of the plants through the holes.

Black plastic films often attract slugs, so watch out for them and take protective measures if necessary.

Although films help to retain soil moisture, watering usually becomes necessary at some point. Either water carefully through the planting holes, or lay irrigation tubing beneath the plastic.

Protected cropping

The term 'protected cropping' embraces all forms of structure used for growing vegetables – whether permanent, semi-permanent or temporary. Structures range from heated and unheated greenhouses, the lean-to, and walk-in polytunnels, to frames, cloches, low polytunnels and 'crop covers' or floating films. Here we are concentrating on the cheaper forms of unheated structure.

Following the lead of commercial horticulture, various plastic materials have been widely adopted for protected cropping in gardens in recent years, and this trend is likely to continue. The most commonly used are the polythene films – strictly speaking thermoplastic films made from ethylene. They have given their name, in abbreviated form, to the walk-in and low plastic film tunnels.

All forms of protective cropping benefit plant growth in two ways: first, by protecting plants from the weather, especially the wind and secondly, by raising soil and air temperatures. It should be stressed that only heated structures give complete protection against frost. However, by protecting plants from wind the damage caused by frost is minimized in protective structures. It is the combination of wind *and* frost which is potentially most damaging to plants and likely to kill them.

General uses of protected cropping

- To extend the season of ordinary garden vegetables such as lettuces, carrots, peas and radishes, so that they can be obtained earlier or, sometimes, later than normal.

- To get improved crops of half-hardy vegetables which do not perform well outdoors in an average British summer, for example, tomatoes, cucumbers and green peppers.

- To improve the quality of hardy winter vegetables such as lettuces, endive and other hardy salads, spinach, chard, parsley, and oriental greens, all of which are toughened by exposure to winter conditions.

- To give an early start to crops which will be subsequently planted outdoors.

- For miscellaneous uses, such as hardening off seedlings, ripening tomatoes and onions, warming up the soil before spring sowings, and providing protection from birds.

Choice of protected cropping

Each of the various forms of protection has advantages and disadvantages. Portable frames, cloches and low polytunnels can be bought in small units: they are flexible in use, easily moved from one crop to another, and ventilation and watering are relatively simple. Among their disadvantages are that they require a fair amount of handling in erecting and moving, many crops cannot be grown to maturity in them because they are low, and only small areas of ground are protected by each unit.

Walk-in polytunnels are a useful half-way house between permanent, but costly, greenhouses, and the flexibility of cloches and low polytunnels. They can be dismantled and moved to a new site relatively easily. The mulching films are used for specific purposes. (See below.)

Cloches

Cloches are made from various materials, glass and plastic being the two most common. Glass transmits light and retains heat very efficiently, at night retaining more heat than plastic materials. As a result crops under glass are usually ready a few days earlier than those under plastic. Glass does not deteriorate with age, but glass cloches are heavy and cumbersome to erect and breakable – a potential hazard in a garden. Glass is expensive initially.

A very wide range of plastic materials is used for cloches, for example PVC sheeting, acrylic sheet or Perspex, glass resin, fibreglass and semi-rigid materials. There are also wire-reinforced plastics. Very cheap cloches can be made by battening polythene film to a wood frame.

Plastic materials can be transparent or translucent, rigid or corrugated. Some of the transparent materials transmit light exceptionally well, but it has also been shown that plants grow surprisingly well in the evenly diffused light beneath some translucent materials. Plastic does not retain heat as well as glass and temperatures under plastic are two or three degrees lower than under glass. Plastic cloches are light in weight and usually need some method of anchorage.

One of the drawbacks of plastic is that it breaks down with age due to the action of ultra-violet light. Plastic should be stored out of sunlight when not in use. If possible buy plastic treated with an ultra-violet inhibitor, which will increase its useful life considerably.

Using cloches

The smallest and simplest cloches are tent-shaped. Larger, higher cloches with a tent roof supported on side pieces are known as barn cloches. Both can be placed in a line to cover a crop row, with the ends

A transparent cloche of corrugated plastic.

Glass barn cloches used on end to protect crops.

Translucent plastic cloche with carrying handle.

Taller crops growing under glass barn cloches.

closed by a piece of glass or rigid plastic held in place with a stick. This is essential, or the cloches become a wind tunnel.

In general the larger the cloche the better for the crop. There must be enough room for plants to grow without being cramped; so barn cloches with their higher roofs are better than tent cloches for tall crops. Ideally, foliage should not touch a glass surface – in summer foliage is liable to be scorched, and in winter it may be frosted. When plants have outgrown the cloche it can be placed on its side and 'wrapped' around the plant, to give at least side shelter.

Ventilation Temperatures build up very rapidly under cloches in sunny weather, and some means of ventilation, such as a panel which can be opened or rolled back, is useful. In some cloches, glass or plastic panels can be removed and replaced with netting, or they are constructed with permanent netting beneath the panel. This allows for ventilation, with protection against birds. Standard barn cloches have a clipping device to facilitate ventilation.

Where there is no ventilation system move cloches slightly apart and remove end pieces, or remove alternate cloches, or take them off the plants altogether during the hottest part of the day.

Watering Plants under cloches must be kept well watered. Larger cloches have to be moved for watering unless irrigation tubing or seep hose has been installed. Smaller cloches can be watered from above, allowing the water to percolate down the sides through to the plants.

Low polytunnels

Low continuous tunnels, made from lightweight (150 gauge) polythene film sheeting stretched over galvanized steel wire hoops, pushed into the ground about 1 m (3 ft 6 in) apart, are the cheapest form of protective cropping for vegetables. The maximum height of the tunnels is usually between 33 and 45 cm (13 and 18 in). Sheeting can be bought in rolls and cut to the length required. It is available in various widths, and it is advisable to err on the wide side to get maximum crop coverage and to allow for burying the sides if necessary.

The film is held taut over the hoops with strings, tied to eyes on either side of each hoop. If a permanent knot is made on one side and an easily untied knot such as a slip knot on the other, tunnels can be moved relatively quickly when the need arises.

Anchor the film at either end of the tunnel, either by burying it in the soil, or bunching it together and tying it in a knot around a short stake. Put the stake in the soil at a 45 degree angle about 60 cm (2 ft) beyond the last hoop.

Unless very securely erected, the sides of low tunnels are apt to be blown up in windy weather. This can be prevented either by weighting the sides with stones, clods or pieces of wood, or burying them in the ground. This does make the crops less easily accessible and less easy to ventilate. A compromise solution is to weight down one side only.

Low tunnels are used and cropped in much the same way as cloches. They are easily moved, and are particularly useful in spring, autumn and winter. In midsummer they tend to create a humid and close atmosphere which will encourage disease. They are relatively low so are best used for low growing crops or for crops in their early stages.

For ventilation, watering and other operations the film is slid up between the hoop and retaining string

Low plastic tunnels

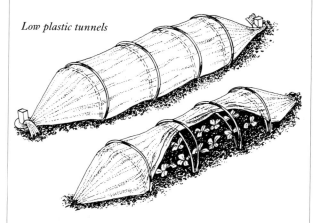

Secure the ends of low tunnels by burying or tying to a stake (above) Slide up the film for ventilation and watering.

– one side only for watering – both sides for maximum ventilation. In winter brush off heavy snow if it is in danger of crushing the plants beneath. Light snow, however, acts as insulation.

Polythene film lasts two or three years if handled carefully. Small tears can be repaired with plastic tape. As with other plastics, store it out of sunlight when not in use. The galvanized hoops last for years.

Strip cropping

The most effective way of using cloches and low tunnels is strip cropping. This is a system whereby, during the course of a year, the cloches or tunnels are moved to and fro between two or three strips of preferably adjacent land, so that they cover three or four different crops at their critical stages.

Numerous plans can be found in specialist books on gardening with cloches. You can easily draw up your own on the assumption that you can sow or plant approximately 10 days to two weeks earlier under cloches than in the open. A simple example of a two-strip system is given below.

Space under cloches and tunnels is so valuable that inter-cropping – growing two or three crops together – should be practised wherever feasible, the faster growing crops being removed before the main crop requires the space. For example, radishes can be sown with most crops; while peas, dwarf French beans or sweet corn can be sown or planted down the middle of the cloches, with lettuces, radishes, early carrots or early turnips sown down either side. The cloches are removed once the larger crops are well established.

Simple strip rotation with cloches
(The same system can be applied to low tunnels.)

STRIP 1	STRIP 2
October to April	
Oct Hardy lettuces and radishes sown at outside edges: intersown (*Nov*) with early peas	————
April to late May	
CLOCHES REMOVED	*April* Dwarf beans sown under cloches.
May/June to October	
late May/early June Bush tomatoes or green peppers planted under cloches. and grown under them as long as practicable.	CLOCHES REMOVED
October to April	
CLOCHES REMOVED	*Oct* Hardy lettuces and radishes sown under cloches.

Frames

Frames can be permanent or portable, free-standing or lean-to. If orientated east to west, they are normally lower at the front and higher at the back to catch the maximum light; from 18 – 30 cm (7 – 12 in) at the front, and 23 – 45 cm (9 – 18 in) at the back.

Traditional frames were built with sides of brick, timber or concrete, many with 'Dutch light' roofs – a standard-sized sheet of horticultural glass in a wooden frame. Most modern frames are glass and aluminium, though some are constructed of plastic.

Frames must be sited away from overhanging trees; for most purposes a south aspect is advisable.

Frames are relatively airtight, and adequate ventilation is extremely important. Some frames have sliding panels, otherwise the glass covers (lights) must be propped open on warm days, and shaded or removed altogether in very sunny, hot weather. Lights must also have some means of being securely fastened, or they may blow off in windy weather. Frames can be covered with sacking or mats to keep out the frost in winter.

In winter water the *soil* in the frame but keep the crop dry, as water left on the leaves will encourage fungus infection.

In spring frames are mainly used for early crops, for raising seeds and hardening off seedlings. In deep or shaded frames, seed boxes may have to be raised off the ground to prevent them becoming drawn towards the light. In summer frames are used for half-hardy crops such as tomatoes and cucumbers using bush cultivars or training plants along the ground. In winter use frames to protect hardy lettuces, over-wintered seedlings (for example cauliflower) and for blanching chicory and endive.

In winter and spring, watch out for mice; they soon discover crops in frames. In summer frames may need to be shaded in bright sunlight.

Walk-in polytunnels

A polytunnel probably offers the keen vegetable grower the greatest area of protection at the lowest cost. The standard polytunnel is essentially a giant semi-circular cloche, consisting of polythene film stretched over galvanized steel tube hoops. For amateur use, polytunnels 2.4 – 3 m (8 – 10 ft) wide, and up to 10 m (35 ft) long are recommended. Longer tunnels require additional ventilation in the centre. It is advisable to use fairly heavy (500 – 600 gauge) film, treated with an ultra-violet inhibitor. With care such film can be used for two to three years before it needs to be replaced.

Polytunnels are erected by sinking the hoops into foundation tubes knocked in the soil. Make a shallow trench alongside, stretch the film over the hoops, laying the sides in the trench, then anchor the film by covering it with soil from the trench. Where possible, orient the tunnel north-south to avoid excessive temperatures, and extend the life of the film.

The serviceable life of the film depends to a considerable extent on how carefully the tunnel is erected, and how taut the film is laid over the framework. When erecting the tunnel make sure the corners of the tunnel are carefully aligned so the tunnel is absolutely straight; insulate the upper curves of the steel hoops with 'anti-hot spot' foam tape (the film is laid over the tape, which protects it from the high temperatures of the metal hoops in midsummer); insulate any rough corners (on doorways, for example), with some kind of padding; put the film over the hoops on a warm day when it is limp, so that it can be pulled very tight.

Ventilation Polythene tunnels heat up very rapidly, and it is most important to ventilate them well to avoid a build-up of pests and disease. The top halves of the end doors should have ventilation panels. In very hot weather, semicircular, dinner plate size 'portholes' can be cut in the plastic along the sides, 30 cm (12 in) above ground level, to improve ventilation. They can be taped up again in winter if necessary. When temperatures are high it is advisable to sprinkle with water once or twice a day, to lower the temperature and discourage pests, such as red spider mite, which can be a problem. There is more natural ventilation where a tunnel is erected on a slope.

Watering Partly because temperatures rise so high during the day, crops in tunnels have to be watered fairly frequently. It is well worth mulching to conserve moisture in the soil.

Polythene film is bound to tear from time to time, especially where it flaps in the wind. Tears can be mended very satisfactorily with the strong plastic tapes made for the purpose.

Polythene film can be attached to, or laid over, any type of framework to make a greenhouse structure. Take care to insulate rough surfaces on the framework so the film does not get snagged, and make sure there is adequate ventilation.

Polytunnels are very versatile structures, and can be in use all year round. If the soil becomes 'tomato sick' after growing tomatoes for several consecutive years, it is relatively simple to move the tunnel to a fresh site when renewing the plastic.

Crop covers

The use of crop covers, formerly known as floating films or mulches, a technique borrowed from commercial growers, is increasingly being taken up by amateur gardeners. In essence crop covers are very light, well-ventilated films which can be laid or draped over a crop, either tucked into the soil on either side or anchored with weights. Because of their 'elasticity', the films are raised by the developing crop, so they can cover crops roughly 10 – 30 cm (4 – 12 in) high, depending on the film and the crop.

The perforated plastic and net films are sometimes used over low wire or plastic hoops to make low tunnels: in this case they can cover taller crops. Their good ventilation is an advantage over the conventional unperforated polythene films normally used for this purpose. (See below.)

The films raise the soil and air temperature around the plants and have a sheltering, windbreak effect. As a result plants may mature up to two weeks earlier, and yield more heavily. They also offer some protection against insect pests and birds. They can be invaluable in a garden with no cloches, frames, or greenhouses. New and improved types of film may well be developed in future, but at present three main types are in use: perforated polythene films; fleecy spun fibre films; fine net films (also known as non-woven films) woven from polyethylene.

Perforated polythene films

The films are transparent, lightweight (100 – 160 gauge) and generally perforated with anything from 200 to 500 holes, of about 10 mm (3/8 in) diameter. They can also be perforated with many very tiny slits.

Their advantages lie in being cheap and warming the soil up rapidly. Their drawback is that they do not let in much rain, will not keep out frost, and at a certain point start to chafe plants. They create higher temperatures than other types of floating film, but in hot weather high humidity and high temperatures can cause disease. The films are used mainly in spring *during the early stages of growth*.

The following are among the many vegetables which can be grown successfully under perforated plastic films: carrots, beetroot, cabbage, cauliflower, calabrese, celery, courgettes, lettuces, spinach, early potatoes, radishes, and outdoor bush tomatoes. Radishes are exceptional in that they can be grown to maturity under perforated films.

On the whole it is easiest to lay the film over a crop after planting rather than when sowing. Let it rest naturally over the plants, neither overstretched nor sagging, and anchor the edges in slits in the soil. Alternatively weight them down with pieces of timber or stones. Keep a close watch on the plants, and as soon as growth under the film appears to be slowing down, the film should be removed.

Fleecy films

These films are soft to the touch; their texture is half way between tissue paper and cotton wool. Compared to the polythene films they are gentler in action, better ventilated and allow more rainfall through. So there is less chafing of plants, temperatures fluctuate less beneath the films, it is easier to water through them, and the time to remove them is less critical. They also offer a little protection against frost (this increases with the thickness of the film) and, *provided they are anchored carefully so there are no gaps*, some protection against flying and crawling insect pests such as aphids, cabbage root fly, carrot fly, flea beetle, and butterflies and moths.

They are used to warm up the soil, to cover early and late crops outdoors, and for additional frost protection in greenhouses. On the whole the films are unsuitable for use in very windy areas. With care they will last for two seasons.

For outdoor use they are best laid after planting, allowing about 50 cm (20 in) of slack for the plants to grow. Fold the edges double and anchor with soil or stones placed about every 50 cm (20 in), or use pur-

Fleecy films can speed up crop maturity and, provided there are no gaps, offer protection against pests.

pose-made pegs. In exposed areas the whole length should be buried. The films can be laid after sowing, but there is the risk that in wet conditions they lie flat on the soil making germination difficult. Seeds are sometimes sown in shallow furrows to avoid this, but some, such as lettuce, do not respond well to being sown in furrows.

On the whole these films are insufficiently ventilated to leave on during hot weather. In most cases plants should only be covered for about four or five weeks in spring, or for longer periods in autumn.

Incidentally these films can be used for extra frost protection in greenhouses. Drape the films loosely over plants. If heavy frost is forecast use a double layer.

Fine net films

Of the various types of floating film the net films are the strongest, the most durable (they will last up to five years), and the best ventilated. They function primarily as a low level windbreak, offering only minimum protection against frost. However, provided they are anchored so there are no gaps, they provide an effective barrier against insect pests, including cabbage root fly, carrot fly, onion fly, cabbage white butterfly, frit fly, flea beetle, pea moth, cutworm, cabbage whitefly, leaf miners and some aphids – in addition to protection from birds and rabbits. Slug and snail damage is said to be less under these films. Of course fine net films offer no protection against any pests *already* in the soil, or in plant debris, when the ground is covered. The good ventilation ensures healthy plant growth beneath these films.

Plants can be watered through the film. Any weeding should be done on a windy day, when flying insects are *not* flying. The films can either be laid flat as a floating mulch or used over low hoops as a tunnel. Because they are so 'airy' most crops can be left under them until maturity. They must, however, be removed to allow for pollination where necessary.

General management of crop covers

Films should only be used on well-prepared, well-drained, weed-free soil. Any weeds in the soil will naturally flourish in the favourable conditions under the films. While the net and fleecy films can be lifted carefully to weed, this is more difficult with the perforated polythene films as weeds grow into the holes.

In general, as the films offer minimal protection from frost, tender crops should not be sown or planted under them any earlier than normal. The gain is in shortening the growing season.

Care has to be taken in removing polythene and fleecy films, or the plants, which make soft growth in the protected environment, suffer a check to growth. Remove the films in the evening, in calm and dull conditions. A 'weaning' process can be carried out by making intermittent slits down the centre of the film several days before removing the covers; finally slit it down the entire length. If necessary water the crop gently after removing the film as the soil is likely to be dry.

Films should be removed from insect-pollinated crops, such as courgettes and tomatoes, when the flowers appear.

Storage

Wherever possible vegetables should be used fresh. Once they are picked they inevitably start to deteriorate through loss of moisture, and to lose flavour. Any method of storage must aim to keep the water loss to a minimum.

A wide range of vegetables is now deep frozen in domestic freezers, so there is less reliance on conventional vegetable storage than there used to be. Consult specialist books for the best methods to deep-freeze vegetables. Conventional storage still has a place, especially for root vegetables, which most people find better flavoured if stored rather than frozen.

Root crops

Many root crops (parsnips, swedes and carrots) are frost tolerant and can often be 'stored' in the soil instead of being lifted, particularly if grown on light, well-drained soils. The advantage of leaving them in the soil is that there is considerably less water loss than when they are lifted. The disadvantages are the risk of slug and other pest damage (worst on heavy soils) and the unpleasantness and difficulty of lifting in wet and cold weather.

Where vegetables are left in the ground, mark the ends of the rows so they can be found in snow, and cover them when soil temperatures have fallen to their winter level of about 5 C (41 F) with a thick layer of straw or bracken, held in place with wire hoops if necessary. This is about mid to late November in the south and the end of October to early November in the north. The covering will protect them from severe frost and make it possible to dig the soil to lift the roots even during frosty weather. Beetroots, swedes and turnips, which protrude out of the soil, need to be covered by about 20 cm (8in) of straw; carrots by about 15 cm (6 in).

Most root vegetables can be stored in boxes, barrels or bins in layers of slightly moist sand or sieved ash. They are easy to get at when needed but the moisture loss is relatively rapid. Handle roots for storage very gently, rub off surplus mud and trim or twist off leaves. Reject diseased and damaged roots or store them separately and use them first.

Place the largest roots at the bottom of the container so that smaller roots, which lose moisture faster, are used first. Cover the top layer so that no roots are exposed. Keep the containers in a frost-proof building such as a cellar, or soundly built shed, where temperatures are as close to a uniform 0 C (32 F) as possible, and mice are not likely to be a problem.

Potatoes are susceptible to frost damage, and cannot be left in the ground. Store them at temperatures between 4 and 10 C (39 and 50 F). Give them extra protection if the temperature is likely to fall any lower. They are best stored in shallow wooden boxes, so that they get enough ventilation, and covered with old carpet or sacks to keep out the light. Double-thickness paper sacks tied at the neck may also be used, but should not be filled too full. Potatoes must be stored away from light, which stimulates the formation of poisonous alkaloids in tubers. Plastic sacks are not suitable as the conditions in them become too humid.

The traditional method of storing root vegetables is in clamps, which can be either made outdoors, or on the floor in outbuildings or cellars. Vegetables in clamps are easier to get at than those left in the open ground, but there may be fairly high wastage. Clamps are used much less today, but swedes, carrots, turnips, Chinese radish and potatoes are among the vegetables that can be stored in this way.

Clamps should be made on well-drained ground. They can be made against a wall for extra protection. They can be round, semicircular or oblong. Roots

Carrots stored in moist sand. Place the smaller roots near the top.

Healthy undamaged roots of beetroot stored in a wooden box.

Swedes being placed in a clamp on a bed of straw 20cm (8in) deep.

are piled up in a neat heap as high as required except for carrots. These should not be piled more than 60 cm (2 ft) high on a layer of straw about 20 cm (8 in) thick. The top of the heap is covered with another layer of straw of about the same thickness, and then a layer of earth about 15 cm (6 in) thick. This is taken from around the outside of the clamp, so making a small drainage ditch around it. For very hardy roots such as swedes the final layer of earth is unnecessary. A watch should be kept for mice and rats which may burrow into clamps.

Leafy vegetables

Spinach, lettuces, spring cabbages, Brussels sprouts, and sprouting vegetables such as broccoli, calabrese and cauliflower lose moisture very rapidly once picked and are difficult to store for any length of time. Apart from lettuces, they can be deep frozen satisfactorily.

To maximize their short-term storage life they are best picked early or late in the day, when at their coolest, further cooled as quickly as possible by being put somewhere cool. Store in a cool, dark, airy place (the old-fashioned larder was ideal), in paper bags rather than plastic bags. If kept in a fridge use the salad drawer, not the coldest area.

Certain hearted vegetables, such as winter cabbages nd to some extent summer cabbages, hearted 'Sugar Loaf' chicories, endive and Chinese cabbage can be stored for periods ranging from several weeks to several months. Temperatures should be as near

0 C (32 F) as possible, and the atmosphere fairly moist. Tolerance to frost varies, but generally they can be kept in a frost-free shed or cellar, either on racks or shelves or hung in nets.

There are several ways of storing non-hardy cabbage, such as red cabbage and the Dutch 'Winter White' types. They need to be kept at a low, even temperature just above freezing. They can be stored in frostproof sheds, either with the heads on raised wooden slats and the stalks dangling below, or piled on a layer of straw on the floor. There is no need to cut off the roots. If temperatures are likely to freeze, cover them with more straw. They are sometimes hung in nets – but in this case it is difficult to give them extra protection if temperatures drop severely. Cabbages are also sometimes stored on wooden slats in garden frames outdoors, but this method is not recommended except in mid-winter as it is difficult to maintain an even temperature on sunny days.

Inspect stored cabbages and other leafy vegetables regularly, gently rolling off any diseased or withered outer leaves with the palm of the hand.

Onions, shallots and garlic

These are best stored in frost-free conditions but at low temperatures, ideally 0 C (32 F), with as much ventilation as possible. Good harvesting is the key to good storage and this is helped greatly if it can be done during dry weather. As soon as the foliage has died down, or started to yellow in the case of garlic, ease the bulbs gently out of the ground, and spread them to dry on sacks, trays or netting raised off the ground outdoors. In a period of prolonged wet weather bring in the bulbs and dry them off in warmth indoors or in a greenhouse.

Aim to dry them as quickly and thoroughly as possible. Handle them carefully to avoid bruises and cuts; damaged, diseased, or thick-necked bulbs should not be stored.

Onions and garlic can be plaited in ropes and hung up after drying. This is rather laborious, but it keeps individual bulbs separate, making it easier to select the size wanted for cooking. There is also less likelihood of disease spreading from one bulb to another. Alternatively, the bulbs can be hung in woven, plastic or nylon nets or stockings, or stored in shallow layers in trays. They must not be put into polythene bags because the atmosphere becomes too humid, encouraging condensation and rotting. Inspect all bulbs regularly and remove any showing signs of disease.

Pumpkins, marrows, winter squashes

Pumpkins and other firm-fleshed gourds, which will keep for several months, are picked when mature but not over-ripe. Pick them with as long a stalk as

Dutch 'Winter White' cabbage stored in nets.

Autumn red cabbage stored on raised slats.

Onions plaited on ropes and hung up for storage.

Onions stored in woven plastic nets.

Pumpkins should be harvested when mature and left in the sun for the skins to harden before storage.

Garlic plaited into a bunch for storage.

Beans for dried seed are uprooted whole.

possible. Dry them off well in the sun to harden their skins before storing them in cool, dry, frost-free conditions. They can be placed on racks or suspended in nets. Cover them with extra sacking if unusually hard frost is expected.

Drying vegetables

Bean and pea seeds can be dried for winter use. A few plants are best reserved for the purpose, leaving the pods on the plants until nearly mature. They can then be uprooted whole and hung to dry in a cool, airy place. If it is more convenient, pick off the individual pods and spread them on trays to dry. Once dry they can be shelled and stored in airtight jars. They will need to be soaked in water for 24 hours before use.

Chilli pepper plants similarly can be pulled up and hung indoors. The desiccated peppers will remain in good condition for several years. Green peppers will keep in reasonable condition for several months if the plants are hung to dry in an airy frost-free shed.

Pests and diseases

There are a number of pests and diseases which attack vegetables. Pests range from rabbits, pigeons, sparrows, mice and moles to slugs, insects, mites and nematodes. Diseases are caused by fungi, bacteria and viruses. Plants can also suffer from physiological disorders, brought about by unsuitable growing conditions.

Birds and animals apart, it cannot be over-emphasized that the first line of defence against the majority of pests and diseases is to grow plants well. Strong plants raised in clean hygienic conditions and grown uncrowded in fertile, well-drained soil with adequate moisture and balanced nutrients are far less prone to pest and disease attack. Moreover, they stand a good chance of outgrowing any attacks that do occur. It is the weaker plants which are most likely to succumb – whether to pests or diseases.

The incidence of pests and diseases varies from one locality to another, and from one season to another. In most seasons it is only necessary to take preventive and control measures against the few most serious problems being encountered.

General preventive measures

As mentioned above, growing plants well, and adopting a number of preventive measures, is the best insurance against pest and disease problems becoming serious.

Soil condition Creating and maintaining a highly fertile and well-drained soil is of paramount importance in growing strong healthy plants. (See Soil fertility, p 10.) Practise rotation as far as is practicable to limit the build-up of soil pests, such as eelworm, and diseases such as onion white rot and various root rots. (See Rotation, p 23.)

Garden hygiene Clear away garden debris, as it often harbours diseases and provides shelter for pests. Pull up old brassica stumps at the end of the season, as they may shelter overwintering pests such as aphids. When a crop is thinned, remove the thinnings to avoid attracting pests: this applies particularly to carrot thinnings, which attract the carrot fly. Diseased leaves should be removed from plants, and diseased material, especially virus infected plants, should be burned. Keep the garden weed free, as weeds and weedy ground provide shelter for overwintering pests such as slugs, leatherjackets and cutworms and may also harbour diseases. Keep water tanks covered, as they provide a breeding ground for diseases.

Healthy plant material Never plant diseased material. Inspect onion, shallot and garlic bulbs carefully for disease; inspect young brassica plants for any signs of clubroot swellings. Take particular care if buying in plants. Wherever possible use cultivars with tolerance or resistance to diseases or pests.

Plant raising Rapid germination and steady growth can prevent pest and disease attack in the most vulnerable early stages. Sow thinly in warm soil, in a well prepared seedbed, to get plants off to a good start. Treated seed can be used in some cases to give protection against seed-borne and damping off diseases. Some pests, such as the bean seed fly, lay eggs in freshly disturbed soil. By sowing in a 'stale seedbed', that is, by allowing 10 days to elapse between preparing the seedbed and sowing, severe damage can often be avoided.

Thin as soon as possible to avoid overcrowding, which encourages pests and disease.

Wherever practicable, raise plants in modules, so that they are well developed with a strong root system when planted out. This is one means of partially overcoming clubroot in infested soils. Keep propagating equipment clean to avoid 'damping off' diseases. Use sterile seed and potting composts where possible, and store them in the dry. (See Sowing indoors, p 33.)

Feeding and watering Don't overfeed plants with nitrogenous fertilizers. This leads to soft, sappy growth, which is vulnerable to pest and disease attack. On the other hand, make sure plants have plenty of water: wilting plants are the most susceptible to aphid attack.

Regular inspection Inspect plants frequently, so that pest and disease outbreaks can be spotted early, when they are much easier to control. Attacks can build up very rapidly in conditions which favour the pest or disease.

Handling Handle vegetables for storage very carefully, as storage rots often start with bruises and cuts. This is particularly true of onions and garlic. Do not try to store vegetables that have been damaged by pests or diseases.

Common types of pest and disease

The chart on pp 58–66 lists the most common vegetable pests and diseases, describes the symptoms they cause, and summarizes the methods of prevention and control.

Here we discuss briefly the main pest and disease groups, and outline some of the specific preventive and control measures which can be taken.

Pests

Mammals Burrowing rabbits can be a very serious problem in rural areas, and it may be necessary to fence in the whole garden with 2.5 cm (1 in) mesh wire fencing, at least 1m (3 ft 6 in) high, buried at least 15 cm (6 in) below ground and turned outwards. Where deer are a problem, high fencing or electric fencing is probably the only answer. Moles can almost literally turn a garden upside down: they should be caught with humane traps set in the main runs. Mice eat pea and bean seeds and various seedlings, especially in spring. They are best caught in mouse traps set beneath tiles or wire to prevent pets being harmed.

Birds Large birds like pigeons, jays and pheasants can seriously damage brassicas, peas and other vegetables, sometimes completely stripping the plants. Smaller birds such as sparrows go for seedlings, young pea plants and tender-leaved plants like lettuces and beetroot.

Bird scarers are effective to some extent, but they must be changed or moved constantly, as birds quickly become accustomed to them. Humming tape erected around a plot has proved fairly successful in some cases. Where there is persistent damage, especially from large birds, it may be necessary to cage in the whole vegetable garden or to erect temporary net cages over vulnerable crops. This should be done only in an emergency, as birds feed on pests and weed seeds, helping to keep them down. Small birds can be deterred from attacking emerging seedlings by single strands of strong black cotton stretched 2.5 cm (1 in) above the row when sowing.

Soil pests There are a number of pests which live in the soil, many of the commonest being the larval forms of familiar insects, given in brackets. Examples are wireworms (click beetles), leatherjackets (craneflies or daddy-long-legs), cutworms (noctuid moths), and chafer grubs (chafer beetles). Along with millipedes they attack the roots and stems of a range of plants causing many casualties.

Soil pests are generally worst in neglected gardens or after grassland has been dug in. Wireworm damage, for example, is worst the second year after digging in grass, as the wireworms feed on decaying grass roots during the first season. Attacks from all these pests gradually diminish, though occasionally, when weather conditions are favourable to them, there is an outbreak.

Various chemicals (see the chart on pp 58) can be worked into the soil before sowing or planting to control soil pests. They may also kill beneficial soil insects so should be used only if really necessary. Soil pests can be attracted to traps made from scooped out potatoes and carrots fixed on skewers just below soil level. Examine these daily, killing any pests found. Cutworms are night feeders and like slugs (see below), can often be caught at night.

Slugs and snails Both these pests can be extremely damaging. They are most active at night in damp weather and on heavy soils. They eat holes in the leaves and stems of many plants, destroying seedlings and young plants and disfiguring mature plants. They can be controlled chemically with methiocarb or metaldehyde pellets. The latter is less effective under damp conditions: neither should be used within seven days of eating crops and both are dangerous to pets. Less toxic, but less effective, are products containing aluminium sulphate.

Traditional deterrents such as lime, soot and broken egg shells scattered around vulnerable plants may have some effect. The much publicized ground level 'slug traps' and 'slug pubs' filled with beer, certainly attract slugs but also attract and drown beneficial predatory beetles. Slug barriers can be made from plastic pots and bottles with the bottoms removed, slipped over young plants and pushed into the soil to protect them at their most vulnerable stage. Probably the single most effective measure is to hunt for slugs and snails at night by torchlight when they are feeding. Many can be caught this way on warm damp nights.

Eelworms More correctly known as nematodes, these minute, unsegmented worms live in the soil and in roots. Some are serious plant pests and so debilitate the crop – a state known as 'soil sickness'. Some make cysts which enable their eggs to persist in the soil for many years. As there are few remedies against eelworms the only practical solution is crop rotation, on a minimum three year cycle, to prevent the problem building up to serious infestations. Use resistant cultivars if available.

Aphids Aphids (including greenfly and blackfly), are a large group of insects with many species attacking a wide range of vegetables. With a few exceptions, each aphid species only attacks one species of plant. Aphids are sucking insects, feeding on the sap of the plant, and weakening it, often transmitting virus diseases in the process. They can build up very rapidly in warm weather, although predators such as ladybirds and hoverfly larvae, various parasites, and fungal diseases help to keep down the population. Ladybirds can be collected and transferred to plants

---

ORGANIC REMEDIES

DERRIS	aphids (greenfly, blackfly), beetles (flea beetle, pollen beetle), small caterpillars, turnip fly, weevils, red spider mite, sucking insects – see aphids, thrips
PYRETHRUM/ PYRETHRINS	caterpillars, beetles (many), greenfly, blackfly, leafhoppers, whitefly, thrips
INSECTICIDAL SOAP	aphids, leafhoppers, red spider mite, whitefly
BORDEAUX MIXTURE	blight, celery leaf spot
SULPHUR	powdery mildew
FINE NET FILMS (well pegged down)	cabbage root fly, carrot fly, bean seed fly, frit fly, onion fly, pollen beetle, cabbage whitefly, cabbage white butterfly, pea moth, cutworm (adult moths), leaf miners, birds, deter aphids and flea beetle

---

attacked by aphids, although there is no guarantee that they will stay there!

There are many chemical and organically approved sprays to control aphids (see chart, pp 58). Aphids can sometimes be cleared from plants by spraying with insecticidal soap. Bright yellow plastic glue-coated traps help to prevent infestations. They are hung slightly above plants in greenhouses or among crops. Well anchored spun fibre films keep out aphids (see Protected cropping, p 46), and shiny mulching films have a deterrent effect.

Beetles and weevils Of several types of beetle and weevil which nibble plants and cause damage, the most serious are flea beetles. These tiny beetles attack the seedlings of brassicas, including radishes, and turnips, especially in dry, warm weather, making small round holes in the leaves. Flea beetles can be destructive if not caught early, though well established plants can tolerate fairly extensive damage. Apart from the use of chemical and approved organic sprays, they can sometimes be caught with grease traps. Coat a piece of wood with heavy grease and hold it 2.5 cm (1 in) above the infested plants. The beetles will jump up and get stuck on the grease when the foliage is disturbed.

Caterpillars Caterpillars are amongst the most common and easily recognized pests, several species mainly attacking members of the brassica family. If a careful watch is kept they can be picked off by hand before they have done serious damage. Adult butterflies and moths can be prevented from laying eggs by growing crops under fleecy and net films. (See Protected cropping, p 46.) A wide range of chemical and approved organic products can be used to control caterpillars, as well as the biological control spray made from the bacterium *Bacillus thuringiensis.*

Root flies Three serious pests in this group are cabbage root fly, onion fly and carrot fly. The first two pests look like house flies and all three flies lay eggs at soil level. These hatch into small white maggots which feed on the roots. Young brassica and onion plants are often destroyed: carrot yields can be affected dramatically and the roots disfigured. Chemical sprays can be applied to the soil but it is better to protect the plants with physical barriers to prevent the flies laying their eggs.

For brassicas, use discs of about 13 cm (5 in) diameter made from rubberized carpet underlay or similar material. Cut a slit in one side to the central point, and open this out so the disc can be slipped around the stem of the plant after planting. These discs also provide cover for carabid beetles which eat the fly eggs. Barriers made from bottomless plastic pots or bottles can also be used. (See slugs above.) Remove them when they are outgrown.

Carrots can be grown within a 60-cm (2-ft) high barrier of clear polythene sheeting, erected around the bed or row. Because they fly low this effectively prevents the adult female flies from laying their eggs on the young plants. In a confined area the barrier may keep rain off the carrots: watch out for this and water if necessary. Fleecy and net films (see pp 49) give protection against root flies.

Bean seed fly The bean seed fly, whose maggots can also attack onions and leeks as well as slow-germinating peas and beans, is attracted to freshly disturbed soil to lay its eggs. It can be deterred by sowing in a 'stale' seedbed, ie a seedbed prepared ten days in advance of sowing.

Greenhouse pests Glasshouse whitefly and red spider mite are two pests which can pose serious problems in greenhouses and walk-in polytunnels. Both attack a wide range of plants, whitefly being most serious on tomatoes and cucumbers, red spider mite on cucumbers, beans, aubergines, tomatoes and peppers. Red spider mite may also attack plants outdoors in hot weather. The mites are tiny, and can be seen clearly only with a magnifying glass.

Both pests build up rapidly under high temperatures under cover, and are difficult to control with sprays as they have largely become resistant. In commercial horticulture, biological control is used instead. With care this method can be used in greenhouses and polytunnels. To some extent whitefly can be kept in check with sticky yellow glue traps, provided they are put up early in the season. Many organic growers have found that French and African marigolds (*Tagetes* spp.), interplanted with susceptible greenhouse crops act as a deterrent.

To prevent the build-up of pests under cover, it is most important to lower temperatures in hot weather. Ventilate as much as possible, and in hot weather, damp down several times a day by spraying plants and the greenhouse floor with water.

Diseases

Plant diseases are caused by fungi, bacteria and viruses. They are infectious, and in favourable conditions can spread rapidly through crops. Fungi cause grey moulds, mildews, the damping off diseases which infect seedlings, blight, rots and galls. They may be spread by airborne spores, and sometimes have resting spores which can persist in the soil for years.

Bacterial infections are often slimy in nature, and frequently occur as secondary infections on plants which are already damaged in some way. They may be spread in soil water, by splashing, and in wind blown soil particles or scattered by other means.

Virus diseases are often typified by stunted, twisted growth and mosaic patterning on the leaves. They may be transmitted by aphids and other insects, eelworms, occasionally by fungi, and sometimes even by hand.

Once a plant disease is well established it is generally too late to eradicate it. Preventive spraying, for example against potato or tomato blight, has to be done as soon as the first symptoms appear.

In all cases, prevention is better than cure. Strict garden hygiene, and burning all diseased materials, are important measures. This is particularly true of virus diseases, for which there are no remedies. Infected plants should be uprooted and burnt.

Thanks to the plant breeders, there are now many cultivars of garden vegetables with tolerance or resistance to common diseases. These should be used wherever possible. Refer to the individual vegetables for disease-resistant cultivars.

Plant disorders

Plants sometimes suffer from physiological disorders, due in the main to inadequate watering, unsuitable growing conditions, poor feeding or mineral deficiencies.

Chemical control

Although chemical sprays offer a quick and simple solution to many pest and some disease problems, their use in the vegetable garden should be kept to a minimum. There are several reasons for this.

- Many chemicals are toxic not just to the pest in question, but to other beneficial and predatory insects which can do much to keep pests in check.
- Most chemicals leave residues on plants and in the soil, so a certain amount of time has to elapse before the plants are eaten. The damage to soil life is difficult to assess.
- In some cases pests and diseases develop immunity and resistance to specific chemicals, so the less any chemical is used, the longer it is likely to be effective. This is a major problem in commercial horticulture, but can arise on a garden scale.
- If wrongly used, chemicals are a hazard to man, domestic animals and wildlife. Serious accidents can occur if they are misused.

A few chemicals are approved for use by organic growers. These are mainly of plant origin, and break down more rapidly than 'inorganic' chemicals into non-toxic components, so making them less harmful from the environmental point of view. They are generally less effective but can be useful as a last resort for organic gardeners.

Using chemicals

Insecticides (chemicals which kill pests) fall into three categories. The *contact* poisons kill pests which are directly hit by them. Most of the approved organic sprays fall into this group. *Stomach* poisons kill pests which eat the plants within a few days of spraying, before the spray has been washed off the leaves. *Systemic* insecticides are absorbed by the plant and kill insects and mites which subsequently feed on the sap.

Fungicides (chemicals which kill fungi), being relatively ineffective once a disease is established, have to be used in advance of an attack. There are two types. *Protectants* kill infective spores which land on the plant surface, but are likely to be washed off by rain. *Systemics* are absorbed by the plant, and kill the fungus once it starts to develop inside the plant.

Chemicals are marketed under brand names, but should be selected according to their *active ingredient*, stated on the bottle or packet. Active ingredients are given in the chart on pp 58–65.

Chemicals are available in various forms. Dusts are applied with puffers, or shaken up with seeds as a seed dressing. They are sometimes sprinkled along the drill before sowing. Granules are applied direct to the soil. Wettable powders and liquid concentrates are made up or diluted in liquid forms, and applied with small hand sprayers or syringes. A 1-litre (2-pt) sprayer is adequate for most garden purposes. Some chemicals are now available in diluted solutions which are ready to spray.

Rules for spraying

These rules apply for all chemicals including those approved for organic gardening, which though less damaging, are still toxic.

- Always follow the manufacturer's instructions, never exceed the recommended dose.
- Never apply in windy conditions, when spray or dusts may drift on to other plants. Never spray in hot sun, which can cause scorching on leaves, and harm pollinating insects. Ideally spray in still, overcast conditions, in the evening.
- Try to avoid spraying plants in flower, again to protect pollinating insects.
- Never spray water in ditches, tanks or tubs.
- Spray so that the leaves of the whole plant are well covered, but avoid holding the spray nozzle so close that the leaves are physically damaged. Never spray wilted plants.
- Only make up the minimum amount of spray, and dispose of any left over. Wash out all equipment after use. Never transfer sprays into ordinary bottles. Store chemicals in a cool place out of sunlight, and out of reach of children and pets.

Biological control

Biological control is the technique of controlling a pest by introducing a natural enemy. Where feasible it is a practical alternative to chemical spraying. The biological agents are specific to their 'host' and will not harm other insects or wildlife. There is little risk involved, as the introduced agent dies out once its 'host' has been cleared. Currently there are only a few cases where biological control is practical for amateur gardeners, but it is quite likely that more will become available in future.

Most of the butterfly and moth caterpillars attacking cabbages and some cutworm caterpillars can be controlled by spraying with products containing the bacterium *Bacillus thuringiensis*. This is sold in sachets which can be kept unopened for two to three years in a cool dry place. Spraying may be necessary at weekly intervals, but should be done no more than necessary, to prevent caterpillars building up resistance.

Glasshouse whitefly can be controlled by introducing the tiny parasitic wasp *Encarsia formosa*, and red spider mite with the predatory mite *Phytoseiulus persimilis*. In both cases, the controls should be ordered from mail order suppliers as soon as the pests are noticed. The beneficial animals require average daytime temperatures in the low 20s C (mid 70s F) to operate, so they may be ineffective if there is a sudden temperature drop. Nor will they be effective if chemical sprays have been used in the greenhouse. Most suppliers send out detailed instructions which should be followed carefully.

PESTS, DISEASES AND DISORDERS

(See also general preventive and control measures, Pests and Diseases pages **53–57**).

PEST AND APPEARANCE	CROP AFFECTED	SYMPTOMS	PREVENTIVE MEASURES	CONTROL

Soil pests

[Controls approved for organic use are shown in brackets]

PEST AND APPEARANCE	CROP AFFECTED	SYMPTOMS	PREVENTIVE MEASURES	CONTROL
CUTWORMS: greenish grey caterpillars up to 5cm (2in) long. (See p 54.)	Wide range, especially those with soft tap roots, e.g. lettuces, beetroots, carrots, parsnips, potatoes.	Cuts off plants at ground level. Makes holes in potatoes and other roots crops. May to September.	Heavy rain or watering in June/July kills young caterpillars. Grow under fine nets.	Chlorpyrifos+diazinon or pirimiphos-methyl granules worked into top 5cm (2in) of soil before sowing or planting.
LEATHERJACKETS: tough skinned, legless, greyish brown grubs, up to 3.5cm (1¼in long. (See p 54.)	Wide range of plants, young ones in particular, e.g. lettuces, brassicas.	Stems bitten through at soil level. Ragged feeding on lower leaves. March to July.	Ensure the ground is well drained. Clear and dig land before end of September, especially if after grassland.	As for cutworm.
SLUGS AND SNAILS: familiar soft-bodied creatures. (See p 55.)	Attack leaves, stems, roots, tubers, of a wide range of plants. Potatoes (maincrop), oriental greens and celery are at risk in particular from slugs.	Make holes in plant tissue. Most active on wet sites and in damp weather, all year round.	Improve drainage. Clear weeds. Lift maincrop potatoes as soon as the tubers have matured. Avoid highly susceptible cultivars, e.g. 'Maris Piper', when slugs are a problem.	Slug pellets containing metaldehyde or, especially in damp conditions, methiocarb. [Aluminium sulphate, applied in spring, helps control newly hatched slugs.]
WIREWORM: yellow wire-like body about 2.5cm (1in) long, with three pairs of short legs. (See p 55.)	Wide range of crops, especially roots, potatoes and lettuces.	Holes in roots and tubers; plants nipped off at soil level. March to September. Worst effects in first three years after cultivation of neglected ground or former grassland.	Avoid growing root crops for three years after digging in turf unless they are used primarily to attract and remove wireworms.	As for cutworm.

Eelworms (nematodes)

PEST AND APPEARANCE	CROP AFFECTED	SYMPTOMS	PREVENTIVE MEASURES	CONTROL
STEM AND BULB EELWORMS: microscopic pests inside leaves and bulbs or stems. (See p55.)	Onions, leeks, and related plants. Can also develop in some common weeds.	Seedlings stunted, bloated and distorted. Later, leek stems thicken and rot: onions become thick-necked and rot. April to August.	Practise three- or four-year rotation. Remove and destroy infested plants. Keep weeds under control. All brassicas and lettuces are immune and can be grown in infested soil.	No chemical treatment available to amateurs.
POTATO CYST EELWORMS: pinhead-sized spherical white or yellow-brown cysts on roots in July to August. (See p 55.)	Potatoes, tomatoes.	Growth stunted and weak. Plants die early with the lower leaves dying first. Potato tubers and tomato fruits small.	Practise at least a three-year rotation. Buy clean potato seed. Some cultivars have some resistance or tolerance of cyst eelworms. (See p 136.) Where soil infested don't plant potatoes or tomatoes for at least six years.	No chemical treatment available to amateurs.

Aphids, thrips and whitefly

PEST AND APPEARANCE	CROP AFFECTED	SYMPTOMS	PREVENTIVE MEASURES	CONTROL
BLACK BEAN APHID (BLACKFLY)	Broad, French and runner beans	Colonies of black aphids appear on stem tips. Late May to August.	Pinch out tops of broad beans after flowering. Transfer ladybirds on to colony.	Spray at dusk with systemic aphicide e.g. dimethoate, heptenophos, or use malathion or pirimicarb. [Derris/pyrethrum, insecticidal soap]

Cutworms affect many crops including lettuce (see p 58)

Leatherjackets attack young plants (see p 58)

Slugs damage on potatoes (see p 58)

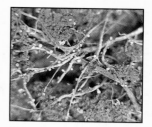

Cysts of potato cyst eelworm (see p 58)

Black bean aphids on broad beans (see p 58)

Cabbage mealy aphid (see p 60)

Root aphid on lettuce (see p 60)

Flea beetle damage on turnip (see p 60)

Pea and bean weevil damage on broad beans (see p 60)

Cabbage root fly damage (see p 61)

Onion fly damage (see p 62)

Parsnip roots affected by canker (see p 62)

Clubroot affects brassicas (see p 63)

Scab on potatoes (see p 63)

Leek rust (see p 63)

Downy mildew on lettuce (see p 63)

Neck rot on onion (see p 63)

Cucumber mosaic virus on marrow (see p 64)

Symptoms of magnesium deficiency (see p 65)

Hormone weedkiller damage on tomato (see p 66)

Continued overleaf

PEST AND APPEARANCE	CROP AFFECTED	SYMPTOMS	PREVENTIVE MEASURES	CONTROL
CABBAGE MEALY APHID	Brassicas including swedes	Mealy grey aphids on leaves and stems. Leaves pucker May to October, worst attack late summer. Can permanently stunt young plants.	Destroy overwintered brassicas by May. Move ladybirds to lightly infested plants.	Spray the underside of leaves with dimethoate, heptenophos, or pirimicarb. [Insecticidal soap, derris, pyrethrum]
CABBAGE WHITEFLY: small, white-winged insects (.5mm (1/16in) long, and pale oval scale-like nymphs on underside of leaves.	All leafy brassicas. Present throughout the year	Adult whiteflies readily fly up when disturbed. Heavy infestations cause stickiness and sooty mould, especially on Brussels sprouts.	Destroy old plants immediately after cropping. Grow under fine nets.	Light infestations not damaging, but if necessary spray underneath leaves with pirimiphos-methyl or permethrin. [Pyrethrum]
LEAF APHIDS (GREENFLY – may also be yellowish green or pink)	Cucumbers, tomatoes, peppers, aubergines	Colonies of aphids on underside of leaves cause stunted growth and mottled puckered brittle leaves throughout growing season.	Brush off and destroy colonies while small. Destroy virus-infected plants promptly.	Spray with heptenophos, pirimicarb or permethrin. [Pyrethrum, derris, insecticidal soap]
	Lettuces, endives, and other crops	Colonies on underside of leaves and in centre of plant: especially under cloches or in greenhouses.	Aluminium foil mulch may deter winged aphids from landing. Also growing under fine nets.	Spray with dimethoate, heptenophos or pirimicarb. [Derris, pyrethrum, or insecticidal soap near harvest]
PEA THRIPS (THUNDERFLIES): black or yellow narrow bodied insects, just under 2mm (1/12in) long.	Peas	Attack young pods and foliage from early June. Worst in hot summers. Pods silvery, distorted. Peas in pods fail to develop. June to August.		Spray with fenitrothion or dimethoate. [Derris, rotenone, pyrethrum]
ROOT APHIDS (several spp.)	Lettuces, runner and French beans, carrots, parsnips, globe artichokes	Yellowish brown aphids secrete a white waxy powder on the roots and soil particles. Plants grow slowly and wilt.	Lettuces: use resistant cultivars. (See p 116.) Rotate crops.	Difficult, but watering infested plants with pirimiphos-methyl may help.
ASPARAGUS BEETLE: grey-green grubs, black and yellow adult beetles up to 7mm (1/4in) long.	Asparagus	Attack leaves and stems. Leaves may be stripped. Late May to October.	Remove beetles and larvae as soon as seen.	Spray with malathion, or pirimiphos-methyl. [Derris]
FLEA BEETLE: bluish or black beetles, 3mm (1/8in) long, sometimes with a yellow stripe down each wing case.	Brassicas, radishes, swedes, turnips and salad rocket	Neat round holes made in seedling leaves. March to September.	Sow early (March) or late (June) to miss most severe attack from first brood. Water seedling rows in dry spells to get seedlings quickly through this susceptible period. Try grease traps and fine nets. (see p 55)	Spray or dust seedlings with gamma-HCH, carbaryl or pirimiphos-methyl. [Derris]
PEA AND BEAN WEEVIL: greyish brown beetles about 5mm (1/5in) long.	Peas and broad beans	U-shaped notches nibbled from leaf margins. March to July.	Plants recover but seedlings may be checked.	If necessary treat as for flea beetle.

PEST AND APPEARANCE	CROP AFFECTED	SYMPTOMS	PREVENTIVE MEASURES	CONTROL
POLLEN BEETLE: black beetle 2mm (1/12in) long	Cauliflower, calabrese, broccoli. Also found in flowers of marrows and related plants, and runner beans, but rarely damaging.	In cauliflower etc flower heads damaged and discoloured where beetles have eaten into them. Found in late spring and summer.	Grow under fine nets.	Difficult due to vast numbers of beetles migrating from oil seed rape fields. Spraying with permethrin [or derris] may protect brassicas. Do not spray flowers of beans or marrows etc or bees will be killed and pollination prevented.

Caterpillars (butterfly and moth)

CATERPILLARS (several types of 'Cabbage Whites' and cabbage moths. (See p 55)	Brassicas	Caterpillars make holes in leaves and bore into cabbage hearts. Frass collects at base of leaves May to October.	Inspect plants twice weekly. Destroy eggs and caterpillars. Grow under fine nets.	Spray or dust with pirimiphos-methyl, fenitrothion or permethrin. [Derris, pyrethrum. Apply biological agent *Bacillus thuringiensis*]
PEA MOTH: small white caterpillars up to 6mm (1/4in) long in the pods.	Peas	Feed on developing peas. June to August.	Sow early (March) for crop to flower before early June. Grow short cvs under fine net.	For cultivars flowering between early June and mid-August spray with permethrin or fenitrothion 7 to 10 days after first flowers open.

Flies

BEAN SEED FLY: white maggots, 8mm (1/3in) long.	Runner beans, French beans	Seeds do not germinate, or seedlings weak and distorted. April to October damage most frequent in cold wet soils, when germination is slow.	Sow into a 'stale' seedbed (see p 56.) Encourage rapid germination. Grow under fine nets.	Apply pirimiphos-methyl or gamma-HCH dust along rows at sowing.
CABBAGE ROOT FLY: white maggots, 8mm (3/8in) long.	All brassicas, including turnips and swedes, and radishes	Maggot damage to roots causes stunting and death of seedlings and transplants. May to October. Adults start to emerge when cow parsley is in flower.	Use a physical barrier round the plant stems after planting (see p 56.) Sow turnips and swedes after May to miss main attack. Grow under fine nets.	Apply chlorpyrifos + diazinon or pirimiphos-methyl to soil around plants within three days of planting or along seed drills.
CARROT FLY: slender creamy white maggots 8mm (3/8in)	Carrots, parsley, parsnips, celery, and celeriac. June to October	Seedlings die. Plants become stunted and foliage reddish. The roots are mined and maggots will be found later, on lifting.	Sow very thinly. Sow early (mid-March) or late (mid-June) to avoid first brood. Lift early carrots before September, parsnips and celery by November. Plant within barriers (see p 56) or grow under fine nets. The cultivars 'Fly Away' and 'Sytan' are less susceptible than other carrots.	Apply chlorpyrifos + diazinon or pirimiphos-methyl dust below or along seed row before sowing. Water rows with spray strength liquid pirimiphos-methyl in early August for late crops.
CELERY FLY OR LEAF MINER: white maggots up to 8mm (3/8in) long, inside the leaves	Celery, celeriac, lovage and parsnips	Large brown blister mines in leaves June to October. Early summer attacks more damaging; slows growth, makes stalks stringy and bitter.	Reject seedlings with blistered leaves. Pinch out and destroy blistered leaves. Grow under fine nets.	Spray with dimethoate or malathion if attack is becoming severe.

Continued overleaf

PEST AND APPEARANCE	CROP AFFECTED	SYMPTOMS	PREVENTIVE MEASURES	CONTROL
FRIT FLY: small white maggot 3mm (⅛in) long inside the stem base.	Sweet corn	Maggots attack base of seedlings causing growing point to wilt and die. May to June.	Seedlings immune after five to six leaf stage. Raise singly in pots in the greenhouse and transplant, or sow late (May). Grow under fine nets until five to six leaf stage.	Spray with fenitrothion or apply gamma-HCH dust as shoots emerge.
ONION FLY: white maggots, 8mm (⅓in) long.	Onions, leeks and shallots	Seedlings die off in groups, with yellow drooping leaves. May to September. Worst on dry soils in hot weather.	Sow into 'stale' seedbed (see p 56), especially for August sowings. Remove and burn infested plants. Grow under fine nets.	If attacks occur frequently apply chlorpyrifos + diazinon or pirimiphos-methyl dust along rows when seedlings at the 'loop' stage.

Greenhouse pests

GLASSHOUSE RED SPIDER MITE: minute, eight-legged, yellowish green, black or reddish mites on underside of leaves. Difficult to see individuals with naked eye.	Cucumber, pepper, aubergine, tomato. In hot summers damages outdoor vegetables, especially French and runner beans.	Fine pale mottling of the upper leaf surface. Leaves dry up and fall prematurely. Fine silk webbing may be seen between the leaves.	Spray the underside of leaves frequently with water, and maintain high humidity.	Resistance to chemicals such as malathion, dimethoate and pirimiphos-methyl now widespread. Biological control: introduce predatory mite *Phytoseiulus persimilis* before a heavy infestation develops.
GLASSHOUSE WHITEFLY: white winged insects 1.5mm (1/16in) long, and flat oval whitish green scale-like nymphs underneath the leaves.	Tomato, cucumber, pepper; less frequent on outdoor crops	Upper surface of leaves becomes sticky and blackened with honeydew and sooty mould.	Avoid buying infested plants. Yellow sticky traps catch some of the adults.	Resistance to chemicals such as permethrin, [pyrethrum] and pirimiphos-methyl frequently occurs. Biological control: introduce parasitic insect *Encarsia formosa* before a heavy infestation has developed. (Indoors only)

Fungal and bacterial diseases

BLIGHT	Potatoes	Brown patches on the leaves (showing in mid to late summer) which on the undersurface have a white fringe.	Cut back haulms of infected potatoes in late August, to prevent blight spreading. Use resistant cultivars (see p 136)	Spray maincrop cvs in early July with a copper fungicide or mancozeb.
	Tomatoes	Brown patches on the leaves which soon die. Russet-brown marbled rotted areas on fruit.		Same chemicals applied to outdoor tomatoes as soon as the plant has been 'stopped'.
BOTRYTIS (GREY MOULD)	Lettuces	Stems may rot completely at the collar, so that plant collapses. May be grey mould on leaves.	Destroy infected plants. Maintain good air circulation.	Spray with benomyl or carbendazim at the first sign of the disease.
CANKER	Parsnip	Tops of roots blackened and cracked, and eventually rotted.	Rotation. Use resistant cultivars, e.g. 'Avonresister'. May/June sowings and closely spaced sowings are often less affected.	No satisfactory chemical control known at present.
CHOCOLATE SPOT	Broad beans	Small chocolate coloured spots or streaks on leaves and stems. In wet springs affected winter sown plants may become blackened and die.	Lime acid soils to pH 7. Apply potash before November sowing. Sow thinly in well drained soil. Burn diseased plants at end of season.	Following year spray developing foliage with benomyl or carbendazim until flowering.

DISEASE	CROP AFFECTED	SYMPTOMS	PREVENTIVE MEASURES	CONTROL
CLUBROOT	Brassicas including swedes and turnips, and radishes	Above ground: discoloured leaves; wilting in warm weather. Below ground: solid swollen galls on roots.	Maintain a slightly alkaline pH by liming. Ensure good drainage. Raise plants in sterile soil. Rotate brassicas strictly. See also Brassicas p **81**.	Dip transplant roots into thiophanate-methyl or carbendazim.
COMMON SCAB	Potatoes	Scabby areas on tubers, with ragged edges to lesions.	May be severe on light dry soils. Dig in organic matter but do not lime before planting. Grow resistant cultivars. Water in dry weather.	
DAMPING OFF	Brassicas, beetroots, carrots, lettuces, peas, tomatoes	Seedlings fail to emerge or keel over and die soon after emergence.	Avoid sowing in cold, wet soil. Sow thinly.	Drench seedlings with a suitable copper fungicide.
LEAF SPOTS	Celery	Small brown spots on leaves and stalks. Yields may be poor in severe cases.	Use fungicide-treated seeds.	Spray with benomyl, carbendazim, mancozeb or a copper fungicide
	Beetroot, spinach beet, brassicas	Brown spots on leaves, which may fall out leaving holes.	Rotate. Apply potash before sowing. Thin out early and/or space well.	
LEEK RUST	Leeks	Orange spots and blotches appear on leaves. Rarely very severe.	Raise plants on a fresh site each year. Remove and burn diseased leaves. Keep plants widely spaced. Avoid high nitrogen fertilizers.	No chemical control known at present.
MILDEW, DOWNY	Brassicas	Usually affects young plants. Leaves yellow with white area on under surface.	Avoid overcrowding. Raise seedlings in new beds.	Spray with mancozeb at first sign of disease.
	Lettuces	Pale green or yellow angular areas on older leaves (white spores on lower surface). Infected areas die and become brown. Occurs mainly in autumn. See p **116**	Use resistant cultivars. Avoid overcrowding. Remove diseased leaves.	After removing infected leaves spray with mancozeb or with a fungicide containing thiram if spotted early.
	Onions	Pale oval areas on leaves; tips of leaves become grey and die back. Leaves often fold downwards at infected area.	Avoid contaminated and badly drained soils. Ensure adequate air circulation.	Spray with mancozeb or a fungicide containing thiram at first signs of disease.
MILDEW, POWDERY	Cucumbers	White powdery spots or patches on leaves.	Maintain good air circulation if under cover.	Spray with benomyl at first sign of the disease. [Sulphur]
NECK ROT	Onions	Grey rots on necks of stored onions.	Grow well! Rotate. Buy good-quality sets or treated seed. Remove all debris. Avoid over-feeding. Dry bulbs well before storage. Remove rotting bulbs as seen. Handle bulbs gently when lifting.	Dust onion seeds or sets with an approved formulation of carbendazim. Spraying foliage with benomyl during the growing season may help.

Continued overleaf

DISEASE	CROP AFFECTED	SYMPTOMS	PREVENTIVE MEASURES	CONTROL
ROOT ROT	Peas, beans	Leaves, stems and pods turn yellow and shrivelled. Roots and stem base become browny black.	Practise a three-year rotation. Avoid sowing on a heavy wet soil (especially early cultivars). Burn diseased plants.	Drench seedlings with a suitable copper fungicide.
SMUT	Sweet corn	'Smut balls' form on the cobs and occasionally on the leaves and stems and are filled with a black spore mass. Most likely to be seen in a hot dry year.	Remove affected areas before the smut balls rupture. Remove and burn crop debris at the end of each year.	No chemical control.
STEM ROT	Tomatoes	Yellow-brown canker at base of stem on mature plants. Black dots in cankered area.	Destroy infected plants.	No chemical control.
WHITE ROT	Onions and sometimes leeks	White fluffy mould at base of onion and roots. Leaves wilt and turn yellow.	Rotation. Remove and burn affected plants.	No chemical control.

Virus diseases

DISEASE	CROP AFFECTED	SYMPTOMS	PREVENTIVE MEASURES	CONTROL
CARROT MOTLEY DWARF VIRUS	Carrots and parsley	Plants become stunted with twisted leaf stalks. yellow bands develop between leaf veins; later become reddish. Root tips and root hairs die.	Dig up and burn affected plants.	Control aphids which transmit the disease.
CUCUMBER MOSAIC VIRUS	Cucumbers, marrows.	Leaves mottled yellow with surface puckered and distorted. Plants become stunted and may die: any fruits which develop are likely to be puckered and blotched yellow.	Remove and destroy infected plants immediately. Grow up to three times as many plants as finally needed. Avoid handling.	Control of aphids will help to reduce virus spread. Grow cultivars showing resistance where available.
LETTUCE MOSAIC VIRUS	Lettuces	Yellow mottling on leaves; veins appear transparent. Plants stunted.	Buy virus-tested seed. Destroy infected plants.	As above.
MOSAIC VIRUSES	Potatoes	Yellow mottling on leaves.	Remove and burn infected plants.	As above.
	Tomatoes	Pale green and yellowish mottling on leaves. Fruit bronzed and blemished. Yields reduced.	As above.	As above.
PARSLEY YELLOWS	Parsley, carrots, possibly parsnips	Plants yellowing occasionally pink; weak. Relatively common, especially in dry years with high aphid population. May be combination of viruses, probably aphid borne.	As above.	As above.
POTATO LEAF ROLL VIRUS	Potatoes	Leaves roll upwards and become hard and brittle. Plants stunted.	Remove and burn infected plants. Use certified seed.	As above.

DISEASE	CROP AFFECTED	SYMPTOMS	PREVENTIVE MEASURES	CONTROL
TURNIP MOSAIC VIRUS	Turnips and swedes	Yellowish and dark green mottling on the foliage.	Destroy infected plants.	Control of aphids will help to reduce virus spread.

Disorders

DISEASE	CROP AFFECTED	SYMPTOMS	PREVENTIVE MEASURES	CONTROL
MAGNESIUM DEFICIENCY	Many, but especially common on tomatoes and other crops fed with high potash fertilizers	Interveinal yellowing (or occasionally orange-brown discolouration). The older leaves affected first. Leaf drop may occur.	Avoid excessive use of potash or high potash feeds.	Dress the soil with Epsom salts or spray the foliage with a solution of Epsom salts to which a wetter has been added.
CALCIUM DEFICIENCY	Common on tomatoes and peppers as 'blossom end rot'	A dark brown-black sunken leathery patch develops at the blossom end of the fruit.	Water regularly and plentifully so that adequate calcium can be taken up.	Remove affected fruit and improve water regime.
BORON DEFICIENCY	Mainly root crops, and celery	Often browning or darkening in concentric rings. Roots may split open and the foliage be discoloured. With celery the stems develop horizontal cracks.	Avoid excessive liming of the soil and water well so that dry soil conditions do not develop.	Deficiencies can be avoided by applying borax at 35g/20 sq metres (1oz/20 sq yds) before sowing or planting.
WHIPTAIL	Brassicas, especially broccoli and cauliflower	Leaves become very narrowed and straplike, and may show distortion. Heads fail to develop.	Deficiency of molybdenum, most likely to be seen on acid soils.	To counteract acidity lime soil prior to sowing or planting. Apply a chelated or fritted formulation containing molybdenum.

Spasmodic watering

DISEASE	CROP AFFECTED	SYMPTOMS	PREVENTIVE MEASURES	CONTROL
FRUIT WITHERING	Cucumbers	Young fruits wither starting at the blossom end and progressing towards the stem.	Poor nutrition or starvation of the fruit due to a root problem or disease such as a foot and root rot. (see p **108**.)	Plants affected by a foot or root rot are best removed. If otherwise healthy, remove withered fruit and foliar feed whole plant regularly.
PREMATURE FRUIT DROP	A wide range, including cucumbers and tomatoes	Fruit starts to form but drop while still immature.	Ensure regular feeding and watering. Try to avoid extremes of temperature.	Withered fruit will not recover.
BLOSSOM END ROT	Tomatoes and peppers	See Calcium deficiency above.		
FLOWER DROP	Especially common on protected crops	Flowers form and may even open, but are shed when flower stalk breaks.	Water regularly and in sufficient quantity. Improve the soil moisture retaining capacity.	As for prevention.
ROOTS CRACKING	Root crops including potatoes	Fissures in the roots, usually longitudinal, and sometimes reaching into the centre of the root. Secondary infections may occur. Symptoms actually develop *after* the crop has received heavy watering or rainfall.	Water regularly and in sufficient quantity. Improve the soils' moisture retaining capacity.	Later developing crops may be saved if conditions are improved.

Continued overleaf

DISEASE	CROP AFFECTED	SYMPTOMS	PREVENTIVE MEASURES	CONTROL
POTATO HOLLOW HEART	Potatoes	Large central cavities develop, often star shaped and in the larger tubers. The plant itself looks normal.	Water regularly and in sufficient quantity. Improve the soil moisture retaining capacity. Do not overfeed.	Later developing crops may be saved if conditions are improved.
FRUIT SPLITTING	A wide range, especially tomatoes	Fruits split open, often becoming affected by secondary infections. Symptoms developing after crop has received heavy watering or rainfall.	Water regularly and in sufficient quantity. Improve the soil's moisture retaining capacity. Do not overfeed.	Later developing crops may be saved if conditions are improved.

Dryness

DISEASE	CROP AFFECTED	SYMPTOMS	PREVENTIVE MEASURES	CONTROL
BEAN POD SET FAILURE	Beans, especially runner beans	Pods fail to set or set and drop off.	Water well, especially in the flowering and pod stages. Prepare the trench thoroughly to maximize moisture retention. Harvest beans as soon as they are ready, to encourage future pod set. Sow white/pink-flowered beans as they are less prone to this problem than those with red flowers.	Later developing crops may be saved if conditions are improved.
BOLTING	Especially common in spinach, beetroot, leeks, onions, celery, oriental brassicas.	Flower stems develop prematurely during the first season.	Water well and regularly so that the soil never becomes too dry. Do not sow seed too early. Can be due to sudden temperature drop, or to sowing at season when daylength triggers bolting. Choose appropriate cultivars.	Later developing crops may be saved if conditions are improved.
BITTER FRUITS	Cucumbers	Fruits appear normal but have a bitter and unpleasant taste.	Water regularly and adequately. Avoid too much high nitrogen fertilizer.	Later developing crops may be saved if conditions are improved.
HORMONE WEEDKILLER DAMAGE	A wide range, but especially common in tomatoes.	The foliage becomes distorted, often narrowed with very prominent and parallel veins. Any fruit which develop may be strangely elongated and hollow inside.	Apply all weedkillers exactly according to the manufacturers' instructions, using equipment kept solely for that purpose. Store weedkillers in a cool safe place away from plants.	Except in severe cases and in brassicas, plants usually grow out of the symptoms.

RECOMMENDED CULTIVARS

The recommendations for the main vegetables have been based on those made by the National Institute of Agricultural Botany (NIAB) as a result of their trials for commercial growers. For crops not covered by NIAB trials, recommendations are based on other trials (eg RHS trials at Wisley), reports and general experience. It should be stressed that there are probably many other equally good cultivars which for a variety of reasons, such as not being included in trials, having been recently introduced, or currently unavailable to amateur gardeners, have not been listed. Inclusion is simply a guarantee of reliability and good quality, not necessarily superiority. Look out for improved new cultivars, which are continually being introduced. All cultivars listed are available from current seed catalogues, but inevitably these change from year to year. The list of stockists, below, all provide a mail order service. (For more detailed information on NIAB recommendations see *Vegetable varieties for the gardener* (Wisley Handbook, Royal Horticultural Society 1992.)

LIST OF SUPPLIERS

BAKKER HOLLAND, PO Box 111, Spalding, Lincs PE12 6EL

J W BOYCE, Bush Pasture, Lower Carter St, Fordham, Ely, Cambs

D T BROWN & CO LTD, Poulton Le Fyle, Blackpool FY6 7HX

CHILTERN SEEDS, Bortree Stile, Ulveston, Cumbria, LA12 7PB

COUNTRY GARDENS, 69-71 Main St, East Leake, Leics LE12 6PF

DIG AND DELVE ORGANICS, Fen Road, Blo' Borton, Diss, Norfolk IP22 2JH

SAMUEL DOBIE & SON LTD, Broomhill Way, Torquay, Devon TQ2 7QW

MR FOTHERGILL'S SEEDS, Kentford, Newmarket, Suffolk CB8 7QB

W W JOHNSON & SON LTD, London Road, Boston, Lincs PE21 8AD

S E MARSHALL & CO LTD, Regal Rd, Wisbech, Cambs PE13 2RF

THE ORGANIC GARDENING CATALOGUE, Coombelands House, Addlestone, Weybridge, Surrey KT15 1HY

PROSEEDS, 26 Chapman Close, Potton, Sandy, Beds SG19 2PL

SUFFOLK HERBS AND KINGS SEEDS, Monks Farm, Pantlings Lane, Kevedon, Essex CO5 9PG.

SUTTONS SEEDS, Hele Rd, Torquay, Devon TQ2 7QJ

THOMPSON & MORGAN, London Rd, Ipswich, Suffolk IP2 0BA

EDWIN TUCKER & SONS LTD, Brewery Meadow, Stonepark, Ashburton TQ13 7DG

UNWINS SEEDS LTD, Histon, Cambridge CB4 4LE

VEGETABLE PLANNING CHART

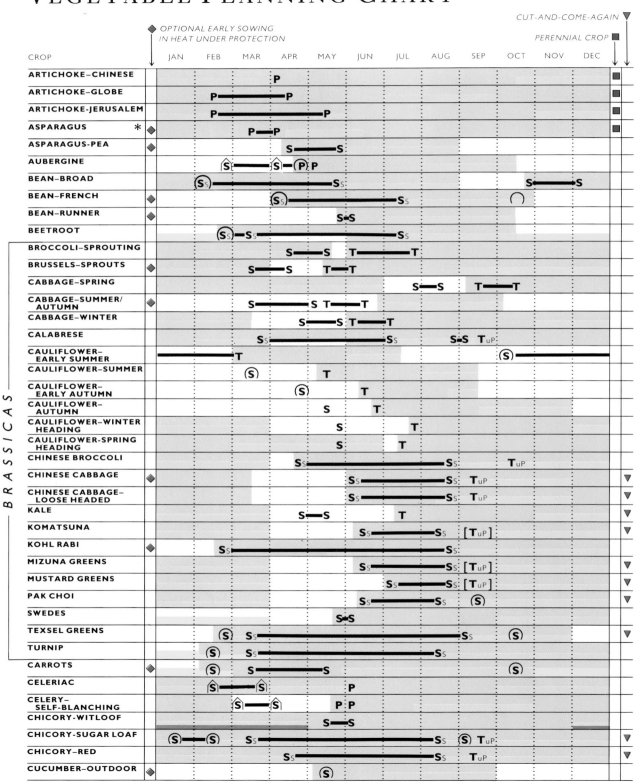

◆ *OPTIONAL EARLY SOWING*
IN HEAT UNDER PROTECTION

CUT-AND-COME-AGAIN ▼

PERENNIAL CROP ■

CROP	JAN	FEB	MAR	APR	MAY	JUN	JUL	AUG	SEP	OCT	NOV	DEC		
ARTICHOKE–CHINESE			P											■
ARTICHOKE–GLOBE		P━━━━P												■
ARTICHOKE-JERUSALEM		P━━━━━━━P												■
ASPARAGUS ✳ ◆			P━P											■
ASPARAGUS-PEA ◆					S━━━S									
AUBERGINE		(S)━━━(S)━(P)P												
BEAN–BROAD	(S)━━━━━━━━━Sₛ									S━━━S				
BEAN–FRENCH ◆			(Sₛ)━━━━━━━Sₛ						⌒				
BEAN–RUNNER ◆					S━S								
BEETROOT	(Sₛ)━Sₛ━━━━━━━━━Sₛ												
BROCCOLI–SPROUTING				S━━S T━━━━━T									
BRUSSELS–SPROUTS ◆		S━━━S T━━T											
CABBAGE–SPRING								S━━S	T━━━T				
CABBAGE–SUMMER/ AUTUMN ◆		S━━━━━S T━━━T											
CABBAGE–WINTER				S━━S T━━T									
CALABRESE		Sₛ━━━━━━━━━━━Sₛ S━S Tᵤₚ											
CAULIFLOWER– EARLY SUMMER	━━━━━━━T								(S)━━━━━━━				
CAULIFLOWER–SUMMER		(S)		T									
CAULIFLOWER– EARLY AUTUMN			(S)		T								
CAULIFLOWER– AUTUMN				S	T								
CAULIFLOWER–WINTER HEADING					S	T							
CAULIFLOWER-SPRING HEADING					S	T							
CHINESE BROCCOLI				Sₛ━━━━━━━━Sₛ					Tᵤₚ				
CHINESE CABBAGE ◆						Sₛ━━━━━Sₛ			Tᵤₚ				▼
CHINESE CABBAGE– LOOSE HEADED						Sₛ━━━━━Sₛ			Tᵤₚ				▼
KALE				S━S		T							▼
KOMATSUNA					Sₛ━━━━━Sₛ			[Tᵤₚ]					▼
KOHL RABI ◆		Sₛ━━━━━━━━━━━Sₛ											
MIZUNA GREENS					Sₛ━━━━━Sₛ [Tᵤₚ]								▼
MUSTARD GREENS						Sₛ━━━Sₛ [Tᵤₚ]							▼
PAK CHOI					Sₛ━━━Sₛ			(S)					▼
SWEDES					S━S								
TEXSEL GREENS		(S) Sₛ━━━━━━━━━━━━Sₛ							(S)				▼
TURNIP		(S) Sₛ━━━━━━━━━Sₛ											
CARROTS ◆		(S) S━━━━━S						(S)				
CELERIAC		(S)━━(S)		P									
CELERY– SELF-BLANCHING		(S)━━(S)	P P										
CHICORY-WITLOOF	━━━━━━━━━━━ S━S										━━		
CHICORY-SUGAR LOAF	(S)━(S) Sₛ━━━━━━━━Sₛ							(S) Tᵤₚ				▼
CHICORY–RED			Sₛ━━━━━━━━Sₛ					Tᵤₚ				▼
CUCUMBER–OUTDOOR ◆					(S)								
	JAN	FEB	MAR	APR	MAY	JUN	JUL	AUG	SEP	OCT	NOV	DEC		

BRASSICAS (vertical label at left, spanning BROCCOLI–SPROUTING to TURNIP)

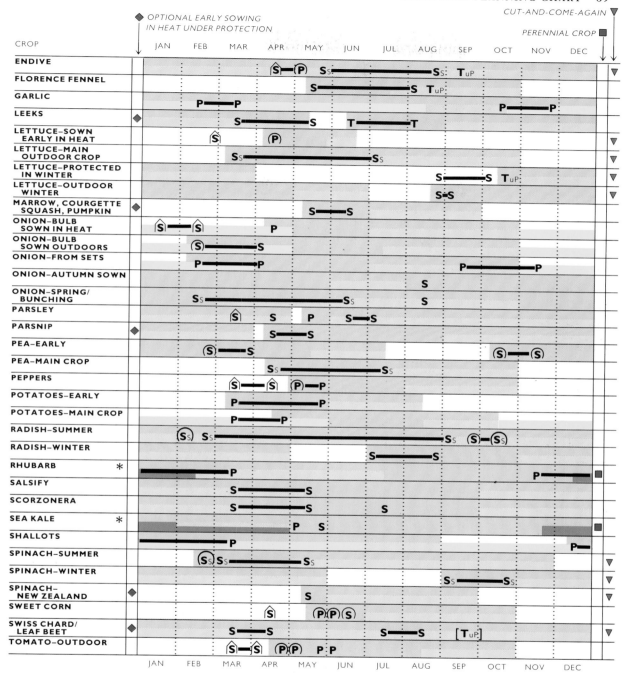

KEY TO CHART SYMBOLS AND COLOURS

* Full cropping begins second season after planting/sowing.   **P** Plant outdoors.   **S** Sow outdoors.   (Ŝ) Sow in heat under protection.

Ss Successional sowing/cropping outdoors.   **T** Transplant to cropping position.   (S) Sow outdoors under protection.   **T**uP Transplant to unheated

protection.   ▬▬▬ Duration of sowing/planting period.   [**T**uP] Transplanting to unheated protection *optional*. Will result in improved yield and

quality.   ⌒ Outdoor protection – cloches, frames, low tunnels.

Fresh harvest period.   Actual period of growth in the *cropping situation*.

Forcing period.   Available from store.   Cropping area *not* occupied.

* *Consult text for appropriate cultivar for sowing/planting times shown.*   * *Salad plants not included in chart (see page 151).*

Artichokes, Chinese

(Stachys affinis)

Chinese artichokes are little ridged tubers, generally not much more than 5 cm (2 in) long and 2 cm (¾ in) wide. They have a beautiful, pearl-like translucency when fresh, and a nutty flavour. They can be used raw or cooked. The somewhat sprawly plants resemble mint, and grow about 45 cm (18 in) high.

The small ridged tubers of Chinese artichoke (top left) and the larger knobbly tubers of Jerusalem artichoke (see p72).

Site / soil

These artichokes need an open, sunny site, and grow best in rich light soils. They need plenty of moisture throughout the growing period.

Cultivation

Chinese artichokes take five to seven months to develop. To get a good crop of tubers of a reasonable size, plant the largest tubers obtainable as soon as the soil is workable in spring. To get an early start they can be sprouted in potting compost in a seedtray or in small pots before planting out.

Plant the tubers upright, 4–7.5 cm (1½–3 in) deep, spaced 30 cm (12 in) apart each way, or 15 cm (6 in) apart in rows 45 cm (18 in) apart. They require little attention other than being kept weed free in the early stages before the leaves form a canopy over the soil. They can be given a general liquid feed in summer to stimulate growth. When the plants are 30–60 cm (12–24 in) high, they can be earthed up about 7.5 cm (3 in) around the stems. If growth becomes very rampant in summer, cut back straggly stems and any flowers which have developed to encourage the development of the tubers.

Harvesting

Chinese artichokes are best lifted just before use, as they quickly shrivel once out of the soil. Start lifting in early winter after the foliage has died back. The artichokes can be normally left in the soil until required, even in fairly wet soils. Cover the soil with straw to make it easier to lift them in heavy frost.

When the ground is dug over in spring take care to remove even the smallest tubers, as the plants can become invasive. Save some large specimens for replanting. Small tubers can be planted up individually in small pots, and can be moved eventually into 20 - 23 cm (8 – 9 in) pots and used to increase stock.

Pests

Slugs may be a problem on young plants.

Detach rooted suckers of globe artichoke with a sharp knife.

Harvest mature globe artichoke heads with a portion of stem.

Artichokes, globe

(*Cynara scolymus*)

Globe artichokes are handsome perennial vegetables. They are grown primarily for their thistle-like flower heads, in which the edible parts are the fleshy pads at the base of the bracts and the 'choke' or receptacle found in the large heads. The heads are green to deep purple in colour, depending on the cultivar. Plants are normally 60 – 90 cm (2 – 3 ft) high, with a 90 cm (3 ft) spread.

Site / soil

Artichokes need an open but not exposed site, with protection from strong winds. The soil needs to be well drained, but the roots must not be allowed to dry out during the summer. Good crops are only obtained on fertile soil. Prepare the site by digging it thoroughly, incorporating plenty of well-rotted manure or compost.

Cultivation

Artichokes are normally raised from rooted suckers (offsets) taken in the spring (or autumn in mild areas) from mature plants of good cultivars. They are planted out between February and April. They can be either purchased or taken from your own plants. In the latter case scrape away the soil from the base of the plant, and with a sharp-bladed trowel or knife slice down between the offset and parent plant. Make sure you leave at least three shoots in the centre of the parent plant. They will produce three stems in the current season.

Select offsets with as much root as possible. Plant them firmly, about 5 cm (2 in) deep, and 75 – 90 cm (2½ – 3 ft) apart. The tips of the leaves can be trimmed back to reduce transpiration. Keep the plants well watered and protected from full sun until they are established. A dressing of general fertilizer or manure can be given before planting, followed by a topdressing of nitrogen or organic liquid feed six weeks later. Plants benefit from mulching throughout the growing season, and this will also help to smother weeds.

Artichokes can also be raised from seeds, sown indoors in February or outdoors in March. Plant seedlings out in their permanent position, after hardening off, if necessary, in May. The problem with raising globe artichokes from seeds is that the resulting plants are very variable, and it is impossible to tell which are the good ones until they have produced heads. It is best to build up stock in the following years by taking offsets from the best plants and discarding the poor ones. Cultivars will not come true from seeds and must be raised from offsets.

During the first season of growth, keep the plants weed-free and well watered. A single head is normally produced towards the end of the first season.

Artichokes vary in their hardiness; they are more susceptible to cold when growing on a heavy soil. Some winter protection is normally advisable on any soil. In the north and in cold parts of the British Isles, earth up the base of the plant, and cover the crown with straw or bracken. In the south it is usually sufficient to leave the dead foliage to give some protection. Remove any covering in the following spring, about mid-April.

In its second season the plant throws up several flowering stalks. Each shoot normally bears one large artichoke at the tip, and several smaller ones lower down the stem. If large heads are required, reduce these shoots to three per plant, snapping off the others at the base. The small artichokes can be removed when about 4 cm (1½ in) diameter to encourage the growth of the terminal bud. They can be eaten but will not have developed a 'choke'.

Plants generally start to deteriorate after their third season though some will go on for many years. However it is sound policy to replace about a third of your plants each year with new offsets to maintain a steady supply of vigorous plants.

Harvesting

Artichokes can be eaten at various stages, but are normally considered mature when heads are plump, and the scales still soft and green, just before starting to open. Cut off the heads with a portion of stem, or snap the stem off at the base if there are no secondary heads. Harvesting stimulates secondary shoots, which may give a second crop later in the season. This is encouraged if the plants are topdressed with a nitrogen fertilizer or organic liquid feed and watered after the primary heads are cut.

As mature plants crop in early summer, often in May in June, and young plants in late summer, from September onwards, a succession is ensured by having plants of various ages in the garden.

Pests and diseases

Lettuce root aphid is sometimes a problem. (For symptoms and control measures see p 60.)

Petal blight fungus occasionally causes rotting of the heads in wet weather. There is no remedy.

Recommended cultivars

The cultivar 'Vert de Laon' (syn. 'Gros Vert de Laon') is generally recommended as the most suitable for this country, and is usually available as offsets. 'Green Globe' is widely available.

Artichokes, Jerusalem
(*Helianthus tuberosus*)

Jerusalem artichokes are very hardy, perennial members of the sunflower family, grown for their nutritious, knobbly tubers (see p 70). The plants grow to over 3 m (10 ft) high.

Site / soil
Jerusalem artichokes tolerate open or shaded sites and a very wide range of soils, including cold, heavy soils. Because of the fibrous root system this is a useful crop for breaking in rough ground and heavy soil. Jerusalem artichokes can be used as a screen, or planted in rows two to three deep, as windbreaks, but remember they will cast fairly heavy shade.

Cultivation
Plant tubers from February to May, 10 – 15 cm (4 – 6 in) deep, about 30 cm (12 in) apart. It is quite satisfactory to use tubers bought from a greengrocer. Those the size of a hen's egg are said to be best; larger tubers can be cut into two or three sections, provided each has a bud. When the plants are about 30 cm (12 in) high the stems can be earthed up to make them more stable. In midsummer cut off any flower heads and shorten back the tops to 1.5 – 1.8 m (5 – 6 ft), to encourage tuber growth and prevent plants being windblown, which lowers the yield. Staking or tying may be necessary sometimes to give extra support. In dry conditions Jerusalem artichoke tubers will become more knobbly, so irrigate them if necessary. When the foliage starts to yellow in autumn cut back stalks to within 8 cm (3 in) of the ground. The stalks can be left lying over the stumps, to help to protect the soil from frost, and make it easier to lift the tubers in hard weather.

Harvesting
Tubers are normally lifted from the soil as required. However, they can be clamped like swedes (see p 51). Reserve a few tubers at the end of the season; they can be lifted and replanted immediately. Dig up all other tubers, however small, as Jerusalem artichokes spread easily and become invasive.

Pests and diseases
A fungal rot occasionally develops on stored tubers. If it should attack growing stems they become rotten for about 30 cm (12 in) or so above the soil surface: the plants should be uprooted and burnt.

Cultivars
'Fuseau' has long, relatively smooth tubers; 'Dwarf Sunray' is slightly less tall than others.

Asparagus
(*Asparagus officinalis*)

Asparagus is a perennial vegetable grown for its delicious young shoots, or 'spears'. Most asparagus eaten in Britain is green, but on the Continent it is often earthed up and blanched to produce white asparagus. A bed can be productive for eight to twenty years. Asparagus takes up a fair amount of ground, and is cut for only a short season, so it is a luxury crop in terms of space. If you like asparagus, plant as much as you have space for.

Asparagus plants are either male or female, the male plants giving higher yields. However, as it is impossible to distinguish between the plants until they are more than a year old, in the past most asparagus beds were a mixture of male and female plants.

In recent years plant breeders, mainly on the Continent, have been developing very productive, all-male cultivars. Although the long-term qualities of these new cultivars have not been assessed yet, they promise to be of good value.

Site / soil
Asparagus thrives on a wide range of soil types, from heavy clay to sand, provided the soil is well drained. It does not need particularly fertile soil. The preferred pH is 6.3 to 7.5, so acid soils need to be limed. Very exposed sites and frost pockets should be avoided. Asparagus should not be replanted where it has been grown before, as serious root diseases can build up in the soil.

Cultivation
Asparagus was traditionally grown on ridged or raised beds to give a long blanched stem. Today most asparagus is grown very satisfactorily on flat beds, though ridged beds give better drainage and larger spears. It is possible to plant on the flat, then to raise the bed by earthing up in the second season.

Prepare the ground by digging thoroughly and incorporating a good dressing of well-rotted farmyard manure or compost. On heavy land do this the previous autumn. It is absolutely essential to rid the ground of all traces of perennial weeds before planting, as it is very difficult to weed asparagus once it is established. (See Weeds, p 42.)

There are various methods of spacing asparagus. The standard method is to grow it in single rows, with plants spaced 30–45 cm (12–18 in) apart. It can also be grown at similar spacing in beds of two or three rows, with the rows about 30 cm (12 in) apart, and a 90 cm (3 ft) path between the beds. Generally speaking closer spacing gives higher yields overall, but wider spacing gives thicker spears and may re-

Plant one-year-old crowns of asparagus by spreading their thick spidery roots over a mound of soil.

duce the risk of root infection. The optimum spacing is 2.5 plants / sq m (2.25 plants / sq yd).

The traditional method of growing garden asparagus is to plant one-year-old crowns (roots) obtained from nurseries. These are preferable to two- or three-year-old crowns, which although larger, transplant less satisfactorily. Crowns must be handled very carefully and never be allowed to dry out. Plant crowns in March or early April. The optimum depth for planting is 10 cm (4 in). The traditional method is to take out a trench about 30 cm (12 in) wide and 20 cm (8 in) deep, making a mound in the bottom of the trench about 10 cm (4 in) high. Carefully spread the roots, which resemble large thick-legged spiders, over the mound, covering them with about 5 cm (2 in) of fine soil. It is now thought best to fill in the trench at the end of the season, after cutting back the fern.

A recent development is for young asparagus plants to be sold in modules ready for planting. They are cheaper than crowns, and can be planted any time, but ideally in or before June. They take no longer to develop to the harvesting stage than one-year-old crowns. Plant them 10 cm (4 in) deep.

Asparagus can also be raised from seeds. Again there are two methods. The traditional method is to sow on an outdoor seedbed in spring, in drills at least 2.5 cm (1 in) deep, thinning plants to 7.5 cm (3 in) apart, then to plant out the largest crowns the following spring. The modern method, which produces a faster-maturing crop, is to sow indoors in February, at a temperature of 13 – 16 C (55 – 60 F). Either sow direct in modules, or sow in a seedtray and prick out into some kind of module, such as a small pot. Harden off and plant out in June in their permanent position.

During the growing season keep the beds weed free by hand hoeing or shallow surface hoeing, so as not to damage the roots. Remove any seedlings which appear. Where fern is liable to be blown over, give it some support with canes and twine. After the fern has turned yellow in the autumn cut it down to within 2.5 cm (1 in) of ground level. If a long-handled spear is preferred, draw 5 – 7.5 cm (2 – 3 in) of soil over the stumps. In heavy soils this can be done in spring.

The ADAS recommendations for feeding asparagus, which is not a hungry crop, tend to be vague. A general fertilizer can be applied in spring, and a nitrogenous topdressing, or organic liquid feed, later in the year when the fern is growing. Research has shown that there is little value in mulching the beds with manure or straw in winter. Nor is there any value in the traditional practice of dressing asparagus beds with salt. To utilize the space taken up by an asparagus bed interplant asparagus with parsley or small salad crops.

Harvesting

The older cultivars of asparagus were not harvested until their third season, that is, two years after planting one-year-old crowns. With module-raised plants, and the new hybrid cultivars, it is possible to cut a few of the larger spears in the second season.

Depending on the season and the cultivar, cutting normally starts in the second half of April. Cut with a sharp knife or an asparagus knife, which has a forked blade so a single spear can be cut without damaging other spears. Cut a few centimetres (an inch or so) below soil level when spears are 13 – 18 cm (5 – 7 in) high. In the first harvesting season cut for no more than six weeks; in following years for no more than eight weeks.

Pests and disease

Slugs can be very damaging to young plants. In some areas the black and yellow asparagus beetles and larvae are very destructive to the fern. (For control measures see Pest and disease summary chart, p 60.)

Beds sometimes become infected with the soil-borne violet root rot fungus, which kills the plants. It can be seen as purple strands on the roots. There is no remedy other than leaving the ground fallow or growing non-susceptible crops. The fungus also attacks weeds, carrots, potatoes and beetroot. The bed can be isolated from the rest of the garden by digging sheets of thick polythene film 30 cm (12 in) deep around it. In recent years a *Fusarium* root root has similarly caused premature death in asparagus. Again the only remedy is to plant in a new site with fresh plants, carefully removing and burning all the infected plants.

Recommended cultivars

Modern all-male hybrids 'Cito', 'Franklim', 'Lucullus'.
Older cultivars 'Connover's Colossal' (for light soils).

Asparagus pea
(*Tetragonolobus purpureus*)

Asparagus pea is a pretty, decorative plant, with delicate foliage and scarlet-brown flowers. It belongs to the pea family, and is grown for the triangular-shaped, winged pods, which are cooked whole and are said to have a flavour of asparagus. The plants grow 30–45 cm (12–18 in) high, spreading to 45–60 cm (18–24 in) across. They make a neat edge to a path.

Site / Soil
These prefer an open, sunny site on rich light soil.

Cultivation
Seeds can be sown outside from mid-April until the end of May, sowing so that plants are about 25–30 cm (10–12 in) apart in rows 38 cm (15 in) apart. Alternatively, seeds can be started indoors in April, and seedlings transplanted outside in May. Protect the plants from pigeons. Otherwise they need only be suported with small pea sticks or twigs, or twine attached to small canes.

Harvesting
Pods are ready for picking from June to August. It is essential to pick them when immature, between 2.5–5 cm (1–2 in) long, otherwise they become tough. Regular picking prolongs the season, as once the seeds in the pods start to harden, the crop is checked. Yields are low in comparison with garden peas, but the flavour is distinctive.

The winged pods should be eaten when young.

Asparagus pea makes a neat path edging.

Note: The asparagus pea above is sometimes confused with the four-angled bean (*Psophocarpus tetragonolobus*), which is also known as 'asparagus pea'. This is a perennial, climbing tropical bean, with edible leaves, flowers, pods and tubers. The winged pods are similar in shape to those of the annual, dwarf asparagus pea grown in temperate climates.

Aubergine
(*Solanum melongena*)

The aubergine is a plant of tropical origin, grown for its fruits. It has a bushy habit, growing 60 – 76 cm (2 – 2½ ft) high, with a spread of up to 60 cm (2 ft). The stems and leaves are prickly. The fruits are round, long, oval, or egg shaped and in the types grown in the West, purple, black, white tinged with purple or pure white. The pure white egg-shaped aubergine probably gave rise to its other popular name, eggplant.

A purple-fruited aubergine is ready for picking.

Site / Soil
Aubergines are deep rooting and require fertile soil. They will normally only grow successfully outdoors in the warmer parts of the country. When grown outdoors, plant them in a warm, sheltered spot. Otherwise they need protection to grow well. (See Protected cropping, p 46.)

Cultivation
Sow seed in heat indoors, ideally at a temperature between 21 – 30 C (70 – 86 F), from mid March to early April. Once the seedlings have germinated aim to maintain minimum night temperatures of 16 C (60 F) and day temperatures of 18 C (64 F) to keep the plants growing. Seedlings are ready for transplanting into pots when about 5 cm (2 in) high. Aim to grow short-jointed sturdy plants with good root

systems. Overheating and forcing lead to spindly plants.

Aubergines are ready for planting when the first flowers have appeared. Plant them under cover in late April (in warm areas) to early May, and outside when there is no longer any risk of frost. Space them 40–45 cm (16–18 in) apart.

The growing plants need plenty of water. Nip out the growing points when the plants are 40 cm (16 in) high, to encourage bushy growth. Plants may need staking and tying if growth is vigorous. Where there are several flowers on one stem, remove all but the largest after the first fruit has set. With most large-fruited cultivars a maximum of four fruits should be allowed on each plant. Once four fruits have set, re-move any surplus side shoots.

Plants will benefit from feeding with a high potash fertilizer (a tomato fertilizer) every 10 to 12 days once the fruits start to set. Alternatively, use an organic tomato feed.

Pests and diseases
Red spider mite, glasshouse whitefly, and aphids can be a problem under cover; aphids and red spider mite may attack outdoors. (For symptoms and control measures, see p 58ff.)

Recommended cultivars
There is little to choose between the F_1 hybrids currently available.

Beans, broad
(*Vicia faba*)

Broad beans are the hardiest of our beans. They are grown primarily for the large green and white beans inside the pods, but some people also eat the young leaf tips as boiled greens; others eat the very young pods whole.

Equidistant spacing of broad beans in a bed.

Support tall types with canes and twine.

Nip out the tops when plants are in full flower.

Types of broad bean: the long podded hardier Longpods (top), and the broader, shorter Windsors (bottom).

Broad beans fall into three main types. The Long-pods, (which include the Sevilles), are the hardiest, with very long pods. The Windsors have shorter, broader pods, are later maturing, and generally believed to be better flavoured. The 'Fan' or dwarf type bear many small pods and are early maturing. There are green- and white-seeded forms within the first two types. The green-seeded forms are considered more tender and the best for freezing. An unusual cultivar is 'Red Epicure', which has distinctly flavoured, reddish bronze beans.

The older cultivars reach heights of 1 – 2 m (3½ – 6½ ft), newer dwarf cultivars, with upstanding pods, are only about 30 cm (12 in) tall. They are very useful where space is limited or for growing under cloches.

Site / Soil

An open site is the best for the spring and summer sowings. A slightly sheltered position and well-drained soil is advisable for late autumn sowings.

Broad beans require a reasonably fertile soil, preferably well dug and manured in the previous winter. They prefer a neutral to slightly acid soil. They should not be grown on the same site two years running, because of the risk of soil-borne foot and rot diseases, which cause plants to collapse.

Cultivation

First sowings can be made as soon as the soil is workable in February or March. Unlike most seeds, broad beans germinate best at low temperature. For successional crops further sowings can be made in April and May.

In most parts of the British Isles autumn sowings from late October to the beginning of December may give very early crops the following year. In some seasons the crop is lost due to soil pests and severe weather, in others they are only marginally earlier than spring-sown beans; but nevertheless it can be worthwhile. The 'Aquadulce' cultivars are particularly suitable for autumn sowing, but in fact most cultivars can be autumn-sown. They need be no more than 2.5 cm (1 in) high at the onset of winter.

Overwintered and spring-sown crops benefit from cloche or floating film protection, particularly in the early stages. (See Protected cropping, p 46). The dwarf cultivar 'The Sutton' is very suitable for autumn or spring sowing under cloches. In very cold areas, or where autumn sowings tend to fail, sow seeds in boxes in greenhouses or frames in December or January, for planting out early in spring.

Sow seeds 4-5 cm (1½ – 2 in) deep, either in drills or using a dibber, taking care not to leave an air pocket beneath the seed. Discard any seeds with holes in them; they are generally caused by bean seed weevils. Maximum yields are obtained at a spacing of two plants per 30 cm² (12 in²). Broad beans are often grown in staggered double rows, the seeds 23 cm (9 in) apart, with 60 cm (2 ft) paths between the pairs of rows. They can also be grown satisfactorily in patches 90 cm (3 ft) wide, with equidistant spacing of 20-30 cm (9-12 in) between plants. Tall cultivars can also be grown 11 cm (4½ in) apart in rows 45 cm (18 in) apart.

Most beans require a support of canes and twine to prevent them being blown over when fruiting. The smaller cultivars can be propped up with twigs if necessary.

It is not necessary to water broad beans between germination and flowering, unless the plants are actually wilting. If rainfall is less than normal, watering once the beans start to flower and throughout the pod-forming and harvesting period, at the rate of 22 litres / sq m (4 gal / sq yd) per week will give improved yields and better quality pods.

When the plants are in full flower, or when small colonies of black aphids are noticed on the tops of the plants, the tips can be nipped out. This both encourages the development of the beans and discourages the blackfly.

Harvesting

Broad beans are often the first fresh vegetables of the season. Overwintered crops are generally ready for picking from May onwards, with later sowings cropping from June to August. Pick the pods before they are too large, or else the beans will have become tough. The very small pods can be used whole, but if many are picked small the total yields will be lowered. Broad beans can be deep frozen or dried for use during the winter.

Pests and diseases

Mice may attack seeds and seedlings; blackfly is a common problem; bean weevils are sometimes a problem. (For symptoms and control, see p 58ff.) The disease chocolate spot, which makes chocolate-like marks on the leaves, is occasionally serious. Vigorous, well-grown, uncrowded plants are the least susceptible to attack.

Recommended cultivars
(*In order of maturity*)
'Aquadulce Claudia' (autumn sowing), 'The Sutton' (dwarf), 'Bonny Lad' (dwarf), 'Express' (very early Longpod), 'Jubilee Hysor' (Windsor), 'Hylon' (Longpod), 'Relon' (green-seeded Longpod), 'Red Epicure'.

Beans, French or kidney

(Phaseolus vulgaris)

French beans are half-hardy and treated as annuals. They are grown mainly for the pods, which are eaten when immature. However, when partially ripened they can be shelled and the fresh beans eaten as 'flageolets'. The mature, shelled, dry beans, often known as haricot beans, can be stored for winter use.

The pods of French beans take many forms. The typical French bean is rounded in cross-section, 12 – 15 cm (5 – 6 in) long, and slightly curved. The filets are exceptionally thin, round beans. There is also a relatively flat and straight type, not unlike runner beans in appearance. More recently a much shorter type has been developed, which is rounded, straight and approximately 10 cm (4 in) long. Pods of this type can be cooked or frozen whole, with the minimum loss of flavour. The pods can be green, purple, purplish flecked or yellow in colour. The yellow-podded cultivars have a rather waxy texture and are known as 'waxpods'. Most of the modern cultivars are stringless if picked young. The filet beans, the waxpods, and the purple-podded cultivars are widely thought to have the best flavour.

The majority of the French bean cultivars are dwarf, bushy plants, but there are a few climbing cultivars. These tend to be more popular on the Continent. The dwarf types mature earlier than the climbing types, but the latter may yield more heavily overall. French beans are self-pollinating, and do not have the setting problems that may occur with runner beans.

Site / Soil

French beans need an open but sheltered site, as they are very susceptible to wind damage. It is best to rotate them because of a possible build-up of root-rotting diseases. They prefer rich light soil, neutral to slightly acid. The soil should be well worked, ideally with manure or compost incorporated the previous season.

Cultivation

Most failures with French beans result from sowing too early in cold soils. Seeds will not germinate successfully until soil temperatures reach about 12 C (53 F), which is normally late April to early May in the south of England, and about two weeks later in the north. If cold, wet conditions occur after sowing, beans frequently succumb to pests and diseases in the soil.

This problem can be overcome by sowing seeds in boxes, blocks or pots indoors, and transplanting them outdoors when 5 – 7.5 cm (2 – 3 in) high. Use healthy seed; dressed seed (see Seeds, p 28) will give protection against soil-borne diseases. When sowing directly outside, sow in a 'stale seed bed', ie prepare the seedbed 10 days before sowing and, if possible, warm the soil beforehand with cloches or a covering of plastic. French beans can be grown under floating films (see Protected cropping, p 49) in the early stages.

Sow the seed 4–5 cm (1½–2 in) deep, making successional sowings from the end of April until the end of June. Slightly earlier sowings can be made under cloches or indoors. The traditional spacing is to sow 6.5–10 cm (2½–4 in) apart, thinning to 23 cm (9 in) apart. But research has shown that the highest yields of bush French beans are produced at

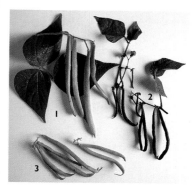

French beans: 1 flat podded; 2 purple podded; 3 filet type.

Earth up young French beans with a draw hoe to give extra support.

Early sowings of French beans can be made outdoors under cloches.

a density of three to four plants per 30 cm^2 (12 in^2), with equidistant spacing between plants. To achieve this grow in staggered rows 22 cm (9 in) apart. No thinning will be necessary later with these populations. For spacing of climbing cultivars see runner beans.

The plants will benefit from earthing up the stems when young for extra support, and by being mulched. For fertilizer requirements, see p 17.

Climbing cultivars need supports (see runner beans), but bush cultivars can be supported with small twigs to keep the lower leaves off the ground and the pods clean.

French beans benefit from extra watering once they are in flower. In dry conditions give 5–11 litres /sq m (1–2 gal / sq yd) ideally twice weekly. Pod set is improved, and stringiness delayed, if the soil is kept moist and the plants well watered.

Harvesting

The earliest cloche sowings are ready in June, while successional sowings can be picked from July until frost, or later if covered by cloches. Pick the pods in their prime, when they can be cleanly snapped in half. Frequent picking will encourage high yields and better quality.

If dried beans are required, select a few plants and leave the pods unpicked until they have turned brown. The whole plant can then be pulled up and hung in a dry, airy shed (see p 53). When the pods have dried to the point of cracking open, shell them and store the beans in air-tight jars.

Pests and diseases

The main pests are slugs, bean seed fly, root aphid and black bean aphid. For symptoms and control, see p 58ff). Various diseases include foot and root rots, anthracnose, halo blight and virus. Rotation, the use of healthy seed and resistant cultivars where available, and good growing conditions are the main precautions against these. Diseased plants should be removed and destroyed.

Recommended cultivars

Green podded 'Aramis' (filet), 'Delinel' (filet), 'Pros' (stringless short), 'Tendergreen' (stringless round dwarf).
Purple podded 'Purple Queen', 'Purple Tepee'.
Yellow podded 'Mont d'Or'.
Climbing 'Blue Lake', 'Climbing Purple' ('Purple Podded').
For drying 'Chevrier Vert' (also used for flageolets), 'Dutch Brown'.

Beans, runner

(*Phaseolus coccineus*)

Originally introduced into this country for its ornamental qualities, the runner bean is one of our most prolific and vigorous vegetables. It bears heavy crops of long, flat-podded beans from July to October. Most cultivars are climbers, reaching heights of 2.4–3 m (8–10 ft), making this a useful screening and decorative plant. The flowers are usually red, but there are white, pink and bicoloured cultivars.

Older cultivars tended to be stringy unless picked young; some recently introduced cultivars are stringless. Runner beans freeze well.

Site / Soil

Runner beans are susceptible to frost, and so are not generally successful in colder parts of the British Isles. They benefit from planting in warm, sheltered positions, for example growing up a fence. A warm site also encourages pollinating insects which help the beans to set. It is better not to grow runner beans in the same position year after year, because of the likely build-up of root-rotting diseases.

They are deep-rooting plants, requiring well-prepared, fertile, moisture-retentive soil. The ground is best prepared in the previous autumn, ideally digging a trench one spit deep and 60 cm (2 ft) wide, into which strawy manure or compost is mixed when replacing the top soil.

Cultivation

Runner beans need relatively warm soil for germination, at least 10–12 C (50–53 F). It is better to wait until the second half of May before sowing, or into June in the north. Runner beans can also be started indoors in early May and transplanted at the end of the month. They can be grown under cloches or floating films in the early stages. (see Protected cropping, p 46).

Highest yields are obtained from planting at a density of two plants per 30 cm^2 (12 in^2). Runner beans are usually grown in double rows, 60 cm (2 ft) apart, with plants 15 cm (6 in) apart in the rows. However, where pollination is a problem it may be advisable to grow them in a block of two or three short rows, rather than one long row, to provide more shelter for insects.

Very sturdy supports need to be erected for climbing runner beans. Traditionally, crossed poles or bamboo canes at least 2.4m (8 ft) long are used, firmly secured to cross members along the top. There should be either one cane per plant, or provided there are canes or poles every 60 cm (2 ft), strings can be substituted for intermediate plants.

Two plants can be trained to grow up each cane.

A wigwam support made of bamboo canes.

Traditional supports using 2.4m (8ft) canes arranged in rows.

Run the strings from the ridge to a horizontal string linking the canes some centimetres (a few inches) above ground level. An alternative means of support is 10 cm (4 in) square wire or nylon netting (beans will not grip plastic-coated netting), or circular wigwams of canes, poles or strings, tied near the apex. Tension wires may be necessary at either end of a supporting structure to bear the weight of the crop.

Climbing forms can be grown without support if the leading shoot is nipped out when the plant is about 23 cm (9 in) high. This will produce several side shoots, which can be nipped off at the first or second joint, so making a small bushy plant. Again, where pollination is a serious problem, runner beans can be grown this way, or naturally dwarf cultivars can be grown. They will produce an earlier crop, but the yields will be lower than with climbing plants.

The problems of getting runner beans to set seems to be increasing, especially in dry seasons. In some cases it is due to birds destroying the buds and flowers. Contrary to popular belief, syringing flowers with water does not seem to help setting. However, watering the soil at the base of the plant has a beneficial effect on flowering and pod-setting. In dry weather water when the first green flower buds appear and again when the first flowers are fully open. Plants will need 5–11 litres / sq m (1–2 gal/sq yd), twice a week during these periods. There may be less of a pollination problem with white-flowered cultivars. In some areas pollen beetle may damage the flowers.

Harvesting
Runner beans crop from about July to October. Beans *must* be picked regularly and thoroughly to obtain the highest yields and to prevent pods from becoming tough and stringy. Mature beans can be dried for winter use.

Pests and diseases
See French beans.

Recommended cultivars
Non-stringless 'Bokki', 'Enorma', 'Liberty', 'Painted Lady' (decorative bicoloured flowers).
Stringless 'Butler', 'Desirée' (white flowered), 'Polestar'.
Dwarf 'Gulliver', 'Hammond's Dwarf', 'Pickwick'.

Nip off shoots to make climbing bean cultivars stay dwarf.

Beetroot
(Beta vulgaris subsp. *vulgaris)*

Beetroot is one of the most useful root vegetables, used fresh from late spring to autumn, and stored or pickled for winter. It comes in many shapes: round, flat, pointed (oval), and long-rooted. The flesh is normally deep red in colour, but there are yellow and white forms, and an old cultivar, 'Chioggia' with very marked white rings. The unusually coloured forms have much the same flavour as red beet: some people think them superior in flavour. The very long slow-growing types are also considered well flavoured.

In practice most types of beetroot can be stored successfully, though traditionally the long-rooted types were grown primarily for storage. Most beet can also be pulled and eaten at almost any stage of development. Beet leaves, especially when young, can be eaten. The old cultivar 'Bulls' Blood', which has deep red foliage, is a colourful potager plant which also produces good beetroots.

Site / Soil
An open, unshaded site is best. Beets prefer rich, light soil, manured the previous season rather than freshly manured. Long-rooted cultivars require deep soil. The pH should be slightly acid to alkaline, so the soil should be limed if very acid.

Cultivation
The beetroot 'seed' is really a cluster of two or three seeds, all of which may germinate, and will need to be thinned out. They contain a natural inhibitor which may prevent germination. If this problem is encountered, soak the seed in tepid water for half an hour before sowing. 'Monogerm' cultivars have been developed which contain only one seed, and therefore require less thinning.

Beetroot seeds will not germinate at soil temperatures below 7 C (44 F), and in cold soils early spring sowings can be slow to emerge. Moreover, some cultivars are very prone to bolt (run to seed) if sown early in the year or in unfavourable conditions.

For early sowings use a bolt-resistant cultivar, and if possible, warm the soil beforehand with cloches. Alternatively, use the fluid sowing method (see Sowing outdoors, p 32), or sow indoors and plant out, though beetroot seedlings can be transplanted only when very small, unless raised in modules. Beetroot responds well to being multi-sown in modules (three seeds per module), then planted out when about 5 cm (2 in) high. (See Sowing indoors, p 36.) Beetroot can also be covered with crop covers in the early stages. (See Protected cropping, p 46.)

Beetroot can be grown in rows, or in patches at

Sow the large 'seeds' thinly, 2cm (¾in) deep.

Early beetroot grown on the bed system.

Thinning should start when seedlings touch.

Twist off the stems when harvesting.

equidistant spacing. Sow as thinly as possible in drills about 2 cm (¾ in) deep. Sparrows are very partial to beetroot seedlings, so net the plants or cover with strong black cotton until they are established. Thin as soon as seedlings are touching. Young thinnings are sometimes large enough to pull and use whole.

In good growing conditions round cultivars of beetroot are ready 11 to 13 weeks after sowing, so beetroot can be a useful catch crop. Various sowings and spacings can be adopted according to the season and type of beet required.

Fresh supplies For a continuous suppy of young, fresh beetroot, sow round cultivars at roughly monthly intervals. The very first sowings can be made under protection (see above) in late February or early March. The roots are usually pulled when still small at the end of May or early June.

Make the first outdoor sowings in March or April: medium-sized roots will be ready in June and July. Use bolt-resistant cultivars for all these sowings. Continue sowing in May and June. In mild areas the last outdoor sowings can be made in July.

Storage beetroot The main sowings of beetroot for storage are made in May and June, using either globe or long cultivars.

Spacing The following recommendations are based on research, and at first sight appear rather contradictory. If adopted they will, however, give the maximum yield of medium-sized roots.

The *early crops* require wide spacing to enable the beetroot to grow very fast. Aim for five plants per 30 cm^2 (12 in^2) ie with the beetroot in rows 23 cm (9 in) apart, thinned to 9 cm (3½ in) apart.

Maincrop fresh or storage beet, should be grown in rows 30 cm (12 in) apart, and thinned to 2.5 cm (1 in) in the rows. The more general practice is to grow beetroot in rows 30 cm (12 in) apart, thinning to 7.5 −10 cm (3−4 in) in the rows. Reasonably sized beet can usually be obtained by growing them at equidistant spacing 13 − 15 cm (5 − 6 in) apart each way.

For *pickling beetroot* aim for a maximum density of 20 plants per 30 cm^2 (12 in^2). This can be achieved by sowing in rows 7.5 cm (3 in) apart, thinning to 6.5 cm (2½ in) apart. The ideal size for pickling is about 5 cm (2 in) diameter.

For steady growth and good quality beetroot water to prevent the soil drying out. In a dry season water at the rate of 11 litres / sq m (2 gals / sq yd) every two or three weeks. Overwatering encourages leaf rather than root growth. For fertilizer requirements see p 17. Apply only part of the nitrogen requirement before sowing.

Harvesting
Beets are pulled when they reach the size required. On well-drained soil in mild areas beetroot can be left in the soil during the winter, but the quality will deteriorate eventually. Cover with a 20 cm (8 in) deep layer of bracken or straw. Otherwise lift the roots in October, or before there is heavy frost. Dig them out carefully with a fork, and twist off the stems a few centimetres (an inch or so) above the roots. Store in boxes of moist peat or sand or in clamps. (See Storage, p 51.) Beetroot normally keep until April.

Pests, diseases and disorders
Cutworm and black bean aphid are sometimes a problem. Diseases include damping off and leaf spots. Beetroot is also susceptible to mineral deficiencies, especially manganese and boron, on alkaline soil. For symptoms and control measures, see p 58ff.

Recommended cultivars
Round red 'Boltardy' (bolt-resistant), 'Detroit–Little Ball', 'Monopoly' (monogerm), 'Regala' (bolt resistant).
Long red 'Cheltenham Mono' (monogerm, good bolting resistance), 'Forono' (good storage).
Miscellaneous 'Albina Vereduna' (white, poor storage), 'Bull's Blood' (dark red leaves), 'Burpees Golden' (yellow), 'Chioggia' (white internal rings, novelty value).
For leaf beet see Spinach and leaf beet, p 143.

Brassicas
(*Brassica* spp.)

The brassicas are the backbone of the vegetable garden. They include cabbage, sprouting broccoli, Brussels sprouts, calabrese, cauliflowers, kales, and more recently Texsel greens, as well as the root crops swedes, turnips and kohl rabi. There is also a large group of oriental brassicas − some remarkably hardy − and these are increasingly being grown in gardens. Headed Chinese cabbage is the best known: others are loose-headed Chinese cabbage, pak choi, komatsuna, various hardy mustards and mizuna greens. The brassicas have many features of cultivation in common. These are summarized here.

Site / soil
Brassicas need an open, unshaded site. The soil must be fertile, well drained and moisture retentive. Most brassicas prefer a slightly acid soil, but a very acid soil will need liming. (See also clubroot below.) The nitrogen requirements of these leafy crops are relatively high, mainly because they are growing over several months. The ground should be well worked and manured, ideally in the autumn before planting, but at least for the previous crop. It is not necessary to fork over the ground before planting: it is enough to clear the ground of weeds and plant debris without disturbing the soil. This gives the firm roothold brassicas need. Most brassicas take a relatively long time to mature, and are likely to need a topdressing of a nitrogenous fertilizer or organic liquid feed during growth. (See Fertilizers, p 17.)

Brassicas are prone to soil-borne infections such as clubroot and brassica cyst eelworm so should be rotated over a minimum three-year cycle to prevent infection build up.

On some soils, especially where brassicas have been grown for many years, the disease clubroot can be a major limitation on growing brassicas. The infection causes the roots to swell and eventually to develop gross lumps. These decay releasing disease spores into the soil. Infected plants become stunted and die.

The soil can remain infected for 20 years, so steps should be taken to avoid introducing clubroot (examine any bought-in plants for lumps). Good drainage, rotation, liming acid soils to a pH of about 7 and, possibly, working in high levels of organic matter, all help to prevent clubroot becoming established. Burn, never compost, any infected plants.

Once soil is infected the only way to grow brassicas successfully is to raise seedlings in modules (see Sowing indoors, p 35), and then pot them on into

10 cm (4 in) pots before planting out. This may give them a sufficient start to come into production before being infected – though they *can* be infected within five weeks of sowing or planting. Alternatively, grow fast-maturing brassicas, such as Texsel greens or cut-and-come-again seedling crops of oriental brassicas. (See Sowing outdoors p 32). For chemical measures which may give some protection to transplants see Pest and disease summary chart, p 58.)

Cultivation

Most brassicas are sown in seedbeds and transplanted into their permanent positions in spring and early summer as ground becomes vacant. They can also be raised successfully in seedtrays or modules and this is recommended on heavy soil to minimize root disturbance. Brussels sprouts, however, should not be raised in modules.

Sow seed 2 – 2.5 cm (¾ – 1 in) deep, as thinly as possible, aiming to space the plants 7.5 cm (3 in) apart. This will give them enough room to grow well and make strong transplants. Before lifting the plants for transplanting, water the seedbed to minimize root damage.

Good anchorage and stability are important factors in growing brassicas successfully. On light soils it is advisable to make drills about 7.5 cm (3 in) wide and 10 cm (4 in) deep, planting in the bottom of the drill. Soil can be pulled up around the plant as it grows until the drill is level. On heavy soil brassicas are planted on the flat (as the drill might become waterlogged), with the lower leaves just above the soil level. In both cases plant firmly, so that if a leaf is tugged, it will tear off, rather than uproot the plant. Again, as the plant grows, soil can be hoed up around the base to give better support.

Where cabbage root fly is a common pest, put discs or barriers around the plants after planting. (See Pests and diseases, p 56.)

Water around the base of the plant immediately after transplanting. If conditions are dry in the following three or four weeks, water each plant, giving about 140 ml (¼ pt) a day, until the plants are well established.

In exposed positions, some of the taller growing overwintered brassicas (especially Brussels sprouts and sprouting broccoli) may need to be securely staked in autumn to prevent 'windrock' at the base.

Keep plants weed free by hoeing during the growing season. Mulching helps to conserve moisture and suppress weeds. Catch crops of radishes, lettuces or seedling salad crops can often be grown between widely spaced brassicas, if sown or planted soon after the brassicas are planted.

Watering

If maximum yields and tender succulent crops are to be obtained, brassicas should never be checked by lack of water or nutrients, so frequent watering is beneficial, up to 22 litres / sq m (4 gal / sq yd) per week in dry weather. Where facilities for watering are limited, the most effective means of watering is a single heavy watering 10 to 20 days before the crop matures.

Pests and diseases

Unfortunately brassicas are prone to a fair number of pests. The most common are flea beetle which attacks the seedlings, cabbage root fly which usually attacks shortly after planting out, caterpillars, cabbage white fly, white mealy aphids which mainly damage the mature crop and pollen beetle, which attacks cauliflower, calabrese and broccoli. Slugs and snails are sometimes very damaging, as are birds, especially pigeons, which may in some areas make it necessary to net the crop. The most serious disease is clubroot (see above). In all cases, see p 58ff for symptoms and preventive and control measures.

On light soils plant in deep drills.

Test firmness of planting by tugging a leaf.

Use discs to give protection from cabbage root fly.

Hoe soil up around plants to give extra stability.

Broccoli, sprouting

(*Brassica oleracea* Italica Group)

The purple and white sprouting broccolis used to be considered amongst the hardiest and highest yielding winter brassicas. However, in recent years the quality of seed, and resistance to frost, have deteriorated. It is hoped that improved stocks will be reintroduced. The purple forms are hardier, and more prolific, than the white. There are early and late selections of both types, though in some seasons there may be little difference between them. In fertile soils good strains of broccoli can grow to dimensions of at least 90 cm (3 ft) across and 90 cm (3 ft) high.

Site / soil
See Brassicas, p 81. Sprouting broccoli does best in a warm, well-drained position.

Cultivation
Sow from mid-April to mid-May, sowing the earliest forms first to give a prolonged season. Plant out 60 cm (2 ft) apart each way in June and July, aiming to complete planting by mid-July.

Sprouting broccoli develops into a large, top-heavy plant, so stalks should be earthed up during the growing season, and the plants may need to be firmly staked in the autumn. They are very likely to need protection from pigeons in winter.

For planting methods, watering, pests and diseases see Brassicas, p 82.

Harvesting
The season for sprouting broccoli normally extends from February to May, depending on area and cultivar. Snap off the flowering shoots abut two-thirds down their length, when they are between 15-20 cm (6-8in) long, and before the flower buds open. New side shoots will be produced. With regular picking, plants may continue cropping for six to eight weeks.

The hardy purple form of sprouting broccoli.

White sprouting broccoli ready for harvest.

Brussels sprouts

(*Brassica oleracea* Gemmifera Group)

Brussels sprouts, the traditional British winter vegetable, can provide fresh pickings from September to April. They survive all but the most severe winters. The modern F_1 hybrids are a great improvement on earlier cultivars, as the sprouts are compact and uniform, few become loose or 'blown', and the plants are more responsive to fertile conditions and less likely to fall over in winter. Small button cultivars are excellent for freezing. The reddish cultivar 'Rubine' has a good flavour and is a colourful plant, but it is a poor cropper.

Site / soil
It is most important to plant in firm ground, which has *not* been freshly manured, as too much nitrogen will cause the sprouts to become loose. But Brussels sprouts need an adequate supply of nitrogen throughout the relatively long period of cultivation: a base fertilizer dressing can be hoed in before planting, and a nitrogenous topdressing supplied in late summer. (See Fertilizers, p 18.)

Cultivation
Brussels sprouts grow over a period of several months and need to be kept growing steadily. Sow from mid-March to mid-April, progressing from early to late cultivars. For a very early crop (ready in August), seeds can be sown under glass in February or in early August of the previous year, planting out in spring. Otherwise, sow well spaced out in a seedbed. For some reason Brussels sprouts do not do well in modules.

Plant out from mid-May to early June. The usual spacing is about 60 cm (2 ft) apart; slightly wider spacing will produce larger sprouts, which can be picked in succession over a long period. Closer spacing tends to induce smaller sprouts, and uniform maturity.

If sprouts are required for freezing, grow the early, autumn-maturing hybrids spaced 50 cm (20 in) apart. Pick them before they become blemished by winter weather.

After planting, water until the plants are established. (See Brassicas, p 82.) Subsequently, because of the wide spacing, little extra watering is required except in unusually dry years. Plants must be earthed up. They can be intercropped in the early stages.

The traditional practice of 'stopping' sprouts by taking out the growing point in late summer, is not now recommended for normal open-pollinated or late-maturing F_1 cultivars. However autumn-

Plants should be earthed up and well staked.

Sprouts are picked from the base upwards.

The decorative red cultivar 'Rubine'.

Sprout tops can be harvested and eaten.

Cabbage
(*Brassica oleracea* Capitata Group)

Using the different types available, cabbage can be picked fresh from the garden all year round. In addition there are the Dutch winter white types, and some of the red cabbages, which can be stored for winter. Red cabbage is also excellent pickled. The recently introduced Abyssinian cabbage, Texsel greens, is very useful for spring and autumn greens and a cut-and-come again seedling crop. (See Outdoor sowing, p 33.)

All types of cabbage are cultivated in much the same way. (For soil, site, cultivation, watering, pests and diseases see Brassicas, p 81.) They are grouped below according to their main season of maturity, though in practice there is considerable overlapping between the groups. Sowing and planting dates vary according to the season of use, and appropriate cultivars must be used for each season. Today there is a wide choice of excellent cultivars, the modern hybrids being notable for their compact heads, and ability to stand without bolting.

maturing F_1 cultivars grown for freezing can be stopped when the lowest sprouts are reaching 13 mm (½ in) diameter, to encourage even development of the sprouts. This gives a uniform crop for picking at one time. If left unstopped a succession of sprouts can be picked over a longer period.

Harvesting
The earliest crops are ready in September. Pick from the bottom of the plant upwards, snapping off mature sprouts with a downward movement. When picking, remove blown sprouts, and yellow and diseased leaves. At the end of the season the sprout tops can be picked. They can become very weighty and are well flavoured.

Pests and diseases
See Brassicas p 82. Clubroot, damping off and downy mildew are the most likely diseases. Of the normal range of brassica pests, attacks of mealy aphid in late summer can be particularly damaging, penetrating and spoiling the sprouts. For symptoms and control measures, see p 58ff.

Recommended cultivars
(*All are F_1 hybrids*; * = *suitable for organic growing*)
Early (September-October) *'Oliver', 'Peer Gynt'.
Maincrop (October-December) 'Roger', 'Widgeon', *'Rampart'.
Late (January-March) *'Troika', 'Fortress'.

SPRING CABBAGE

These are mostly small cabbages, ready for use in April or May. In the past most of the spring cultivars were pointed; now some are round-headed. Most cultivars can also be eaten as 'spring greens', before they heart up.

For most cultivars the main sowing is towards the end of July in the north, and in the first two weeks of August in the south. Sow in a seedbed or in modules (See Sowing indoors, p 33), planting out from mid-September to mid-October. Where both spring greens and heads are wanted, plant in rows 30 cm (12 in) apart, with cabbages 10 cm (4 in) apart in the rows. Use the two intermediate cabbages as spring

A bed of equidistant spaced spring greens.

The pointed head of a hearted spring cabbage.

greens, leaving the third to mature as a hearted cabbage. Alternatively, cabbages can be planted at equidistant spacing 30 cm (12 in) apart. Spring cabbages can be protected with floating films in spring, or covered with cloches, to bring them on sooner. For a succession, sow in a cold frame or under cloches in September, planting out in spring.

A base fertilizer dressing is unnecessary when planting spring cabbage, but a nitrogenous topdressing (watered in well) or organic liquid feed can be given in March or April. (See Fertilizers, p 17.) Spring cabbage should be earthed up well during the winter.

Providing the plants are healthy, the main heads can be cut leaving the stalks in the ground. If a shallow 13 mm (½ in) deep cut is made in the stalk several small cabbages will usually develop on the edges of the cut, giving a second crop. This is only successful in fertile, moist soil.

Recommended cultivars

(In order of maturity, from April to June)
'Greensleeves' (spring greens only), 'Durham Early', 'Avoncrest', 'Dorado', F_1 'Spring Hero' (sow late August to avoid bolting).

SUMMER AND AUTUMN CABBAGE

The earlier summer cabbages generally have pointed heads, and the later maturing cultivars compact round or oval heads with few outer leaves. Summer cabbage is used from the end of June until September or October. Summer cabbage can be sown and planted in succession to give mature heads over a long season. Cultivars which stand well without deteriorating are especially useful. 'Minicole' is an outstanding example: it will stand for two to three months after maturing.

Spacing can be varied according to the size of head required. Plant 35 cm (14 in) apart for small

A late maturing cultivar of summer cabbage with a compact round head and few outer leaves.

heads; 45 cm (18in) apart for large heads. A general fertilizer can be worked in before planting, and in most conditions plants will benefit from a nitrogenous topdressing or organic liquid feed later in the growing season. (See Fertilizers, p 17.)

For a succession make several sowings, starting with the early summer cultivars and progressing to the late summer and autumn cultivars.

Very early crops are obtained by sowing under cover in heat at the end of February in the south, or the second week of March in the north. Seedlings are pricked out into pots or modules, and planted outside in April or May. They must be hardened off very carefully or there is a risk of bolting. The next sowings can be made under cloches or frames, planting out in April and May. The main sowings are made outdoors in seedbeds from March to early May.

The early summer cabbages can be cut across the stalk, (see spring cabbage above), to induce a late second crop of small heads.

Recommended cultivars

(In order of maturity, June to October)
'Hispi' (high-quality pointed), 'Spivoy' (savoyed leaves), 'Spitfire' (long standing pointed), F_1 'Golden Cross' (earliest round), 'Derby Day' (round), F_1 'Stonehead' and F_1 'Castello' (stand well), F_1 'Minicole' (exceptional standing quality).

A cabbage stem cut to give a second crop.

Second crop of small heads following cutting.

WINTER CABBAGE

There are several types of cabbage grown for use between November and March. They are sown in succession from late April to late May, and planted early June to early July. Average spacing is 50 cm (20 in) apart. Slightly closer spacing will produce smaller heads; slightly wider spacing larger heads. Winter cabbage should be earthed up well, and rotten leaves removed regularly. The main groups follow, in order of increasing hardiness.

Dutch winter white storage type These smooth-headed cabbages have densely-packed white inner leaves, which are excellent for coleslaw salads. Sown in late April, they mature from the end of October to November, and will stand into the following year in mild winters. For storage they should be lifted before frost. They can be uprooted whole, and stored either with roots intact, or cut off leaving a stem 15 cm (6 in) long. Cabbages for storing should always be handled very gently to prevent bruising, which may lead to rots developing during storage. (For storage see p 52.)

January King type The original 'January King' had purple-tinged foliage; the hybrid cultivars are greener. They are reasonably hardy, maturing from October to December, and often standing into February. Sow in late May.

White cabbage × savoy hybrids These tend to have the texture of the Dutch winter whites but are hardier. They mature from October to December, and may stand into March. Sow in late May.

Savoy type These crinkly-leaved cabbages are the latest to mature and the hardiest. They mature from October to January, and may stand into March or even April. Sow in late May.

Recommended cultivars
(*In order of maturity*)
Dutch winter whites F$_1$ 'Hidena', F$_1$ 'Polinius'.
January King 'January King – Hardy Late Stock 3', F$_1$ 'Aquarius'.
White cabbage × savoy hybrids 'Celtic', 'Tundra'.
Savoys F$_1$ 'Ice Queen', F$_1$ 'Wirosa', F$_1$ 'Wivoy'.

RED CABBAGE

There are summer and autumn types of red cabbage which are grown in the same way as summer and autumn cabbages, above. The main sowing for the summer types is in mid-March, and seedlings are planted out in early May. They can be spaced 23 cm (9 in) apart in rows 45 cm (18 in) apart, or at an equidistant spacing of about 33 cm (13 in) apart each way. The crop matures July/August, but will stand into October.

For an early summer crop, sow in seedtrays or modules (see Sowing indoors, p 33) in September, overwintering seedlings in a cold frame, and planting out in spring. The summer types will resprout if the stalks are left in the ground after the heads are picked. (See spring cabbage above.)

The autumn types of red cabbage are sown in late April and planted out in early June at the spacing given for winter cabbage above. The crop matures in October to November but will stand until December. However, autumn red cabbage can be lifted before heavy frost and stored in the same way as Dutch winter white cabbage.

Recommended cultivars
(*In order of maturity*)
Summer 'Langedijk Red Early–Norma'; F$_1$ 'Ruby Ball'.
Autumn F$_1$ 'Autoro', F$_1$ 'Hardoro'.

Hardy winter cabbage 'January King' has purple-tinged leaves.

Crinkly-leaved savoy cabbage is the hardiest and latest to mature.

Red cabbage 'Ruby Ball' is a useful and decorative brassica crop.

Calabrese

(*Brassica oleracea* Italica Group)

Calabrese is also known as American, Italian or green sprouting broccoli. It produces bluish green heads up to about 15 cm (6in) diameter, and smaller spears on sideshoots. It is a fast-growing brassica, being ready 75 to 95 days after sowing, depending on the cultivar. The plants are more dwarf than the purple and white sprouting broccolis, rarely more than 60 cm (2 ft) high. Calabrese has an excellent flavour, and freezes well.

Site / soil

See Brassicas, p 81. Calabrese grows well on less fertile soil than most brassicas.

Cultivation

Calabrese can be sown in succession from late March to early July for crops from early summer to autumn. Unlike most brassicas, calabrese is best sown direct, as transplanting may encourage the premature production of very small heads. However, it can be raised in pots or modules (see Sowing indoors, p 33), planted out carefully in moist conditions.

Sow two or three seeds together and thin seedlings to one per site. Unlike most brassicas again, calabrese is remarkably unresponsive to spacing. Plants can be as close as 7.5 cm (3 in) apart in rows 60 cm (2 ft) apart. Spacing does, however, affect the *type* of head produced. Close spacing suppresses the sideshoots, and results in the development of small terminal spears. These tend to be ready at the same time, which is useful where calabrese is grown for freezing. Wide spacing results in larger spears, with more of the yield coming from sideshoots. For the highest overall yield, and a good balance of main head and sideshoots, plant two plants per 30 cm^2 (12 in^2). This can be achieved by spacing 15 cm (6 in) apart in rows 30 cm (12 in) apart.

For an early spring crop of calabrese, sow an early-maturing cultivar in modules in late August or early September, and transplant seedlings into an unheated greenhouse or frame. The plants should be no more than about 13 cm (5 in) high before the onset of winter. There is a risk that very severe weather will·kill them, but it is a gamble worth taking, as survivors will mature from February to April, when fresh vegetables are very scarce. In mild areas seedlings can be planted outdoors in the autumn.

To produce a good quality crop, calabrese requires plenty of water, that is, about 2.5 cm (1 in) – 22 litres per sq m (4 gal per sq yd) – every fortnight.

A firm central head of calabrese should be cut first to allow smaller sideshoots to develop.

In the absence of rain it should be watered accordingly. Where resources are limited, a single heavy watering two to three weeks before harvesting is the most beneficial use of water. Calabrese can be top-dressed with a nitrogenous fertilizer or organic liquid feed after the central head is cut, to encourage the development of sideshoots.

Harvesting

Although the main calabrese season is from June to September, picking can continue until the plants are damaged by frost. Cut the central head first, while it is still firm and before there are any signs of flowers opening. This will stimulate the development of smaller sideshoots which are cut in turn. Early crops may give three pickings during the season.

Pests

Calabrese is subject to the usual brassica pests. (See Brassicas, p 82.) Mealy aphids are a fairly common pest. Caterpillars are a particular nuisance as they conceal themselves inside the heads. Soak the heads in salted water before cooking to flush them out.

Recommended cultivars

(*In order of maturity, the earliest cultivars maturing fastest. All are F$_1$ hybrids*)
'Mercedes', 'Green Comet', 'Citation', 'Shogun'.

Cauliflower

(*Brassica oleracea* Botrytis Group)

In the British Isles it is possible to produce fresh cauliflower from early spring to November, using a succession of cultivars adapted to different seasons. (See also Winter heading cauliflower below.) In the past cauliflowers maturing in winter and early spring were known as 'broccoli': now they are simply known as winter cauliflower.

The typical cauliflower has a cream or white 'curd' or head, but there are purple- and green-headed cultivars, which many think have outstanding flavour. Different again is a perennial form (see below). Cauliflowers are large plants, some growing nearly 90 cm (3 ft) across, and occupying ground for up to a year in the case of spring heading cauliflowers. For small gardens the early summer cauliflowers and mini cauliflowers are the most worth growing.

Cauliflowers are among the more difficult vegetables to grow, mainly because they need plenty of rainfall throughout growth, and normal summer rainfall is often inadequate. For this reason the autumn and spring heading types are the easiest to grow, as there is generally more rainfall in the period when they are maturing.

Site / soil

See Brassicas, p 81. Cauliflower must be grown in deeply dug, fertile, moisture-retentive soil. They prefer a more alkaline soil than most brassicas, with a pH of 6.5 – 7.5. On very acid soils they may suffer from boron or molybdenum deficiency. The latter causes the malformation 'whiptail' when the growing point fails to develop. (See Plant disorders, p 65.)

Cauliflowers need only moderate levels of nitrogen (see Fertilizers, p 18), to obtain the right balance between the growth of leaf and curd. The key to success undoubtedly lies in keeping the soil moist, both in the early stages and during the growing season. Checks in growth result in the formation of small, premature, and deformed heads.

Cultivation

See Brassicas, p 82. Cauliflowers are very susceptible to being checked when planted, so should be transplanted as young as possible, about six weeks after sowing. Although cauliflowers are normally transplanted, they can also be sown *in situ*, thinning to the spacing required, to eliminate the transplanting shock. They also respond well to being raised in modules. (See Sowing indoors, p 35.)

Spacing varies according to the season in which the cauliflower matures. As a general rule, the later the planting, the larger the cauliflower will grow and the wider the spacing it will require. For summer and early autumn cauliflowers, the spacing can be increased to some extent to reduce the amount of water required.

Mature curds of cauliflowers which head during winter and early spring may be damaged by severe frost, especially if they thaw out quickly. This can be prevented by leaning the cauliflower over towards the north and earthing it up on the south side. Alternatively, draw up the leaves and tie them above the head to protect the curd. In summer curds which are nearing maturity can be protected from the sun by bending a large leaf over the curd.

The principal sowing and planting dates, spacing and suitable cultivars for the main groups are given below. There is some overlapping between the groups, but as far as possible, cultivars are listed in order of maturity. The actual maturing dates will also, in practice, be affected by the weather during the growing season. (For Pests and diseases, see Brassicas p 82.)

Early summer cauliflower

(For cutting June/early July) Sow in the ground in a cold frame or under cloches in early October, thinning seedlings so they are at least 5 cm (2 in) apart each way. Alternatively, sow or prick out into small pots or modules (see Sowing indoors, p 35.), and overwinter the seedlings in frames or under cloches. They must be ventilated well on warm days in autumn and late winter and hardened off well before

An unprotected mature curd of cauliflower.

Protect cauliflower curds from frost.

Mini-cauliflowers are grown closely spaced.

Cauliflower 'Purple Cape' has attractive curds.

planting out. Plant out in early to mid-March, as soon as soil conditions are suitable. Plant 53 cm (21 in) apart each way, or 45 cm (18 in) apart in rows 60 cm (2 ft) apart. The crop can be protected with crop covers. (See Protected cropping, p 49.) Alternatively, sow in heat in early February, pricking out into pots or modules as soon as the seedlings are large enough to handle. Harden off before planting out.

Suitable cultivars
'Montano', 'Alpha Paloma', 'White Summer'.

Summer cauliflower

(For cutting August to mid-September) Sow in a cold frame in March (see early summer cauliflower above), or in a sheltered seedbed in the garden. Plant out in mid-May at the same spacing as early summer cauliflower. Water in carefully if the soil is dry. (See Brassicas, p 82.)

Suitable cultivars
'Plana', 'Dok', 'White Rock'.

Early autumn cauliflower

(For cutting late August to mid-September) Sow as for summer cauliflower in late April, planting out in mid-June. Plant 55 cm (22 in) apart each way, or 50 cm (20 in) apart in rows 60 cm (2 ft) apart. Water in carefully if the ground is dry.

Suitable cultivars
'Plana', 'White Rock'.

Autumn cauliflower

(For cutting mid-September to late November) Sow as for summer cauliflower in mid-May, planting in late June. Plant 64 cm (25 in) apart each way, 60 cm (2 ft) apart in rows 66 cm (2 ft 2 in) apart.

Suitable cultivars
'Plana', 'White Rock', 'Wallaby', 'Barrier Reef', 'Canberra'; 'Rosalind' and 'Violet Queen' (purple), 'Romanesco' (green; often listed under broccoli).

Winter heading cauliflower

For coastal areas of the south, south west and Wales, for cutting December to March. Sow late May in a seedbed outdoors, spacing seedlings out well. Plant out at the end of July 70 cm (2 ft 4 in) apart each way. Cultivars in this group are damaged by frost, so can be grown only in frost-free areas.

Spring heading winter cauliflower

(For cutting March to June) Sow in a seedbed outdoors in late May, spacing seedlings well apart. Plant in mid-July, spacing plants as for autumn cauliflower.

These plants need to be grown 'hard' to survive the winter, so only a little nitrogen, if any, should be applied at planting. A nitrogenous topdressing can be applied in late winter or early spring, or an organic liquid feed in spring, to stimulate growth.

Suitable cultivars
(WW = 'Walcheren Winter')
'Asmer Snowcap March', 'WW–Armado April', 'WW–Thanet', 'WW–Markanta', 'WW–Maystar', 'Asmer Pinnacle', 'Vilna'; 'Purple Cape' (purple).

Mini-cauliflowers

Mini-cauliflowers are cauliflowers which are grown so close they make miniature heads only 4–7.5 cm (1½–3 in) in diameter. If grown well they are of good quality and ideal for freezing, or for serving as single portions. The plants are only in the ground for about 13 to 18 weeks (the earlier sowings maturing fastest), so they take up far less garden space than other types of cauliflower. Their disadvantage is that all the heads mature over a few days, and deteriorate if not picked soon after maturing. This can be overcome by sowing small batches in succession during the summer, or by making several sowings of different cultivars at the same time.

Sow early summer cultivars from April until early July. Sow several seeds per 'station' *in situ* and thin to one after germination, or sow in modules and transplant. The most even results are obtained with equidistant spacing: plant 15 cm (6 in) apart each way. Alternatively, plant 10 cm (4 in) apart in rows 23 cm (9 in) apart. It may be necessary to water the seedlings to help them to get established, but further watering is only necessary in dry weather.

Perennial cauliflower

This is a vigorous, spreading plant, which in spring produces a central head, surrounded by smaller, but good quality heads, rather like a sprouting broccoli. It requires fertile soil.

Sow in spring, either *in situ* (sowing several seeds per station and thinning to one after germination), or in a seedbed or in modules for transplanting. Space plants so that each has about 1 sq m (1 sq yd) of space. When cropping is finished straggly shoots can be pruned back. Prune off any shoots which show signs of flowering. Perennial cauliflower is fairly hardy, and may last two or three seasons before it starts to deteriorate. The only cultivar available at present is 'Nine Star Perennial'.

Chinese cabbage

(*Brassicas rapa* Pekinensis Group)

Of the many types of Chinese cabbage two headed types have become popular in Europe: the hearted 'barrel', and the cylindrical 'Michihili'. They are widely known as 'Chinese leaves'. (See also Oriental greens, p 93.) The typical barrel type has a compact head of light green, closely wrapped leaves, is about 20–25 cm (8–10in) high, and is either a stout or elongated barrel shape. The cylindrical type is longer and more erect with a looser heart, and grows 38–45 cm (15–18 in) tall. It tends to be a darker green in colour. Chinese cabbage leaves have a very prominent white midrib (which is edible), and often prominent veining on the leaves. Mild and refreshing in flavour, they are excellent in salads and stir-fried. They should not be boiled.

Site / soil

See also Brassicas, p 81. Chinese cabbage needs an open site, though it will tolerate light shade in mid-summer. It is a very fast growing crop, and for this reason needs fertile, well-drained soil with a high level of organic matter so the roots can run freely. Avoid poor soil, and very light or heavy soils.

Cultivation

Chinese cabbage is naturally a 'short day' plant, so is likely to bolt if sown before the longest day in mid-June. Recently cultivars of the barrel type have been introduced which have considerable resistance to bolting, and can be sown earlier. The main sowings however, are made from mid-June to August. This makes Chinese cabbage a convenient crop to follow early crops of potatoes, peas or broad beans.

Chinese cabbage is easily checked by transplanting, which may result in premature bolting; so either sow in pots or modules (see Sowing indoors, p 35), and plant out when seedlings have about five or six leaves, or sow *in situ* in moist conditions. Sow in rows 45 cm (18 in) apart, thinning plants to 30 cm (12 in) apart, or grow at equidistant spacing about 35 cm (14 in) apart each way.

If earlier crops are required choose a bolt-resistant cultivar, and sow in modules in a heated propagator in late April or early May. A minimum temperature of 18 C (64 F), but preferably 20–25 C (66–77 F) must be maintained for the next three weeks to prevent premature bolting. Plant out after hardening off well. Early outdoor crops of Chinese cabbage can be grown under crop covers. Chinese cabbage responds well to being protected with net films throughout growth. (See Protected cropping, p 49.)

A final late crop can be obtained in early winter by sowing in August and transplanting under cover, preferably into an unheated greenhouse or polytunnel, in September. Choose cold-resistant cultivars where available, and plant closer than normal. The plants may not heart up, but can be used as 'semi-mature' cut-and-come-again plants: cut the leaves 2.5–5 cm (1–2 in) above the base, and leave the stump to resprout. It will continue to produce leaves for much of the winter and in spring, unless affected by very severe frost. Eventually very tender flowering shoots will be produced, and these can be eaten in salads or cooked.

Most Chinese cabbage cultivars will stand only very light frosts. Outdoor plants can be protected with cloches or low polytunnels in autumn to improve their quality and extend their useful season.

Chinese cabbage requires plenty of moisture throughout growth and may need watering in dry seasons to yield a good crop. However, it has a shallow root system, so unlike most brassicas, should be watered little and often. Keep the crop mulched whenever possible. (See Mulching, p 44.)

Harvesting

Heads are often ready for cutting nine to ten weeks after sowing. Cut just above ground level, leaving the stumps to resprout and produce further leaves. The heads can be stored in a refrigerator for several weeks. They are best stored in *paper* bags, or loose, out of contact with other foods, to minimize the risk of listeria.

Pests and diseases

Chinese cabbage is susceptible to all the common brassica pests and diseases, and is particularly vulnerable to slug and caterpillar damage – perhaps because its leaves are so tender. (See also p 82.)

Recommended cultivars

Barrel type hybrids, maturing about 55 days after sowing 'Kasumi' (very good bolting resistance), 'Tip Top' (moderate bolting resistance). *Michihili type* 'Jade Pagoda'.

Chinese cabbage cut to show the dense heart.

A typical barrel type cultivar of Chinese cabbage.

Kale

(Brassica oleracea Acephala Group)

Kale is the hardiest of our winter vegetables, suriviving severe weather and producing young side shoots in spring. Both the leaves and the young spring shoots of curly kale (borecole) are eaten; only the shoots of broadleaved kale are eaten.

Unfortunately many of the older types of kale are no longer available. Some new hybrids of the curly types have been developed, which are very compact and even with finely curled leaves. The highly productive cultivar 'Pentland Brig' is a cross between the curly and broadleaved types, and produces a mass of leafy shoots in spring. The old cultivar 'Ragged Jack' has rather pretty, reddish leaves, but is only moderately hardy. The ornamental kales have highly coloured leaves and are grown primarily for decoration, garnishing or to add colour to salads. They are less hardy than other types.

The dwarf forms of curly kale are about 30 cm (12 in) tall; tall forms are 76–90 cm (2½–3 ft) tall. Both are very decorative during the winter months. The kale season extends from November to April, but kale is undoubtedly most useful in the early months of the year – especially after a severe winter – when fresh vegetables are in short supply.

Site / soil

See also Brassicas, p 81. Although kale will tolerate poorer soil than most brassicas, it does best in rich,

Pick individual leaves of curly kale.

Snap off shoots of broadleaved kale.

well-cultivated, well-drained soil, prepared the previous autumn. A topdressing of nitrogenous fertilizer or organic liquid feed can be applied in spring to stimulate the production of side shoots. (See p 17.)

Cultivation

See also Brassicas, p 82. Sow in late April and May in a seedbed outdoors, spacing seeds out well. Transplant seedlings into their permanent position six to eight weeks later, in June and July, planting firmly. Water in dry conditions to get the plants established. The more dwarf forms can be 45 cm (18in) apart each way, taller forms 60–76 cm (2–2½ft) apart each way. The ornamental kales can be dug up in late autumn and replanted deeply, up to their lower leaves, under cover. This prevents their leaves being damaged by frost and winter weather and provides pickings during winter.

Curly kale can also be grown closely spaced for an early crop of cut-and-come-again spring greens. Sow under cover, in late January or February in mild areas if the soil is workable, or outdoors in March and early April. Sow thinly, either broadcast or in wide parallel drills. Seedlings can be cut when no more than 5–7.5 cm (2–3 in) high, or thinned out to 7.5–10 cm (3–4 in) apart, and cut when up to 15 cm (6 in) high. (See also Sowing outdoors, p 33.)

Harvesting

In the cases of curly kale and the ornamental kales, pick a few young leaves from several plants. Ornamental kales may remain productive over at least 12 months if flowering shoots are removed as they develop. The young shoots of broad and curly types can be simply snapped off in spring.

Pests and diseases

See Brassicas, p 82. Kale is relatively free of pests and diseases. It is less susceptible to clubroot than most brassicas, and is rarely attacked by pigeons in winter.

Recommended cultivars

F₁ 'Fribor' (curly), 'Thousandhead' (broadleaf), 'Pentland Brig'.

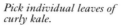

Different types of kale: **1** *curly;* **2** *plain or broadleaved;* **3** *ornamental;* **4** *'Ragged Jack' with reddish leaves.*

Kohl rabi

(*Brassica oleracea* Gongylodes Group)

Kohl rabi is a curious-looking member of the brassica family, grown for its ball-like swollen stem, which develops 2.5–5 cm (1–2 in) above ground level. It is often used as a turnip substitute, as it withstands drought and heat better and is more resistant to clubroot. There are purple and green skinned forms, the latter often known as 'white' kohl rabi. It is an undervalued, tasty, and highly nutritious vegetable, which can be grated raw in salads or cooked. The young leaves can also be eaten as greens.

Site / soil

Kohl rabi does best in fertile, light, sandy soil, but tolerates heavier soil. The soil should be limed if acid. Kohl rabi should be rotated in the same way as other brassicas. Its nitrogen requirements are not high. (See Fertilizers, p 18.) Kohl rabi makes a useful catch crop, as in rich soil and moist conditions it can be ready seven or eight weeks after sowing.

The curious ball-like swollen stems of kohl rabi develop above ground. This example has a green skin.

Cultivation

For a continuous supply sow small quantities outdors in succession from late February and early March (in mild districts) until August. Early outdoor crops can be covered with crop covers. (See Protected cropping, p 49.) Kohl rabi tends to bolt if sown at temperatures below about 10 C (50 F). Generally speaking the green forms mature fastest and are sown until June for the main summer crop. The purple skinned types mature later and are hardier, and are sown from June until August for winter use.

Sow outdoors in drills 30 cm (12 in) apart, thinning to 15 – 23 cm (6 – 9 in) apart. It is most important to thin early or development is checked.

An early sowing can be made in gentle heat indoors in February or early March, for transplanting outside in April for a June crop. Sow in modules if possible (see Sowing indoors, p 35); if not transplant seedlings when they are no more than 5 cm (2 in) high or they are liable to bolt prematurely.

Harvesting

It was essential to use the older cultivars of kohl rabi young, between golf-ball and tennis-ball size, as they became woody if any larger. The new hybrid cultivars will grow larger but remain tender. Kohl rabi is fairly hardy (again cultivars are being developed with improved hardiness), and can be left in the ground during winter in most parts of the country. Quality is lost by lifting and storing, but where it is necessary, store kohl rabi in boxes in sand. (See Storage, p 51.) Trim off the outer leaves, but leave the central tuft of leaves attached to the swollen stem to help keep it fresh.

Pests and diseases

Flea beetle and cabbage root fly are the most common pests; clubroot the most likely disease. For symptoms and control, see p 58ff.)

Recommended cultivars

'White Vienna' ('Green Vienna'), 'Purple Vienna' (old cultivars); F₁ 'Rowel', F₁ 'Lanro', F₁ 'Kolpak' (new hybrids).

Oriental greens

In recent years seed of several types of oriental greens, all members of the brassica family, have become available in this country. In the main oriental greens are fast growing, attractive, and nutritious vegetables, suitable for use raw and cooked. They deserve to be better known and more widely grown.

They are most likely to find a niche in the vegetable garden as late summer, winter and early spring crops. This is because some, like headed Chinese cabbage, will bolt unless sown after the longest day; others are very hardy, and useful either as outdoor winter crops or, if grown under cover, as very tender winter and early spring greens. The following are brief notes on some of the more productive and easily grown oriental brassicas. For Further reading, see p 158.

For soil/site, general cultivation, pests and diseases, see Brassicas, p 81. Oriental greens are often grown as cut-and-come-again seedling crops, (see Sowing outdoors, p 33). For this purpose different oriental brassicas can be mixed together and sown for cutting as salads or spring greens. Most oriental brassicas can also be harvested as a cut-and-come-again crop at a semi-mature stage. (See Chinese cabbage.) In addition, the flowering shoots of bolted plants are normally sweet and tender, if picked before the flowers open, and can be eaten raw or cooked. The flowering shoots of the various mustard types tend to be too peppery for most people's taste.

Most of the oriental brassicas require plenty of moisture during growth, but are fairly shallow-rooted. Therefore, they should be watered little and often, and wherever practical, kept mulched.

LOOSE-HEADED CHINESE CABBAGE
(Brassica rapa Pekinensis Group)

This is a type of Chinese cabbage which forms open heads of light green, mild-flavoured, often prettily serrated or wavy leaves. The 'fluffy top' types develop creamy coloured centres and are excellent in salads. There are many cultivars but on the whole, compared to Chinese cabbage, the loose-headed cabbages tend to be slightly faster growing, somewhat more resistant to bolting and cold but lower yielding.

They can be harvested at any stage from cut-and-come-again seedlings to mature heads, and respond well to cut-and-come-again treatment as semi-mature plants. (See Chinese cabbage p 90.)

Cultivation
Mature heads For cultivation methods and spacing see Chinese cabbage, p 90. Sow from mid-June to August; late sowings can be planted under cover in September, as for Chinese cabbage, and harvested similarly.

Cut-and-come-again seedlings Make the first sowings under cover in spring, and follow by outdoor sowings in late spring. Midsummer sowings may develop too fast and become fibrous, so it is recommended that the next outdoor sowings be made in late summer, followed by early autumn sowings under cover. These cut-and-come-again seedling crops can often be cut four or five weeks after sowing.

Recommended cultivars
'Minato Santo', 'Eskimo' (fluffy top.)

Mizuna greens form clumps of decorative, finely divided leaves.

Related to Chinese cabbage, pak choi has smoother, glossier leaves.

Vigorous-growing komatsuna produces leaves up to 30cm (12in) long.

PAK CHOI
(*Brassica rapa* Chinensis Group)

Pak choi is closely related to Chinese cabbage, but has much smoother, glossier leaves, light to deep green in colour. The leaves have very wide midribs, which often broaden out at the base into a spoon-like shape. The midribs and leaf stems contrast strikingly with the leaves and are usually very clear white, but in some cultivars are a beautiful green. There are many types of pak choi, the smallest little more than 7.5–10 cm (3–4 in) high; the largest 60 cm (2 ft) high. Like Chinese cabbage, pak choi tend to bolt if sown early in the year, but hybrids have been developed with considerable resistance to bolting. Generally speaking, they are more frost-tolerant than Chinese cabbage. They can be harvested at any stage, from small seedlings to mature plants, and respond well to all cut-and-come-again treatments. The flavour is somewhat stronger than that of Chinese cabbage; seedling leaves are crisp and juicy.

Cultivation
Sow as for loose-headed Chinese cabbage above. Use bolt-resistant cultivars where available for spring sowings, and cold-resistant cultivars where available for the late sowings. Spacing of mature plants depends on the cultivar: small types can be grown 10–13 cm (4–5 in) apart; large types up to 45 cm (18 in) apart.

Recommended cultivars
(*Fairly bolt-resistant hybrids*)
'Mei Qing Choi' pronounced 'May Ching Choy', 'Chingensai,' (green stem); 'Joi Choi' (white stem).

KOMATSUNA (SPINACH MUSTARD)
(*Brassica rapa* Perviridis Group)

The komatsunas are a very diverse group of large-leaved brassicas, closely related to turnips. Individual leaves of mature plants can be up to 30 cm (12 in) long and 18 cm (7 in) wide, though they can be harvested at any stage from young seedlings to large plants. The flavour and texture are closer to European than Chinese cabbage, with a hint of spinach to them. Komatsunas are naturally very vigorous and 'healthy' looking, and very adaptable, tolerating both high and low temperatures. They are also more drought-tolerant than most of the oriental brassicas. While they survive most English winters outdoors, it is worth having some plants under cover in winter. They will be of better quality, and will continue growing in sunny spells. Young and shredded leaves can be used in salads; otherwise they are cooked as greens.

Cultivation
The following are the most useful crops:

Mature and 'semi-mature' crop Sow in midsummer for the outdoor autumn and winter crop. Either raise plants in modules and transplant, or sow *in situ* thinning to the required distance. Precise spacing depends on the cultivar, and also determines the size of the ultimate plant. Plants can be spaced as close as 5 cm (2 in) apart for harvesting very young, or 25–30 cm (10–12 in) apart to harvest large. Cut individual leaves and allow the plants to continue growing.

Make a second sowing in late summer to transplant under cover for a top-quality winter crop.

Cut-and-come-again seedlings Make the first sowings under cover very early in spring, followed with outdoor sowings in spring and early summer. Make final sowings outdoors in late August or under cover in September.

Recommended cultivars
'All Top', 'Komatsuna', 'Tendergreen'.

MIZUNA GREENS
(*Brassica rapa* var. *nipposinica*)

Mizuna greens are exceptionally decorative vegetables, forming rosette-like clumps of glossy, deep green, finely divided leaves, about 23 cm (9 in high). As they have a long growing season, they make an attractive edge to vegetable or flower beds. Mizuna greens are also useful for undercropping sweet corn, or, when grown as a seedling crop for intercropping.

Mizuna greens are adaptable plants being both neat and cold tolerant, and also very vigorous; the clumps can often be cut four or five times before they run to seed. Young leaves are used raw, but older leaves are best lightly cooked.

Cultivation
Mizuna greens can be grown either as mature plants or as a seedling crop. The first cut of seedlings can sometimes be made two or three weeks after sowing. Where mature plants are grown, keep cutting regularly to produce a continuous crop of small young leaves.

For sowing times and systems, see Komatsuna.

A red-leaved example of mustard greens.

Mustard 'Green in the Snow' is very hardy.

Chinese broccoli, grown for its flowering shoots.

spring. Plants will also grow larger under cover.

Sow either *in situ*, or in modules for transplanting. Spacing depends on the cultivar, but average spacing would be 30 cm (12 in) apart each way. To get smaller plants for harvesting younger, closer spacing can be used; wider spacing would be appropriate for potentially large cultivars or when grown under cover.

Recommended cultivars
'Amsoi' (moderately hardy), 'Green in the Snow' (very hardy), 'Miike Giant' (very hardy).

CHINESE BROCCOLI
(*Brassica oleracea* var. *alboglabra*)

Also known as Chinese kale, this oriental brassica is grown for its flowering shoots, which could be described as being halfway between calabrese and purple sprouting broccoli in size. They are very succulent and well flavoured, though the stems may need peeling in mature plants.

Cultivation
Chinese broccoli can be sown throughout the growing season, from late spring to early autumn, but it crops best from July to August sowings, which mature in late summer and autumn. It can be grown either as young plants, which are harvested whole, when the flowering shoots start to appear, or as large plants producing shoots over a longer period.

For young plants sow broadcast or in rows about 10 cm (4 in) apart, thinning plants to 10 – 15 cm (4 – 6 in) apart. For large plants sow *in situ* or in seedbeds, transplanting when about 7.5 cm (3 in) tall. Space plants 25 – 38 cm (10 – 15 in) apart. They can be grown closer if you are short of space, as Chinese broccoli, like calabrese, is relatively insensitive to spacing. Harvest the main flowering shoot first and the sideshoots subsequently as they develop. Pick them before the first flowers open. As with calabrese, pollen beetle is sometimes a pest. (See Pests and diseases, p 61.)

Recommended cultivars
F$_1$ 'Green Lance'.

For mature and semi-mature plants use the following spacing: small plants 10 cm (4in) apart; medium plants: 20–23 cm (8–9in) apart; large plants: 30–45 cm (12–18 in) apart.

Recommended cultivars
'Mizuna Greens' ('Kyona'), F$_1$ 'Tokyo Beau' (productive hybrid with increased cold resistance).

MUSTARD GREENS
(*Brassica juncea*)

The oriental mustards are another very large group of rather coarse-leaved brassicas, generally with a spicy flavour. Some of the hardier types have beautiful purplish colouring in the leaves. They are very robust, tolerate a wide range of soil types, and most are exceptionally hardy. They grow more slowly than the milder flavoured oriental greens already covered, so are less suited to cut-and-come-again seedling crops. Mature and semi-mature plants can, however, be cut and left to resprout. Mustard greens are mostly used cooked.

Cultivation
The principal sowings are in midsummer (July and August) for an autumn to winter crop. Like komatsuna and mizuna greens, mustard greens are hardy enough to withstand most English winters outdoors, but if planted under cover in September, will produce a high quality, more tender crop from winter to

Texsel greens
(*Brassica carinata*)

Texsel greens, developed from Ethiopian mustard, is a useful newcomer to our gardens. This vegetable is a fast-growing, shiny-leaved brassica, notable for its nutritional value and good, slightly spinachy flavour. It is reasonably hardy, and can be harvested at any stage from seedlings 5 cm (2 in) high, to 'greens' 20–30 cm (8–12 in) high. It is generally used as a salad vegetable when young, and cooked at the later stages. Texsel greens has superseded the earlier cultivar 'Karate'. For site, soil and fertilizers, pests and diseases see Brassicas, p 81. As Texsel greens is fast growing, it is among brassicas most likely to succeed in gardens where clubroot is a problem. It is also a useful catch crop.

Cultivation
Seeds can be sown outdoors from mid-March to early autumn, at two to three week intervals for a continuous supply. Sowing is probably most valuable in spring and in the late summer to autumn period, when growth is best. Texsel greens is normally sown *in situ* in drills 13 mm (½ in) deep. For a seedling crop sow broadcast or in wide parallel drills. It is normally possible to make one or two cuts.

The highest yields are obtained by sowing in rows 30 cm (12 in) apart, thinning to 2.5 cm (1 in) apart in the rows. Or sow in rows 15 cm (6 in) apart, thinning to 5 cm (2 in) apart. Another option is to broadcast the seed, and to thin to 15 cm (6 in) apart. When growing fast Texsel greens can reach a height of 25 cm (10 in) within about 48 days. Cut or pull the plants when they reach the required size.

Seeds can also be sown under cover, in cloches, frames, polytunnels and so on, in autumn and early spring. Undercover crops are usually grown as cut-and-come-again seedling crops. (See p 33.) To avoid bolting make sure Texsel greens does not dry out during growth.

The nutritious shiny leaves of fast growing Texsel greens.

Turnips and swedes

Turnips and swedes are grown chiefly for their roots. Swedes are milder and sweeter than turnips and raised mainly for winter use, while turnips, by selecting appropriate cultivars, can be available for use all year round.

TURNIPS
(*Brassica campestris* Rapifera Group)

Turnips are flat, round or long in shape, with white or yellow flesh, and their leafy 'tops' can also be used and make excellent spring greens.

Site / soil
Turnips like cool moist conditions; summer sowings can be made in light shade, provided there is plenty of moisture in the soil. Turnips, particularly the early crops, have higher nitrogen requirements than swedes, so the soil should have plenty of organic matter worked in for the previous crop, or a top-dressing of general fertilizer applied before sowing. (See Fertilizers, p 17.) Turnips should be rotated as other brassicas. (See p 23.)

Cultivation
Well-grown early turnips are a fast maturing crop, normally ready within six to ten weeks of sowing. Some of the round white Japanese cultivars can be pulled small 35 days after sowing. Turnips are useful for intercropping and catch-cropping.

Early maturing cultivars deteriorate rapidly once mature, and are best used when small. It is advisable to make successional sowings at three-week intervals from early spring onwards. The hardy cultivars, which may take three months to mature, are grown for autumn use and storage, and will stand longer without deteriorating.

The earliest sowings of summer turnips, using early cultivars, can be made under frames or cloches in February, followed by outdoor sowings in March and April; these will be ready in May and June. Turnips run to seed rapidly in dry weather, so sowings in May and June may not succeed if conditions are dry. Some cultivars are more likely to bolt than others from early sowings.

The main sowings of hardy cultivars for autumn and winter use and storage are made in July and August.

Range of turnip types: **1** *long white;* **2** *round green top;*
3 *round red.*

Sow turnips very thinly on a well-prepared
seedbed, sowing seed about 2 cm (¾ in) deep. Sow
early cultivars in rows 23 cm (9 in) apart, thinning to
10 cm (4 in) apart in the rows. Sow winter cultivars in
rows 30 cm (12 in) apart, thinning to
15 cm (6 in) apart. As turnips grow very fast, any
thinning must be done early, when the seedlings are
no more than about 2.5 cm (1 in) high.

Turnips grown for tops are sown in August and
September, or as early in spring as soil conditions
allow, either under cover or in the open. Sow thinly
in rows 15 cm (6 in) apart, or broadcast in a small
patch. Use hardy cultivars for autumn sowings and
early ones for spring sowings. Even if the seedlings
are small at the start of winter, they will make rapid
growth in spring. The first cutting can be made
when the seedlings are 13 – 15 cm (5 – 6 in) high,
about 2.5 cm (1 in) above ground level. If left longer
they become tough. Provided the ground is not
allowed to dry out, several further cuttings can be
made before the plants run to seed. Growth will be
checked if the soil is allowed to dry out, so watering
will be needed in rainless periods, watering at the
rate of 11 litres / sq m (2 gal / sq yd) when necessary.
This will improve the size and quality of the roots,
but may reduce their flavour. This crop is particularly useful in early spring after a hard winter.

Harvesting
Early cultivars of turnips will be ready when about
4 – 5 cm (1½ – 2 in) diameter. Hardy turnips can be
left in the soil until Christmas. They need a soil
covering if clamped. (See p 51.)

Pests and diseases
The most common pest is flea beetle. Other likely
pests include mealy cabbage aphid and cabbage root
fly. Turnip gall weevil may cause hollow swellings on
the roots (sometimes mistaken for clubroot), but is
not generally serious. Discard any galled seedlings.
Mildew is the most common disease. For symptoms
and control of other pests and diseases, see p 58ff.

Some recommended cultivars
Early 'Purple Top Milan', 'Snowball', F₁ 'Tokyo
Cross' (very fast maturing, but may bolt if sown
before June).
Hardy 'Golden Ball 'Orange Perfection'/'Orange
Jelly' (orange flesh), 'Manchester Market' 'Green
Top Stone'.

SWEDES
(*Brassica napus* Napobrassica Group)

Swedes are one of the hardiest of the root crops, and
often succeed where turnips fail. The flesh is
normally yellow, but in some cases white. The
'purple top' cultivars – the purple referring to the
skin colour – are considered best for home use.
Roots often display considerable variation in shape,
some being thin and narrow, others bulbous. This is
largely due to the quality of the seed.

Site / soil
Swedes need an open site, and do best on light, fertile soils, which suffer neither from waterlogging nor
drought. The soil should have been manured for the
previous crop and be limed if acid. Swedes must be
rotated as other brassicas (see p 23).

Cultivation
Swedes take 20 to 26 weeks to mature. They are
generally sown in early May in the north, and late
May and early June in the south. Sow *in situ* about
2 cm (¾ in) deep, in rows at least 38 cm (15 in) apart.
Sow thinly, and thin in stages until plants are at least
23 cm (9 in) apart.

Apart from keeping the crop weed-free little
attention is required. (For fertilizer needs see p 17).
Growth will be checked if the soil is allowed to dry
out, so watering will be needed (see Turnips).

*Swede 'Marian' is a purple-topped cultivar with good
resistance to clubroot.*

Harvesting

Roots are generally ready for use by September or October in the south and October or November in the north. They can be left in the ground until Christmas, but it is advisable to lift and store them then, or they become coarse and woody. They can be stored in clamps outdoors or in boxes under cover. (See Storage, p 51.)

Forcing

It is not always realized that swedes can be forced for the young blanched shoots, which are excellent raw in salads.

After lifting the roots in early winter, plant a few in the soil under the greenhouse staging. Exclude light by any of the methods suggested for forcing rhubarb indoors. Alternatively, put them into a wooden tray or box covered with a thick layer of straw, upturned box or black polythene to exclude light. Leave them in a cellar, shed, or sheltered spot outdoors. The shoots take three weeks to a month to develop, depending on the temperature. Cut them when 10 – 13 cm (4 – 5 in) long.

Pests and diseases

See Turnips, above. Swedes are susceptible to club-root. The new cultivar 'Marian' has some resistance to both. Swedes are sometimes affected by various root rots, especially when grown for more than one year on one site. Burn diseased roots and practise rotation.

Recommended cultivars

'Acme', 'Marian', 'Devon Champion'.

Barriers protect against carrot rootfly.

The natural canopy of carrot foliage suppresses weeds.

Carrots

(Daucus carota)

There are several different types of carrots, classified according to maturity, size and shape. However, root shape and colour can be affected by soil and growing conditions. Early cultivars mature relatively quickly and are used fresh. Maincrop cultivars take longer to mature and are used freshly dug or stored

The following are the main types of carrots suitable for amateur use, given in order of maturity. In each group there are various selections, claimed to be improvements on the original type.

Paris Market Small round or square carrots. Used for early and quick crops, and on difficult soils.

Amsterdam Small, slender carrots with cylindrical, stump-shaped roots and smooth skins. Used for early crops and forcing.

Nantes Cylindrical stump-rooted carrots similar to the Amsterdam type, but slightly broader and longer. Used for early crops and forcing, and in the case of some cultivars, for late crops.

Chantenay Medium-sized roots, broader and shorter than Nantes, stump-rooted but conical rather than cylindrical in shape. This maincrop type is widely grown for summer use.

Berlicum Large, late-maturing carrots, cylindrical and stump-rooted: very much the same shape as Amsterdam but longer and of better quality. Used for winter storage.

Autumn King Very long, very large, late-maturing carrots, stump-rooted but slightly tapering in shape. These need a long period of growth. Used for winter storage.

Site / soil

Early sowings require a warm sheltered position; later sowings may be made in a more open site. Carrots grow best on rich, well-drained, light soils such as coarse sands or friable loams, rather than heavy clay soils. The roots cannot expand in soils which get compacted or waterlogged: they become stunted and fanged. Good soil structure should be encouraged by preparing the soil thoroughly the previous autumn, working in plenty of organic matter. Carrots prefer a soil pH in the range of 6.5 to 7.5, that is slightly acid to slightly alkaline.

Cultivation

Carrots are normally sown *in situ*, as they do not transplant well unless raised in modules. They lend themselves to being grown in fairly close rows on the bed system (see p 21). In preparing the seedbed aim to create a very fine tilth without consolidating the soil. You should be able to push the fingers right into the soil. Work from the path wherever possible.

Weeding between carrots is difficult, so if possible prepare the seedbed two to three weeks before sowing. Allow the first flush of weeds to germinate and hoe weeds off before sowing. Carrots have a low nitrogen requirement, but an appropriate base-dressing can be worked into the seedbed before sowing. (See Fertilizers, p 18.)

Sow carrot seeds 13-20 mm (½ – ¾ in) deep, as thinly as possible. The seeds are fairly small and can be mixed with sand, or used and redried tea leaves, to make it easier to sow them evenly.

The main sowings are given below.

For very early crop, maturing end of May, early June Use Nantes hybrids, and sow in an unheated greenhouse or polytunnel, or outdoors under floating films (see Protected cropping, p 49) in October.

Early sowings for June and July crops Use Paris Market Round, Amsterdam Forcing and Nantes types. Make the first sowings in frames or under cloches in February (in warm areas) or March, followed by outdoor sowings in a sheltered spot as soon as the soil is workable. Early outdoor sowings can be covered with cloches, low tunnels, or perforated polythene film, which should be removed when plants have four to six true leaves. Carrots can also be grown to maturity under fleecy film (see p 50).

Carrots germinate poorly at soil temperatures below 7.5 C (45 F), so for outdoor sowings warm the soil beforehand with cloches or polythene film. Early sowings can be made more thickly than later sowings as only half the seeds are likely to germinate. Alternatively, use fluid sowing. (See Sowing outdoors, p 32.) There is likely to be some bolting with these early crops.

Another way of growing an early crop is to multi-sow the round Paris Market type in modules.(See Sowing indoors, p 35.) Sow four seeds per module indoors in early February. Plant out after hardening off in April. This method is unsuccessful with long-rooted types.

For August and September crops Use early types mentioned above and Chantenay cultivars. Sow outdoors in March and early April. The Amsterdam Forcing and Nantes types can be pulled while still young for use as 'finger carrots'.

Maincrop sowings for October and November crops Use Chantenay, Berlicum and Autumn King types. Sow outdoors in late April and May.

Late crop, maturing December onwards Use Berlicum, Autumn King, and some Nantes cultivars. Sow in May and June.

Spacing Research aimed at obtaining the highest yield of usable carrots suggests wider spacings then traditionally used for early crops, but closer spacings for later crops. Some carrots will always grow larger at the expense of others, so when high overall yields are obtained a proportion of carrots will be too small to use: the weight of the larger carrots will more than compensate.

Carrots are best grown in rows 15 cm (6 in) apart. With early cultivars aim to space plants 10 cm (4 in) apart in the rows. This wide spacing minimizes competition and enables the carrots to put on weight rapidly in a relatively short time.

With maincrop carrots aim to space plants 4 cm (1½ in) apart if medium-sized carrots are required, or somewhat further apart for larger carrots. These crops naturally grow larger as they are in the ground for a longer period.

For carrot thinning see measures against carrot fly, below.

Where carrots are grown in 15 cm (6 in) rows, weed them by hand until they reach the stage of having two 'true', feathery leaves. After this the natural canopy of foliage will virtually suppress further weed growth. If carrots are grown further apart the canopy is slower to suppress the weeds and the crop will have to be hoed. It is always possible to mulch between the rows in the early stages to keep down weeds and conserve moisture in the soil.

If carrots are over-watered or there is excessive rainfall the leaves, rather than the roots, develop. However, root quality will be poor if the soil dries out. In dry weather watering every two or three weeks will keep the crop growing steadily: 16-22 litres / sq m (3–4 gal / sq yd) will be sufficient. In a mature crop splitting can result from watering or heavy rainfall after a prolonged dry spell; keeping the soil reasonably moist will prevent this.

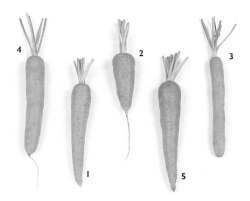

A range of carrot types: **1** *Berlicum;* **2** *Chantenay;* **3** *Amsterdam forcing;* **4** *Nantes;* **5** *Autumn King.*

Harvesting

On light soils early crops of carrots can be pulled as required for use; on heavy soils they may need to be loosened with a fork. The longer maincrop carrots are left in the soil, the larger they grow.

As a general rule, avoid lifting after very heavy rain or watering, as this will encourage splitting.

For winter use, carrots can be either lifted and stored or left in the soil. The flavour is best if they are left in the soil, but this is only advisable in light, well-drained soils, and if carrot fly has been controlled. The carrots can be ridged over with soil to give them extra protection. If leaving them in the ground allow the tops to die down in late November, sprinkle the ground with slug bait, and cover with a layer of bracken, straw or leaves about 15 cm (6 in) deep. Anchor this covering with wire hoops in exposed situations.

Carrots are not generally damaged by the first light frosts, but if heavy frost is expected they should be covered earlier than suggested above.

Roots for storage can be lifted from October to December. Cut the tops about 13 mm (½ in) above the crown, reject diseased or twisted roots or roots with carrot fly damage (they can be used first), and store in clamps outside or boxes indoors. (See Storage, p 51.) Inspect stored carrots periodically and remove any that are rotting.

Pests and diseases

Lettuce root aphid is sometimes a problem. Carrot fly is far and away the most serious carrot pest, sometimes making it very difficult to grow good crops in established gardens. Various measures that can be taken to lessen the risks of serious damage are outlined below. Where carrot fly is a serious problem adopt as many of these measures as possible.

In addition to carrot fly, carrots are sometimes attacked by root aphids and leaf aphids (carrot-willow aphid). For symptoms and control, see p 58ff.)

Measures to avoid carrot fly

Timing of sowings There are several hatches of carrot fly during the year, and to some extent sowings can be timed to avoid the worst attacks.

In the south early sowings in mid-March, and late sowings in June, will avoid the first attack. These sowings should be 10 days later in the north.

Thinning The egg-laying female carrot flies are attracted by the smell of carrot thinnings, and lay eggs in the cracks in the soil where thinnings have been pulled out. Sow as thinly as possible to eliminate or minimize the need for thinning. Where thinning is unavoidable, do it in the evening, preferably on still, overcast or showery days. Water drills before and after thinning, nip off surplus seedlings just above ground level, firm the soil around the base of the plant after thinning, and bury the thinnings in the compost heap. Carrots can be pulled to thin, but nipping off is preferable when carrot fly attacks are likely.

Intercropping There is some evidence that intercropping rows of carrots with onions reduces carrot fly attacks. Mixing carrot seeds with the seeds of annual flowers and sowing them together also seems to discourage attacks. They look attractive growing together, so this method can be used for sowing in a flower bed.

Barriers As the carrot fly does not fly high, the most effective means of control is to grow carrots beneath or within a barrier which screens off the fly. Either grow carrots in low tunnels covered with fine mesh nets (see Crop covers, p 50), or surround them with a 60 cm (2 ft) high screen of clear polythene film. This should be buried 5 cm (2 in) deep in the soil. Water plants within the barrier if it is effectively shielding them from rain. Growing carrots raised off the ground, for example in deep boxes, may also deter carrot fly.

Timing of harvest Lift roots of early carrot crops by the end of August or early September, and maincrop roots by October, to cut short the carrot fly cycle and lessen next year's attacks.

Hygiene Never leave infested roots on the ground, in sheds, or on the surface of the compost heap. They will encourage the flies to breed.

Resistance So far there are no cultivars of carrots with complete resistance to carrot fly. Some fodder carrots (which are surprisingly palatable), and the cultivars 'Fly Away' and 'Sytan' have some resistance.

Recommended cultivars
* suitable for organic gardeners

Maturing June to September 'Amsterdam Forcing–Sweetheart', 'Amsterdam Forcing–Amstel', 'Fly Away,' F₁ 'Nanco' and F₁ 'Nandor' (Nantes), 'Nantes–Express', *'Nantes–Tiptop', 'Parmex' (round), 'Sytan'.

Maturing October to November 'Chantenay Red Cored–Supreme'.

Maturing December onwards 'Autumn King–Vita Longa', 'Berlicum–Berjo', 'Camberley' (Berlicum), F₁ 'Cardinal' (Berlicum), F₁ *'Narman' (Nantes).

Celeriac

(Apium graveolens var. *rapaceum)*

Celeriac is grown primarily for the rather knobbly swollen bulb at the base of the stem, which can grow to 13 cm (5 in) diameter. Celeriac is a useful alternative to celery, being hardier, less prone to pests and diseases, easy to grow, and providing a bulky, well-flavoured winter vegetable.

Site / soil

By nature a marshland plant, celeriac requires fertile, moisture-retentive soil, rich in organic matter. It can be grown in damper parts of the garden, and will tolerate light shade.

Cultivation

Celeriac must have a long, unchecked growing season, and adequate moisture throughout growth if it is to develop to a worthwhile size. Start growing it early, sowing seeds if possible in February or March in gentle heat in seed boxes, or sowing several seeds per pot or module. (See Sowing indoors, p 35.) Alternatively sow in March/April in a cold frame. Germination is often erratic.

Prick out the seedlings when large enough to handle, or thin to one per pot or module. Harden them off gradually before planting outside in May, 30 – 38 cm (12 – 15 in) apart each way taking care not to bury the crowns.

Celeriac needs ample water throughout the summer, so water the plants if rainfall is short. Remove the outer leaves at the end of July to expose the crown. Mulching is usually beneficial.

Harvesting

Celeriac is ready from October until April or May the following year. The roots tend to deteriorate if lifted, so are best left in the ground in winter, protected from severe frosts with a layer of bracken or straw 15 cm (6 in) thick, tucked around the plants.

If the ground in which they are growing is required in spring, they can be lifted and temporarily heeled in until used. Alternatively, they can be lifted for convenience and stored in boxes indoors, leaving the central tuft of leaves attached to the bulb.

Pests and diseases

See celery, p 103.

Recommended cultivars

'Balder', 'Marble Ball', 'Monarch', 'Snow White', 'Tellus'.

To enjoy the best flavour eat the knobbly roots of celeriac fresh from the ground.

Plant celeriac with the crown at soil level.

Remove outer leaves to expose the crown.

Celery

(Apium graveolens var. *dulce)*

The traditional English trench celery is grown for its crisp, white, blanched stems, which are mainly used around Christmas. It requires considerable space and skill to grow well.

The more recently developed self-blanching and American green types are less hardy and have smaller stalks, but they are easily grown, and form a practical alternative for use from about the end of July until the first frosts. Their flavour is not quite as distinctive as trenched celery, but is nevertheless good. The American green type is generally considered the best flavoured of the two.

Leaf, cutting, or soup celery is a small plant with fine leaves and slender stems. It is exceptionally hardy, often remaining green all winter. It is widely grown on the Continent as a flavouring and salad herb.

The leaves of all types can be dried and used to flavour soups.

SELF-BLANCHING AND AMERICAN GREEN CELERY

Most of the self-blanching cultivars have off-white or yellowish stalks, which can be rendered whiter and slightly sweeter, by planting close so light is partially excluded, and by tucking straw around the plants. This is unnecessary for the green types, which otherwise are grown in the same way as self-blanching celery.

Site / soil
Celery requires an open site and very fertile, moisture-retentive but well-drained soil, into which plenty of organic matter has been worked. It does not grow well in acid soils, so if necessary lime the soil so the pH is between 6.6 and 6.8. Celery was originally a marsh plant, so benefits from plenty of moisture during growth.

Celery needs to be grown steadily without any checks, such as might be caused by a sudden change in temperature or a lack of water. Either may induce bolting, or result in stringy stems.

Treated seeds (see Seeds, p 28) can be sown as a precaution against celery leaf spot. It is often a mistake to sow celery too early, as there is a higher risk of bolting with early sowings. Some cultivars are more prone to bolting than others. Sow in seedtrays or modules (see Sowing indoors, p 35) in early March in a heated propagator, or March and early April in a greenhouse or under cover. Sowing in modules is recommended, to lessen the transplanting shock which can result in bolting.

Celery germinates best at soil temperatures between 10 and 15 C (50 and 59 F.) Sow on the surface or very shallowly, as celery needs light to germinate. (Note that germination rates are lower for celery than for most other vegetables.) Try and maintain an even temperature after germination. If seedlings are subjected to temperatures below 10 C (50 F) for more than 12 hours the mature plants are liable to bolt. If the right conditions are difficult to fulfil, it is better to buy in plants. Celery is also a good subject for fluid sowing, which improves germination potential. (See Sowing outdoors, p 32.)

It is important to prick out seedlings when they are as young as possible, or thin to one per module. Harden off carefully before planting out. Celery can be covered with crop covers after planting. (See Protected cropping p 49.) Perforated plastic films should be removed after about four weeks.

Celery has a high nitrogen requirement during growth. Fertilizer can be incorporated into the soil before transplanting. (See Fertilizers, p 17.) Plant in frames in early to mid-May, or outside after all danger of frost has passed at the end of May or early June. Reject any plants with blistered leaves, as these will be infected with celery fly. Plants are ready for transplanting when they have five or six true leaves.

Celery should be planted in a block formation to encourage the self-blanching process. (The ground can be marked out in squares beforehand.) Plant so that the crown is at soil level. There is a choice of spacings, as follows: a maximum of 28 cm (11 in) apart each way gives high yields with good blanching of the sticks. Spacing 15 cm (6 in) apart each way gives a higher total yield of smaller sticks with slender, good-quality hearts, but this close spacing is expensive if plants are bought. Spacing 23 cm (9 in) apart each way is a compromise. Once the plants are established, straw can be tucked around those on the outside of the block to assist in blanching.

Celery needs to be watered generously during its growing period to obtain the best size and quality of stems; up to 22 litres / sq m (4 gal / sq yd) per week in dry weather. Mulching after watering is beneficial. A topdressing of nitrogenous fertilizer or an organic liquid feed can be applied about four to six weeks after transplanting. (See Fertilizers, p 17.)

Harvesting
Self-blanching celery is ready for cutting from about the end of July, continuing until the frosts. It may be necessary to discard some of the outer stalks.

Self-blanching celery is much easier to grow than trench celery.

Plant self-blanching celery in a block to encourage blanching.

Trench celery blanched on the flat using black polythene collars.

Pests and diseases

Celery fly or celery leaf miner is the most serious pest, causing blistering. If possible avoid planting near parsnips, which may also be affected. Slugs are a very serious problem, and preventive measures should be taken as soon as celery is planted out. Leaf spot is a debilitating seed-borne disease. For symptoms and control measures see p 58ff.

Recommended cultivars

SB = *Self-blanching*
'Celebrity' (SB), 'Greensleeves' (SB green cross), 'Hopkins Fenlander' (green), 'Ivory Tower' (SB), 'Lathom Self-Blanching' (bolt-resistant)

TRENCH CELERY

There are white, pink and red stemmed cultivars of trench celery. Traditionally, celery stems were blanched by planting the celery in a trench and earthing up the stems in stages as the plants grew. The easier modern method is to plant celery on the flat and blanch the stems with collars.

Site / soil

See self-blanching celery. As trench celery needs very fertile, moisture-retentive but well-drained soil, it pays to prepare the ground by digging a trench, whatever system is used for blanching. Dig the trench 38 – 45 cm (15 – 18 in) wide and 30 cm (12 in) deep, preferably in the autumn, working plenty of manure or compost into the soil. If celery is being grown on the flat fill in the trench: if it is being earthed up fill it to 7.5 – 10 cm (3 – 4in) below the surface, leaving the rest of the soil alongside for earthing up.

Cultivation

Sow the seeds as for self-blanching celery above. Sow in heat in March, at a minimum temperature of 10 C (50 F). Prick out and harden off before planting out in late May or early June. It is easiest to work the celery if it is planted in single rows, and the plants are spaced 30 – 45 cm (12 – 18 in) apart. Trench celery is sometimes planted in double rows: if you choose this option, plant in pairs rather than staggered, to make it easier to earth up or collar the plants. (Where celery is being earthed up, plant in the prepared trench, below ground level.) Several sowings can be made at three-week intervals for a continuous supply of very tender celery.

Plant in moist conditions, and water after planting if necessary. Subsequently water as for self-blanching celery.

Blanching with collars For collars use 23 cm (9 in) strips of lightproof heavy paper. Black polythene can be used, but it should be lined with paper to prevent sweating.

Start blanching when the plants are roughly 30 cm (12 in) high, usually about mid-August. Tie the paper collar around the stem with raffia or soft garden twine, leaving about one third of the plant exposed. The collar should be fairly loose to allow the stems to bulk up and expand. In situations that are at all windy it is advisable to stake each plant with a cane, tying the paper and plant to the cane. (Cover the top of the cane with something like a paper cup, to avoid stabbing yourself in the eye!) If long stems are required further collars can be added at two- to three-week intervals as the plant grows. Exhibitors aim for about 60 cm (2 ft) of blanched stem, but at this point the stems will become tougher. Unwrap the collar occasionally and remove any slugs hiding beneath.

Blanching by earthing up Start similarly when the plants are about 30 cm (12 in) high. Before earthing up, tie the stems loosely just below the leaves, remove any suckers, and water the soil so it is moist. Draw the soil up about 7.5 cm (3 in) around the stems. Repeat this operation twice more at intervals of about three weeks until only the tops of the plants are exposed. Never earth up higher than the base of the green leaves, and take care not to let any soil fall into the heart of the plants.

In late winter place bracken or other protective material over the plants to protect them from heavy frost. This will help to keep them in good condition as long as possible.

Harvesting

Lifting usually starts in November, using the white cultivars first, until about Christmas. The pink and red cultivars are slightly hardier and can be used later.

Pests and diseases

See self-blanching celery.

Recommended cultivars

'Giant White', 'Giant Pink' ('Clayworth Prize Pink'), 'Mammoth White', 'Mammoth Pink', 'Martine' (red).

CUTTING CELERY

Sow seeds in seed boxes in late spring or summer, planting 13 cm (5 in) apart. A late sowing can be made in August or September to plant under cover for a tender winter crop. Cutting celery can also be multi-sown in modules, with about eight seeds per module. (See Sowing indoors, p 35.) Plant seedlings as a clump about 20 cm (8 in) apart. The plants will have very fine stems.

Cutting celery can be cut frequently; sometimes the first cut is made about four weeks after planting. If plants are left to run to seed in their second season they will often sow themselves. Transplant self-sown seedlings into convenient places. Cutting celery is very hardy and normally free of pests and diseases.

Chicories

(*Cichorium intybus*)

The chicories are a robust group of vegetables, grown mainly for use during the winter months. They tend to have a bitter taste, but this is modified, in some cases by blanching the growing plants, and in others by shredding the leaves finely for salads, or by cooking.

WITLOOF CHICORY

(*Belgian chicory*)

Witloof chicory is a hardy vegetable, very much like dandelion in appearance. It is grown for its 'chicons', the tight conical buds of young white leaves, obtained by forcing the roots in the dark in winter after lifting them from the open ground. This blanching process removes their bitterness. Chicory has a distinct flavour, and is an excellent winter vegetable.

Site / soil

Chicory should be grown in an open site. The soil needs to be fertile, but not freshly manured or the roots are liable to fork.

Cultivation

Sow in rows 30 cm (12 in apart) in May or early June. Sow thinly as the germination rates are very high. Thin to about 20 cm (8 in) apart. During the summer keep the plants weeded, and water to prevent the soil drying out. Leave the plants growing until late autumn.

Forcing in the garden

This is feasible in light or sandy soils. The heads are ready later than those forced indoors, but the flavour is said to be better. In late October or early November cut the leaves off the plant about 2.5 cm (1 in) above the neck. (These leaves can be eaten, though they are a little bitter.) Earth up the stumps so they are covered with 15–18 cm (6–7 in) of soil. This ridge can be covered with straw or cloches to bring the heads on more quickly. The heads will slowly force their way through the soil, and will be ready for cutting between January and March, depending on temperature.

Forcing indoors

Roots are lifted any time between late October and December, and any which are fanged or very thin discarded. The ideal size for forcing is 3.5–5 cm

(1½–2 in) diameter across the top; smaller roots make an insignificant head, and larger roots a very loose head. Trim the leaves off 2.5 cm (1 in) above the neck. The leaves can be eaten, see above. Store roots until needed for forcing flat in boxes in a shed, covered with sand to prevent them drying out, or outside covered with straw.

For a regular supply of heads between December and April it is best to force a few roots at a time. They need to be forced in total darkness with a little warmth. The temperature can be between 10 and 18 C (50–64 F), but the lower the temperature the longer it takes. At 18 C (64 F) heads are generally ready in three weeks.

The simplest method is to plant up to about six roots close together in moist soil in a 20–23 cm (8–9 in) flower pot. The roots can be trimmed to a length of 18–20 cm (7–8 in) if necessary. Invert another pot of the same size over the first, blocking the drainage holes to keep out the light. Put the pots in an airing cupboard, or other suitable place for forcing. The stumps can also be covered with an upturned box, or with some kind of frame or low tunnel covered with heavy duty black polythene. Anchor or attach the film carefully to exclude all light. Give the plants plenty of headroom as rots may develop in a stagnant atmosphere.

Alternatively, roots can be planted in the soil under greenhouse staging, or in a cold frame, devising some method of excluding light. Traditionally light was excluded by covering the roots with a 20 cm (8 in) layer of soil, sand, leafmould, or any material through which the heads could force their way.

With older cultivars this soil covering seemed to be necessary to encourage the formation of nice compact heads. (Loose heads, however, have much the same flavour.) Modern cultivars are naturally compact, and it is only necessary to create darkness.

With all blanching methods, water the soil if it is becoming dry.

Harvesting

The heads of earthed-up chicory are ready when the tips are visible through the soil, and forced heads when they are 10–13 cm (4–5 in) high, and look nice and sturdy. Cut them with a sharp knife 2.5 cm (1 in) above the neck. The roots will then sometimes resprout to give a second, smaller head. Keep the heads covered or in a dark place until required, as they become green and bitter on exposure to light.

Pests and diseases

See Sugarloaf chicory, below.

Recommended cultivars

F_1 'Zoom' and other modern hybrids.

Mature Witloof chicory prior to being forced.

Cut leaves off 2.5cm (1in) above the neck.

Earth up roots for outdoor forcing in situ.

Lift and trim roots for indoor forcing.

Plant several roots together for forcing.

Cover with a similar pot to keep out the light.

Well-forced heads ready for harvesting.

Sugar loaf chicory (see p 106).

SUGAR LOAF CHICORY

This type of chicory looks rather like a cos lettuce when mature. The inner leaves are tightly packed and so naturally blanched and sweetened, hence its name. Even so, it is sharper-flavoured than lettuce, but makes an excellent appetizing salad. Mature sugar loaf chicory is grown mainly for an autumn crop, but if protected it can often be used throughout winter. Plants will withstand light frosts. Sugar loaf chicory is also highly productive as a cut-and-come-again seedling crop.

Cultivation
Mature heads For the main outdoor autumn crop, sow in fertile, moisture-retentive soil in June and July in rows 30 cm (12 in) apart. Thin to about 25 cm (10 in) apart. Keep the plants well watered during the summer: good heads will be formed by the autumn. Protect them with cloches before the onset of severe weather, or cover them loosely with bracken or straw, held in place with wire hoops.

A second sowing can be made in July or August, for transplanting under cover in autumn for a winter crop. This may not form large heads, but can be treated as a useful cut-and-come-again semi-mature crop. (See Chinese cabbage, p 90). Sow in seedtrays or in modules. (See Sowing indoors, p 33.)

Seedling crop Make the first sowing under cover in January or February, either broadcast or in wide or narrow drills. The seeds will germinate rapidly, and provide a most useful cut-and-come-again seedling crop, regenerating several times. (See Sowing outdoors, p 33.) Follow this with outdoor sowings as soon as the soil is workable. Sowings can continue throughout the growing season, though midsummer sowings are less tender. Make the last sowing in September under cover. If the leaves become large and coarse in summer thin out to 25 cm (10 in) apart, allowing the remaining plants to heart up and develop into large plants.

Harvesting
Always cut the heads 2.5 cm (1 in) above the soil, leaving the stump to resprout. Traditionally, sugar loaf chicory was stored in autumn in frost-free sheds or cellars, or outdoors in circular heaps about 90 cm (3 ft) high, with the heads pointing in towards the centre. The heap was covered with straw. Storage is less common now as winter crops are often grown under cover.

Pests and diseases
Sugar loaf chicory is naturally robust, and is rarely attacked by pests or disease, though it may start to rot in cold, wet weather. Remove any decayed leaves, but leave the stump, as it may recover.

Recommended cultivars
'Bianca di Milano' (for summer), 'Pain de Sucre' 'Sugar Loaf' (old cultivars), 'Biondissima di Trieste' (small heads, mainly for seedling crops), 'Poncho', 'Snowflake' ('Winter Fare') (new cultivars).

RED CHICORY

Red chicory (often known as *radicchio*) is characterized by its red and, in some cases, strikingly variegated colouring. It develops a small crisp heart, with inner leaves which are part white or yellow, part deeply coloured. The older cultivars tended to have loose green heads in summer, which started to form tighter hearts and develop reddish colour in the colder nights of autumn. The newer cultivars have naturally redder leaves and denser hearts earlier in the season, and are larger.

Cultivars vary in their frost-hardiness, the slender-leaved, non-hearting 'Red Treviso' type being the only one that is extremely hardy. Red chicory is mainly used as a salad vegetable as it is so decorative, but can be cooked. The flavour is naturally slightly bitter, but this is less marked in the crisp inner leaves, when the leaves are shredded, and when they are cooked.

Note that chicory seeds are very variable, and not all plants will form really tight hearts. The newer

The red chicories have strikingly coloured leaves which turn redder in autumn as temperatures fall.

cultivars are an enormous improvement on the old in this respect, and it is likely that more improved cultivars will be introduced in future.

Site / soil
Red chicory tolerates a wide range of soil types and situations, and a wide range of temperatures.

Cultivation
Using appropriate cultivars, red chicory can be sown from April to August. Sow early-maturing cultivars in late April and May for a summer crop. Make the main sowing for the outdoor autumn crop in June and early July. Sow in August for transplanting under cover in September for a protected winter crop. Plants grown under cover in winter tend to grow larger and form good hearts.

Sow thinly either *in situ* or in seedtrays or modules for transplanting. Space plants 20 – 35 cm (8 – 14 in) apart, depending on the cultivar. Traditionally, red chicory was broadcast, then thinned to the correct distance apart. This method is still appropriate for the more upright 'Red Treviso' type. Early crops benefit from being covered with crop covers mulches. (See Protected cropping, p 49).

Some of the 'Verona' types of chicory, and 'Red Treviso' can be lifted and blanched in the same way as Witloof chicory. This produces beautiful pink, tender leaves, though with the currently available cultivars the chicons will not be as substantial as those of Witloof chicory.

In late autumn plants can be protected with low tunnels, cloches, or straw to prolong the season. Indeed, judging from the way good heads are often uncovered from beneath the foliage of a neighbouring plant, it seems that the quality of red chicory heads in winter is improved if they are lightly covered with straw, bracken or foliage. In mild winters plants may last through to spring.

Harvesting
Either pick individual leaves as required, or cut the hearts as for sugar loaf chicory, leaving the stumps to resprout.

Pests and diseases
Red chicory is rarely seriously attacked by pests or disease, though leaves can rot in damp winter conditions, or when temperatures fluctuate under cover. Remove decaying leaves: the plants often recover in warmer weather.

Recommended cultivars
'Alouette' (early), 'Cesare' (early), 'Red Devil', 'Red Treviso', 'Verona Palla Rossa'.

Cucumbers, outdoor
(*Cucumis sativus*)

There are two distinct types of cucumbers. The greenhouse or frame cucumber is very long and smooth, while the outdoor or ridge cucumber, so-called because it was originally grown on ridges to ensure good drainage, is shorter with rougher skin. (Gherkins are a type of ridge cucumber, as is the unusual, round, 'apple cucumber'.) Nowadays the gap in appearance and quality between the two types has closed, as plant breeders have developed longer and smoother outdoor cucumbers. Most notable of these are the Japanese hybrid cultivars, which often grow over 30 cm (12 in) long. They are naturally vigorous and healthy, and very tolerant of low temperatures.

A further difference between the two types is that outdoor cucumbers need to be pollinated by insects to set fruit, whereas the greenhouse cucumbers set fruit without pollination. Indeed if they are pollinated they become misshapen and bitter. With traditional greenhouse cultivars it was necessary to remove male flowers, or to net greenhouse ventilators to keep insects out. Today this problem is largely eliminated by the development of all-female cultivars, which only occasionally produce male flowers.

Outdoor cucumbers are easier to grow and less prone to pests and disease than greenhouse cucumbers, the majority of which require high humidity and high temperatures to grow well. This usually means heating the greenhouse in spring and early summer to maintain a minimum night temperature of about 20 C (68 F). (For cultivation of greenhouse cucumbers, see Further reading, p 158.) Greenhouse cucumbers with improved tolerance to cold are being bred, and they can be grown successfully in unheated greenhouses. So can outdoor cultivars, but they must not be mixed with all-female greenhouse cultivars, or the latter will be pollinated. No cucumbers are frost-tolerant.

Site / soil
A sunny sheltered site is required for outdoor cucumbers, though they tolerate light shade in summer. They can also be grown in 25 cm (10 in) pots or growing bags. The outdoor crop always benefits from cloche or similar protection in the early stages of growth.

Cucumbers require very fertile and moisture-retentive soil, rich in organic matter, and slightly acid to neutral. Prepare individual holes for each cucumber, about 30 cm (12 in) deep and 45 cm (18 in)

To ensure good drainage, plant cucumbers on a slight mound.

The vigorous Japanese cultivars can be trained up tripods of canes.

Ridge cucumbers have short, rough-skinned fruits.

wide. Work plenty of very well-rotted manure, compost or rotted straw into the hole, and cover it with 15 – 20 cm (6 – 8 in) of soil to make a slightly raised mound on which the cucumbers are sown or planted. This ensures good drainage and so helps to prevent the root rots to which cucumbers are prone.

Cultivation

Ridge cucumbers can be either grown flat on the ground, or, preferably, trained to some support such as a trellis or wire netting. Naturally bush cultivars have been introduced recently, which make compact, non-climbing plants. The Japanese cultivars can be trained successfully on tripods of canes. Gherkins are usually grown on the flat.

Cucumbers are adversely affected by transplanting, so it is best to sow them in their cropping position, or to raise plants in small pots or modules (see Sowing indoors p 35), to minimize the transplanting shock. Do not sow outdoors until mid-May (south) or end of May (north), as seeds will not germinate at temperatures below 23 C (73 F). Sow seeds on their sides 2 – 2.5 cm (¾ – 1 in) deep. Sow two or three seeds per site, thinning to one after germination. Cover with individual jam jars or cloches after sowing.

Alternatively, sow indoors in gentle heat in April, planting outside when danger of frost is past, usually about the end of May or early June, after hardening off. Cucumbers are normally ready for planting four to five weeks after sowing.

Cucumbers can be planted 45 cm (18 in) apart if climbing and 60 – 75 cm (2 – 2½ ft) apart if grown on the flat. In the latter case pinch out the tip of the leading shoot after six leaves have formed to encourage bushy growth. Water well after planting. Lay straw around plants grown on the flat to keep the fruits clean, or use a plastic film mulch.

Cucumbers require plenty of water, especially once they have started flowering and the fruits are setting and growing. Irregular watering can be one reason for fruits withering and failing to form. Pinch out the tops of climbing plants when they reach the top of the support; growth will continue on laterals arising from the main stem. It is not necessary to remove the male flowers from ridge cucumbers to prevent the fruit being fertilized and becoming bitter, as is the case with the traditional greenhouse cultivars.

Harvesting

The outdoor crop is ready between July and September. Keep picking the fruits once they have reached a reasonable size, to encourage further production. Gherkins can be picked small for pickling, or allowed to grow larger for use as cucumbers.

Pests and diseases

The most serious outdoor pests are aphids. In unheated greenhouses red spider mite can be a problem. The commonest diseases are cucumber mosaic virus and powdery mildew. (For symptoms and control, see p 58ff.) Root rots are occasionally a problem; rotation and careful watering are the best preventive measures.

Recommended cultivars

Outdoor cucumbers 'Burpee Hybrid', 'Burpless Tasty Green'.
Gherkin 'Conda'.

Endive

(Cichorium endivia)

Endive is a salad vegetable which has always been more popular on the Continent than here. In appearance it resembles lettuce, forming a rosette of leaves with a loose heart. The outer leaves are green and sharp-flavoured, but the inner leaves are partially blanched and whiter, as well as sweeter in taste.

There are two distinct types. Curly endive is a low-growing plant with finely serrated leaves (this is the French *chicorée frisée*), while the broadleaved, Batavian endive (*escarole* or *scarole*) has much broader leaves and makes a more substantial and generally more upright plant. A number of productive cultivars with intermediary characteristics between the two types have been bred in recent years.

Most of the broadleaved types can resist a little frost, and grow much better than lettuces in the low light of winter. So they were traditionally cultivated as an autumn to early winter crop. If grown under cover in unheated greenhouses the cutting period can often be extended into spring.

The curly-leaved forms were generally more heat-resistant and were mainly grown in summer, with the more cold-tolerant cultivars being grown in autumn.

With improved new cultivars of endive it is possible to grow either type for much of the year, sowing appropriate cultivars, though unfortunately these are not always available to amateur gardeners.

Endive was traditionally blanched to make it sweeter, but whether or not this is done is largely a matter of taste. Certainly it is less necessary with some of the new cultivars, which have relatively dense, deeply curled heads and are often described as self-blanching. Blanching is more commonly practised with the broadleaved types, which can produce most attractive looking crispy white leaves. (For blanching methods, see below.) Although mainly used in salads, endive can also be cooked.

Endive is a vigorous plant, and after the initial cut, mature plants will re-sprout over a long period. This is especially useful when endive is grown under cover between autumn and early spring. It can also be grown as a seedling crop, most successfully in the case of curly endive.

Site / soil

Endive tolerates a wide range of soil types. Autumn crops, however, should be grown on a light, well-drained soil to minimize the risk of rotting in wet weather. Endive requires less nitrogen than lettuces (see Fertilizers, p 18); too much nitrogen encourages lush growth which again makes plants susceptible to rotting diseases. The soil pH should be around neutral. Although an open situation is usually recommended, the summer crop can tolerate light shade.

Cultivation

Endive can be sown *in situ* and thinned out to the correct distance, or sown in seed trays or modules and transplanted, which is the best method for early spring sowings. (See Sowing indoors, p 33.) Spacing varies according to the cultivar, from 25 – 30 cm (10 – 12 in) apart for medium-sized curly cultivars, up to 38 cm (15 in) apart for the larger broadleaved types. Plants take about three months to grow from sowing to maturity. The following are the principal sowings.

Main sowing for outdoor autumn crop Sow in June or July using any type.

For winter crop under cover Sow August, using broadleaved type or hardy curled cultivars.

For early summer Sow in April in gentle heat at a temperature of 20 C (68 F). Sow in seed trays or modules. (See Sowing indoors, p 33.) These sowings are liable to bolt prematurely if low temperatures are experienced, that is if temperatures fall below about 4.5 C (40 F) for more than 20 days. Use suitable curly types and bolt-resistant broadleaved types such as 'Golda'. Make the first plantings outside under cloches or low tunnels, or protected by

The broad leaves of Batavian endive.

Low growing curly endive with serrated leaves.

Use a dinner plate to blanch the central heart.

The hearts are well blanched after ten days.

crop covers. (See Protected cropping, p 49.) Follow this with a May sowing, for planting out in the open. For this sowing it is probably still advisable to sow indoors and transplant.

Cut-and-come-again seedling crops (See Sowing outdoors, p 33), These can be made throughout the growing season. In some cases it may be possible to take only one cut before the plants run to seed. Make the first sowing under cover in spring and the last in late August or early September under cover, using the hardier cultivars.

Blanching

The main purpose of blanching is to make the leaves sweeter; blanched curly endive leaves also look very decorative. Plants are blanched when nearing maturity, about three months after sowing. The leaves must be dry before blanching or the plants will rot when covered. If necessary cover them with cloches for a couple of days beforehand to dry them. Blanch a few plants at a time in succession, as they will not stand long after blanching without deteriorating. Blanching normally takes about 10 days. Use plants immediately or keep them in a refrigerator after cutting; they will become green and bitter rapidly on exposure to light.

To blanch the whole plant cover it with an upturned bucket or large flower pot with the drainage hole blocked to exclude light. Alternatively, place a large dinner plate or slate over the plant: this generally blanches the central heart, but not the coarser outer leaves. Plants can be partially blanched simply by pulling the leaves upright, and tying them together above the plant. Take precautions against slugs.

Traditionally endive was lifted before heavy frost, and replanted in a cold frame, under the greenhouse staging or in boxes, and some means of excluding light was devised. (See Witloof chicory, p 104.) It is unnecessary to trim back the leaves, as is done with Witloof chicory.

Pests and diseases

Although endive is susceptible to the same range of pests and diseases as lettuces, it tends to be a healthy crop. Slugs, and sometimes leaf aphids, can be problems. For symptoms and control, see p 58ff.

Recommended cultivars

Curled 'Fine Maraîchère', 'Ione' (early and summer sowings), 'Pancalière' (early to summer; fairly hardy), 'Ruffec Green' (hardy), 'Wallonne' (hardy; syn. 'Scarola Verde').
Broadleaved 'Golda' (any sowings), 'Cornet Bordeaux' (hardy), 'Full Heart Italian' (hardy).

Florence fennel

(*Foeniculum vulgare* var. *azoricum*)

Florence or sweet fennel has fine, feathery foliage, and is one of the most decorative of garden vegetables. It is grown for the succulent, aniseed-flavoured bulb, which develops from the swollen bases of the leaf stalks. The foliage and stems can also be used in salads, though the perennial herb fennel is normally grown for this purpose. Fennel is used both raw and cooked.

Site / soil

Fennel does best on fertile, well-drained, light sandy soils but will grow in any fertile, well-drained soil into which plenty of organic matter has been worked. It needs plenty of moisture throughout growth.

Cultivation

It is not easy to grow first-class fennel in this country, as plants tend to bolt rather than swell at the base. Some cultivars are very sensitive to day length, and bolt if sown before mid-June. Growth checks, which can be caused by shortage of water, low or fluctuating temperatures, or transplanting shock, may also result in premature bolting. Improved cultivars are continually being developed which have better resistance to bolting: though none is infallible. Pleasantly warm summers with plenty of moisture are the ideal conditions for fennel.

Florence fennel will withstand light frost towards the end of the season. For early winter supplies a late sowing can be made for transplanting under cover. This will not always 'bulb up', but the leaves and stems will be usable in salads.

Florence fennel does not like root disturbance, so either sow *in situ*, thinning eventually to about 30 cm (12 in) apart each way, or sow in small pots or modules (see Sowing indoors, p 35), planting out after hardening off. The latter method is recommended for earlier sowings, and for late sowings transplanted under cover. If fennel is sown in seed-trays, be sure to plant out no later than the three-to-four leaf stage, or the plants may bolt prematurely. The first outdoor plantings can be covered with crop covers. (See Protected cropping, p 49.) Fennel germinates best at a temperature of 15 C (60 F).

For the outdoor summer crop Sow May to early July, using bolt-resistant cultivars for sowings before mid-June.

For planting inside under cover Sow mid-July to early August.

The succulent aniseed-flavoured bulb of Florence fennel develops from the swollen bases of the leaf stalks.

Fennel grows fast in suitable conditions, and can be ready about 15 weeks after sowing. It needs little attention, other than being kept well-watered and weed-free but watch for slugs in the early stages. Mulching to conserve soil moisture is advisable. Once the stems start to swell they can be earthed up halfway with soil. This makes them whiter and sweeter.

Harvesting

Harvest them about 15 or 20 days after earthing-up. When the bulbs have formed cut them just above ground level, leaving the stump in the ground. This will usually throw up further small feathery shoots, which can be used in salads. Plants that have been cut back this way withstand more frost than a whole plant.

Recommended cultivars

'Perfection', 'Sirio', 'Sweet Florence', 'Cantino' (bolt-resistant), 'Zefa Fino' (bolt-resistant).

Leeks
(Allium porrum)

Leeks are one of the most useful of the hardy winter vegetables: their season extends from late summer until late spring the following year. They are grown for the white shank at the base of the leaves, which is to some extent naturally blanched, though further blanching is encouraged by deep planting or earthing up. Modern cultivars are notable for their long white shank and improved hardiness.

Site / soil

An open site is required. Leeks do best in rich, well-worked, light loamy soils, into which plenty of well-rotted manure or compost has been worked. If necessary this can be done shortly before the crop is planted. Leeks will not grow well on compacted soil. Preferred pH is slightly acid to slightly alkaline (6.5 – 7.5).

Leeks have a fibrous root system and help to improve soil structure. They should be rotated as part of the onion group. There is some evidence from Belgian experiments that including leeks in a rotation may help to reduce the incidence of clubroot in brassicas.

Cultivation

There are early, mid-season, and late cultivars of leeks, maturing approximately September to November, December to February, March to early May respectively. The earlier cultivars tend to be taller, with longer white shafts and paler foliage; later ones are thicker, with a shorter area of blanched stem and darker green or nearly blue leaves, or 'flags', as they are known. They are also hardier. As a general rule, the longer the growing season, and the larger the leek at transplanting, the larger the leek will be eventually.

Soil temperatures of at least 7 C (44 F) are necessary for leek seeds to germinate well. The very earliest sowings can be made indoors in gentle heat in February, pricking out and hardening off the leeks before planting them out in May. These sowings can also be made in modules. Leeks respond well to multi-sowing with three to four seeds per module. (See Sowing indoors, p 35.) The main sowings outdoors are made in a seedbed from March to early May, provided the soil is warm enough. Early outdoor sowings can also be made under cloches. Early outdoor sowings and plantings can be covered with crop covers. (See Protected cropping, p 49.)

The optimum sowing depth is 2.5 cm (1 in) deep. Leeks can also be sown *in situ*, thinning to the required spacing when the seedlings have two to three leaves.

The main planting season is June, though planting can continue into July and early August as ground becomes available. Water the seedbed thoroughly before lifting the seedlings. The best size for transplanting is when the leeks are about 20 cm (8 in) tall, between 10 and 15 weeks old. The tips of the leaves can be trimmed back slightly to prevent them dragging on the soil after planting. On the whole trimming the leaf tips and root ends, though a traditional practice, reduces yield.

The highest yields of average-sized leeks are obtained by planting 15 cm (6 in) apart in rows 30 cm (12 in) apart. Closer spacing, at 7.5–10 cm (3–4 in) apart in the rows, will not reduce the total yield, but will give small, more slender leeks. Reasonable yields can also be obtained with equidistant spacing at 18 cm (7 in) apart. Multi-sown modules can be planted 23 cm (9 in) apart each way, using any method suggested for single plants below.

Leeks have high nitrogen requirements because of their long growing season. A nitrogen fertilizer can be forked into the soil immediately before planting. (See Fertilizer, p 18.) Alternatively, apply organic liquid feeds during growth if necessary.

There are several methods of planting. The first two facilitate blanching by planting relatively deeply, though plants should not be planted so deeply that they are buried. The simplest method is to make holes 13–20 cm (5–8 in) deep with a dibber, dropping one plant into each hole. The soil will fall back naturally into the hole during the growing season. The second method is to plant in a V-shaped drill, 7.5 cm (3 in) deep, which is subsequently filled in to blanch the stems.

Leeks can also be planted on the flat, though this is generally done only on very shallow or very heavy soils. In all cases, a further area of leaf can be blanched by earthing up several times during growth. To do this draw dry soil around the shank, taking care none falls between the leaves. Nowadays earthing up is done mainly for show leeks.

Water in well after transplanting, and if dry weather follows, water daily (about 70 ml/⅛ pint per plant) until the plants are well established. Additional watering is necessary only if very large leeks are required.

Make holes for leeks with a dibber.

Drop one plant in each planting hole.

Water leeks in after transplanting.

Late hardy leeks reaching maturity.

A freshly harvested crop of leeks showing long blanched shanks at the base of the leaves.

Harvesting

Leeks can be lifted as required, but mid-season and late cultivars are hardy enough to stand outside in winter. If the ground where they are growing is required in late spring they can be lifted and heeled in temporarily in an out-of-the-way corner. Even early leeks stand for three months when mature.

Pests and diseases

Leeks are relatively trouble free, the most serious pest being stem and bulb eelworm and sometimes onion fly. In some seasons leek rust is a troublesome disease. Onion white rot can be a problem. For symptoms and control measures, see p 58ff.

Recommended cultivars

(In order of maturity, * = especially suitable for organic growing.)

Early 'King Richard', 'Gennevilliers–Splendid', 'Swiss Giant–Pancho'.

Early-mid 'Swiss Giant–Albinstar'.

Early to late 'Autumn Mammoth–Goliath'.

Late *'Wintra' (formerly 'Winterreuzen') 'Blauwgrone Winter–Alaska'

Lettuces and stem lettuce

(*Lactuca sativa*, *Lactua sativa* var. *angustana*)

In many parts of the country lettuces can be cut from the garden from early spring until November. The season can be extended with the use of frames, cloches, floating films and unheated greenhouses. To have lettuce *all* year round usually requires some greenhouse heating in midwinter. Appropriate cultivars have to be used for each season, seed catalogues generally giving an indication of when any particular cultivar can be sown.

Where possible it is worth growing cultivars with pest and disease resistance. (See Pests and diseases, below). The use of mosaic-tested seed lessens the risk of plants being infected with lettuce mosaic virus.

There are several distinct types of lettuces. The main division is between 'headed' and 'non-hearting' types.

Headed lettuces

Butterhead/round-leaf These have soft, rather buttery leaves. The best of the modern cultivars have good firm hearts, and resistance to the disease downy mildew, which frequently disfigures the outer leaves of lettuces. They are mainly grown in summer, but some cultivars are suitable for growing in unheated greenhouses in winter.

Crisphead The heads are usually larger than butterheads, and the leaves crisper and wrinkled in texture. Some have an excellent flavour, others are notable more for their crunchy texture than their flavour. Recently the old cultivar names 'Iceberg' and 'Webbs' have come to be used to describe certain crisphead cultivars. With the Iceberg types, which can grow very large, the outer leaves are trimmed off, leaving only the white, solid heart. Only certain cultivars are suitable for this type of production, and generally they are difficult to grow well in British summers. The Webbs type, like the original 'Webb's Wonderful' cultivar, has a less dense heart but more green outer leaf. Most crisphead cultivars can be grown as Webbs, and they are more suited to our climate. Crispheads are mainly grown for summer, but a few are suitable for winter cultivation in unheated greenhouses.

Cos These are upright, thick-leaved lettuces, with a fairly loose heart in most cases. They are widely considered to have an excellent flavour. The large cos lettuces take longer to develop than other lettuces. The popular, medium-sized, sweet-flavoured let-

Butterhead lettuce with soft round leaves.

The Webbs type of crisphead lettuce.

The non-hearting Salad Bowl type of lettuce.

The thick upright leaves of cos lettuce.

tuce 'Little Gem' is sometimes described as a 'semi-cos'; it has a very compact, crunchy heart. While cos lettuces can be grown throughout the summer season, they generally grow better in cool weather and are among the hardier lettuces, some cultivars being suitable for overwintering outdoors.

Non-hearting lettuces

The non-hearting types are essentially loose-leaved forming only very insignificant, if any, hearts.

Salad Bowl These typify the non-hearting types, in forming a rosette of leaves rather than a heart. Individual leaves are picked as required, or the plants can be cut across the head and left to resprout. These lettuces are much slower to run to seed than the heading types. Generally speaking they are both heat- and cold-tolerant, and can be grown outside for much of the year, and in unheated tunnels or frames during the winter. Some very decorative cultivars, such as the deeply indented 'Oak Leaf' types, and the recently introduced frilly red- and green-leaved 'Lollo', cultivars, belong to this group. It contains several cultivars with reddish leaves, such as 'Marvel of Four Seasons', all of which are decorative in salads.

Cutting lettuces These are old European cultivars of the loose-leaf type, which were traditionally grown for a cut-and-come-again seedling crop (see Sowing outdoors, p 35.) In the past they were often forced in frames early in the year. For current use, see below. There are curly- and smooth-leaved cultivars.

Stem lettuce

Some times misleadingly called 'celtuce', this is an Asiatic type of lettuce, grown not for its leaves, but for its thick central stem, which can be sliced and cooked, or used raw in salads like cucumber.

Site / soil

Lettuces must have an open site and light, fertile, moisture-retentive soil. They will not grow well on poor soil, or soil which dries out in hot weather. The preferred pH range is slightly acid to slightly alkaline. Wherever possible, rotate lettuces to avoid the build-up of fungus diseases. Ideally the ground should be dug over the previous autumn, and plenty of manure or compost worked in. A base dressing of a general fertilizer can be applied 10 days before sowing or planting. (See Fertilizers, p 17.) Organic gardeners can apply liquid feeds during the growing season if growth seems slow, but it is not normally necessary on reasonably fertile soil.

The smaller lettuce cultivars, such as 'Little Gem', 'Tom Thumb', and the 'cutting lettuce' seedlings, can be used for intercropping. The various 'Salad Bowl' types make very attractive edges to vegetable or flower beds.

Cultivation

Lettuces can be sown either *in situ*, or in seedtrays or modules (see Sowing indoors, p 35), for transplanting. Unless modules are used, summer sowings – those made generally between May and mid-August – or sowings in very hot weather, are best *in situ*, as lettuces will not transplant well in dry conditions. In cool weather lettuces can also be sown in a seedbed for transplanting, but other methods are generally preferable.

High temperature dormancy While lettuces germinate well at low temperatures, germination is often erratic if soil temperatures are over 25 C (77 F), especially during a critical period a few hours after sowing – a phenomenon known as 'high temperature dormancy'. These temperatures are quite often reached in late spring and summer. Butterhead cultivars are the most susceptible, but overwintering types sown in late summer can be affected. The problem can be overcome in various ways:

- by watering after sowing to reduce the soil temperature;
- by covering the seedbed with reflective white material after sowing;
- by sowing between 14.00 and 16.00 hrs so that the critical period falls during the cooler hours of evening and night;
- by sowing in seedtrays or modules put somewhere cool to germinate;
- by fluid sowing (see p 32), as the seeds will be past the sensitive stage when sown.

Sow lettuces in drills about 15 mm (⅝ in) deep, and thin to the required spacing apart. In cool weather the thinned seedlings can be transplanted to give a successive crop, maturing about 10 days later. Reject any poor seedlings. Plant seedlings at the four- to five-leaf stage with the seed leaves just above soil level. Lettuces should never be planted deeply.

Spacing varies according to the cultivar. Small lettuces such as 'Little Gem' can be grown 15 – 20 cm (6 – 8 in) apart in each direction. Standard butterhead cultivars can be spaced 25 cm (10 in) apart in rows 30 cm (12 in) apart, or at equidistant spacing about 28 cm (11in) apart each way. Crispheads need to be about 30 × 38 cm (12 × 15 in) apart, or 38 × 38 cm (15 × 15 in) to produce large heads. The large types of cos and 'Salad Bowl' types can be spaced up to about 35 cm (14 in) apart each way.

In dry periods lettuces will need to be watered frequently to obtain good quality heads of a reasonable size. They can be given up to 22 litres / sq m (4 gal / sq yd) every week. If water is in short supply watering should be concentrated on the period seven to 10 days before maturing.

Summer lettuces take an average of about 12 weeks to mature. Butterheads mature fastest; crispheads and cos slowest. Butterheads will stand only a few days after maturing before they start to deteriorate and run to seed: crispheads stand about a week longer. Cos lettuces stand reasonably well in cool weather. So for a continual supply of headed lettuce it is advisable to make successive, small sowings every two weeks or so, or to rely on the 'Salad Bowl' types which can often be picked over several months.

The main sowing periods for lettuces are given below. In practice there is considerable overlap between the different sowings. See also recommended cultivars for the different sowings.

Principal sowings

Early sowings under cover These mature from late May to early June. Sow mid-February (in the south), or early March (in the north). Either sow direct into frames or under cloches, or sow in boxes or modules for transplanting outdoors in a sheltered position or into frames or under cloches at the end of March or early April.

Watch out for high temperature dormancy (see above) if high temperatures are being experienced under cover in spring, and take appropriate

Thin lettuce by hand to the required spacing. In cool weather the spare seedlings can be transplanted.

Early sowings in frames mature from late May.

Stem lettuce is grown for its thick stem.

measures. Lettuces planted outside in spring can be covered with fleecy films or perforated polythene films. Remove them about three weeks before maturity or earlier in hot bright weather or plants may be scorched.

Main outdoor summer sowings These will crop between June and October. Sow from late March until early July, depending on the cultivar. Sow *in situ*, or in seed boxes or modules for transplanting. Plants can be protected with cloches in the autumn to improve the quality.

Protected winter crop This is grown in unheated greenhouses or frames to mature either in November or December, or in February or March the following year. It is important to sow at the optimum time for each cultivar. Sow between late August and October for transplanting into permanent positions during the autumn. The earlier sowings can be made in seedtrays or a seedbed outside; later sowings should be made under cover. This crop can also be grown under perforated films, left in place during the winter but removed a couple of weeks before the crop matures in spring, or earlier in hot bright weather or plants may be scorched. These overwintered lettuces are often attacked by fungus diseases. Keep the greenhouses or tunnels as well-ventilated as possible to discourage disease.

Outdoor overwintering hardy lettuce These mature in May and June the following year. Sow *in situ* at the end of August or early September, thinning to about 7.5 cm (3 in) apart. These hardy cultivars will normally overwinter in the open. Thin them to their final spacing the following spring. They can be covered with cloches or crop covers (see early sowings under cover, above) to improve quality, and

make them mature two to three weeks earlier. Give a nitrogenous topdressing or organic liquid feed in March to encourage growth.

Cut-and-come-again seedling lettuce
For cultivation methods, see Sowing outdoors, p 33. Use continental 'cutting' lettuce cultivars and 'Salad Bowl' types. Seedling crops can normally be cut within three or four weeks of sowing, so they are most valuable early and late in the year. The first sowings can be made under cover in late February or March, followed by outdoor sowings as soon as the ground is workable. Generally two or three cuttings can be made before the plants coarsen and run to seed. Summer sowings are apt to run to seed very rapidly. Useful late sowings can be made outside in late August and under cover in September.

Leaf lettuce
This is a method of growing certain cultivars of cos lettuce densely, to get a high yield of unhearted, crisp leaves. It was originally developed by Horticulture Research International, Wellesbourne, to provide the catering trade with lettuces which required minimum preparation. It can be a useful and productive method for amateurs requiring a continuous supply of lettuces from a relatively small area.

The crop must be grown in fertile, weed-free soil, and be kept well watered. Seed is sown in rows 13 cm (5 in) apart, aiming to get plants about 2.5 cm (1 in) apart. The leaves are cut when 7.5 – 13 cm (3 – 5 in) high, about 2.5 cm (1 in) above ground level. A second cut can be made three-and-a-half to eight weeks later, depending on the time of year.

The following are the Wellesbourne recommendations for producing a continuous supply of lettuce leaves from mid-May to mid-October. They assume that a family of four could be kept supplied by sowing approximately 1 sq m (1 sq yd) at each sowing.

- Sow weekly from mid-April to mid-May. The first cut can be made about seven-and-a-half weeks later, from late May until the end of June. A second cut can be made a further seven-and-a-half weeks later, from early July to mid-August.

- Make three further sowings weekly in the first three weeks in August. Growth is rapid at this time, so the first cut can be made three-and-a-half weeks later in September, and the second four-and-a-half weeks later, in the first three weeks in October.

Stem lettuce

Stem lettuce requires fertile soil and plenty of moisture, especially in the early leafy stage, to grow well. Sow seeds in spring, either *in situ*, or in seedtrays or modules for transplanting. Seedlings should be planted no larger than the three- to four-leaf stage. Space plants 30 – 35 cm (12 – 14 in) apart. Mulch after planting to conserve moisture in the soil. The stem is generally ready for harvesting within four months of sowing, when it is about 30 cm (12 in) high and at least 2.5 cm (1 in) in diameter. It can be left until just before the plant starts to bolt, without becoming bitter. Strip off the leaves, and if the outer skin is tough, peel it off before use.

Pests and diseases

The principal insect pests on lettuces are greenfly and root aphids. Cutworms, leatherjackets, slugs, snails and birds are other common pests. Several good butterhead cultivars have considerable resistance to root aphids: these include 'Avondefiance', 'Musette' and 'Sabine'.

The principal diseases are *Botrytis*, downy mildew, lettuce mosaic virus, and in seedlings, damping off disease. An increasing number of cultivars have varying degrees of resistance or tolerance to downy mildew and lettuce mosaic virus.

For symptoms and control measures, see p 58ff.

Recommended cultivars

Early sowings under cover Butterhead: 'Hilde'
Cos and semi-cos: 'Little Gem', 'Winter Density'.
Main outdoor summer sowings Butterhead: 'Avondefiance', 'Clarion', 'Sabine', 'Musette'.
Crisphead (for use as 'Webb's Wonderful' and 'Iceberg' types): 'Minetto', 'Malika', 'Saladin'.
Cos and semi-cos: 'Bubbles', 'Little Gem', 'Lobjoit's Green Cos', 'Valmaine', 'Wallop', 'Winter Density'.

Protected winter crop Butterhead: 'Columbus', 'Cynthia', 'Kwiek', 'Magnet', 'Pascal'.
Crisphead: 'Kellys', 'Marmer', 'Novita' (curly leaved).
('Salad Bowl' types, 'Lollo' cultivars and 'Marvel of Four Seasons' can be used for any of the above sowings, though growth is slower in the winter months.)
Outdoor overwintering hardy lettuce
Butterhead: 'Valdor'.
Cos: 'Winter Density'.
Leaf lettuce 'Lobjoit's Cos', 'Valmaine'.

A range of different types of squash: **1** *'Onion Squash';* **2** *'Golden Nugget';* **3** *'Baby Blue';* **4** *mature 'White Scallop Bush';* **5** *mature 'Bush Yellow Scallop';* **6** *'Gem Squash'.*

Marrows, courgettes, squashes and pumpkins

(Cucurbita pepo, C. maxima, C. moschata)

These plants all belong to the immense, diverse, and interbred gourd family. Enormous confusion surrounds the many types in the group and their names. They are all grown for their fruits which are used mature and immature, fresh and stored. It is less well known that the young leaves and shoots are also edible, (boiled like greens), as are the flowers, which can be stuffed or used in salads or soups. The seeds of some types of pumpkin are also eaten. The following are the types of gourd most widely grown in Britain. The decorative 'ornamental gourd' is not edible.

Marrows

Also known as 'vegetable marrow', these form cylindrical fruits, which are usually harvested about 30 cm (12 in) long and about 13 cm (5 in) in diameter. There are green, white, gold, striped and round-fruited cultivars. Mature marrows can be stored for a couple of months. Marrow plants are either trailing, in which case the shoots can grow several metres (yards) long, or they make compact bushes about 90 cm (3 ft) in diameter. Bush types are more practical for small gardens.

Courgettes

These are marrow plants grown for the use of the young, immature fruits, which are harvested when about 10 cm (4 in) long. Only certain types of marrow (mainly hybrid cultivars) are suitable for use as courgettes. This is because courgettes must have tender skins and should be smooth and shiny. Some marrows are tough-skinned and hairy even when young. Many cultivars of courgettes have been bred recently, their colours ranging from pale green to dark green or yellow. There are also striped forms and a round, Italian form. They are all bush types.

Summer squashes

This is an American term for members of the marrow and pumpkin family which are generally eaten fresh in summer rather than being stored for winter. It has become adopted here for some of the more curiously shaped marrows, such as the fluted yellow or white forms of 'Patty Pan' ('Custard Marrow')

Various types of marrow: **1** *golden;* **2** *round;* **3** *striped;* **4** *green. Young fruits can be used as courgettes.*

and the fluted, green-skinned 'Scallopini'. Although these can be allowed to grow to about 15 cm (6 in) diameter for stuffing and cooking, their flavour is best if cooked whole, without peeling, when about 7.5 cm (3 in) diameter. 'Crookneck Squash' is another popular type in this group. Most are trailing in habit.

Pumpkins

The best known pumpkin is the large, orange-fruited type grown for Hallowe'en and storage. From the culinary point of view the traditional French types, and the modern greenish-orange Japanese types, are superior as they are far denser in texture. In the USA the term 'winter squash' is applied to these pumpkins and to all gourds grown for winter storage. These include the bun-like, 'Turk's Cap', the club-shaped 'Butternut Squash', 'Acorn Squash', the squat, striped 'Sweet Dumpling' and the well-known 'Spaghetti Squash', amongst others. This last is marrow-shaped and notable for the spaghetti-like texture and appearance of its flesh when cooked. All these gourds can be stored. They are becoming increasingly popular in this country, and new types are being introduced continually. Most are trailing in habit, but a few, such as 'Acorn' are bush types.

None of the gourd family is hardy. Its members are all cultivated in much the same way.

Site / soil

The gourds like an open sunny site, and very rich,

moisture-retentive but well-drained soil, slightly acid to neutral. Make an individual hole for each plant, working in plenty of well-rotted organic matter, as for cucumbers. (See p 107.) The practice of growing marrows and pumpkins on manure or compost heaps is sometimes successful, but there is a risk of the plants growing so lushly, especially early in the season, that leaves are produced rather than fruit.

Trailing types can be allowed to trail over the ground, or they can be trained over *strong* fences or supports, or up tripods of canes or poles. Where space is limited train the shoots into a circular form, pinning down the mainshoots as they grow with wire or wooden pegs. Allow space for the stems to thicken. Many of the gourds throw out roots from the stems, and these can be earthed over to encourage rooting and increase the plant's supply of nutrients and water.

Cultivation

The gourds as a group germinate poorly at soil temperatures below 13 C (56 F), but they grow very rapidly in warm conditions. So little is gained by sowing early. As a general rule, sow three to four weeks before the last frost is expected in your area.

Gourds do not transplant well, so should be either sown *in situ*, or sown in gentle heat indoors in late April or May, for planting out after the last frost. Very good plants can be obtained by sowing in small pots or modules (see Sowing indoors, p 35), allowing only one plant to develop in each module or pot. Seeds can be soaked overnight before sowing, to encourage fast germination.

Sow seeds on their side, pointed end downward, about 2.5 cm (1 in) deep. If sown indoors plants must be hardened off well before planting out. They can be covered with cloches or perforated or fleecy films in the early stages of growth outside.

If seeds are sown *in situ* wait until the danger of frost is over. Sow two to three seeds per site, perferably under a cloche or jam jar, to encourage germination. Thin to one seedling per site after germination. Bush types can be grown about 90 cm (3 ft) apart, and trailing types about 1.2 m (4 ft) apart, though very vigorous types such as large pumpkins can easily be 1.8m (6ft) apart. Put in canes when planting, as it may be hard to find the centre of the plant for watering once it has made a lot of growth.

All the gourds are hungry and thirsty plants. They should be watered lightly after planting so that they become established rapidly, and during growth as frequently as practical, especially in dry seasons, up to about 11 litres (2 gal) per week. Water is particularly important when the plants are flowering and the fruits are setting and starting to swell. It is always advisable to mulch the plants heavily both to conserve water and keep down weeds. Where the soil is not very fertile plants can be given supplementary liquid feeds during growth, especially when the fruits are swelling.

Members of the gourd family have separate male and female flowers. The female flowers can be identified by the tiny embryonic fruit seen at the base of the flower. Sometimes plants seem to produce masses of male flowers early in the season, before the female flowers appear: nothing much can be done about it! The flowers are insect-pollinated, and in cold seasons, if fruits do not seem to be setting and starting to swell, it may be necessary to pollinate the flowers by hand. Pick off a male flower, remove the petals, and press the flower firmly into the centre of a female flower. A 'parthenocarpic' courgette has been introduced in which fruits develop without being pollinated.

Where large pumpkins are required allow only two to three fruits to develop on each plant. Remove surplus fruits while still small; the tips of the shoots can be removed towards the end of the summer, to concentrate energy into the development of the fruits.

Harvesting

Courgettes and other gourds which are harvested young should be picked regularly, to encourage the formation of more fruit. Courgettes are normally ready any time from July to September. Marrows can be picked at any length from about 15 cm (6 in) long. A few can be left on the plant to grow larger for storage. Marrows and most storage gourds should be stored in well-ventilated conditions at a temperature between 7.5 – 10 C (45 – 50 F).

Pumpkins and gourds required for storage should be left to mature on the plant. At the end of summer cut away any foliage which shades them. Although they can be used after being lightly frosted, frosted fruits will not store.

Fruits for storage are ready for harvesting when the stems are starting to dry and the skins to harden. Cut them before frost, with as long a stalk as possible. Most winter squashes need to be 'cured' in the sun for about 10 days, to allow the skin to harden and the stems to seal. Cover them at night if frost threatens. The 'Acorn' types can be stored immediately they are harvested. Store at the temperatures given for marrows above. Depending on the cultivar and conditions, they may keep for four to six months. (See also Storage, p 53).

Pests and diseases

The gourds are relatively pest-free when grown outdoors, provided they are growing in well-drained

Female flowers with embryonic fruits.

The 'Custard Marrow' or 'Patty Pan' squash.

A pumpkin trained in a circle using pegs to hold down the stem.

Harvest courgettes when they are 10cm (4in) long, otherwise they will grow into marrows.

soil. Slugs may attack young plants. Cucumber mosaic virus can be serious in some seasons. (For control and symptoms, see p 58ff.) With marrows withering of the fruit, starting at the blossom end, sometimes occurs, usually due to unsuitable growing conditions. Check that the plant has not been affected by rots on the lower stem or roots. If it has destroy the plant. Otherwise rest the plant by removing the fruit, water carefully, and if the leaves are a poor colour, apply a liquid feed. The plant should regain its vigour and start to fruit normally.

Recommended cultivars

Marrow 'All Green Bush', 'Long Green Trailing', F_1 'Zebra Cross' (bush).
Courgettes F_1 'Ambassador', 'Brimmer', F_1 'Early Gem' (also suitable for marrows), F_1 'Gold Rush' (yellow). Also recommended are F_1 'Defender', F_1 'Supremo', F_1 'Tiger Cross' (also suitable for marrows) which have reasonable resistance to virus.

*Summer squash** 'Custard White', 'Tender and True'.
*Winter squash** 'Hubbard's Golden'

---

* Many other excellent cultivars are listed in general and specialist catalogues.

Onions, shallots and garlic

(*Allium* spp.)

Many types of onions are grown in gardens. The principal type is the bulb onions, which are used fresh and stored for winter. Most of the bulb onions grown in Britain are yellow – or brown - skinned with white flesh, but there are also red-skinned types with reddish pigment in the outer layers. Very small bulb onions are used for pickling. The 'Egyptian' or 'tree onion' is a curious type which forms small aerial bulbs. Bulb onions are used both raw and in cooking.

Spring onions are onions harvested small and immature, for use of the white stems and young leaves, and tiny immature bulbs. There are also several types of perennial evergreen onion, such as the 'everlasting onion' and 'Welsh onion' which are grown for the green leaves. The oriental or Japanese bunching onions are types of Welsh onion. They can be grown both for their white stems, which can develop to the size of leeks, and their green leaves. Green onions are mainly used raw and for seasoning.

Soil / site
Onions require an open site and fertile, well-drained soil. Acid soils will need liming. The soil should be thoroughly dug several months in advance; in the case of spring-sown onions in the autumn before sowing. Work in plenty of well-rotted manure or compost. Onions should not be sown on freshly manured ground. They should be rotated on at least a four-year cycle to avoid the build-up of various soil-borne pests and diseases. Most types have low nitrogen requirements. (See Fertilizers, p 18.)

BULB ONIONS
(*Allium cepa*)

Bulb onions are raised either from seeds or from sets, which are specially produced, very small bulbs. Raising from sets (see below) is much easier than raising from seeds and has several advantages for the amateur gardener.

A long growing season is required where large bulb onions and storage onions are required: the latter need time to develop, mature and be dried before storing. With the types of onions grown here, the ultimate size is determined by the amount of leaf the plant has developed *before* the days start to

A selection of onions: **1** *'Egyptian' or 'tree' onion;* **2** *garlic;* **3** *Welsh onion;* **4** *shallots;* **5** *bulb onions.*

shorten in mid-June. At this point no more leaf is developed but the bulbs start to swell. Any measures to hasten early growth, such as sowing very early or in autumn, or by using sets (which have large food reserves) instead of seeds, help to produce large bulbs.

For an almost all-year-round supply of bulb onions it is necessary to make two sowings or plantings. The first is made in spring, for onions which will be harvested from August until mid-September, and then stored for winter use. Carefully stored onions normally last until about April. (Shallots will last into May, and sometimes June.)

To fill most of the gap between April and July make a second sowing in autumn, using the hardy Japanese overwintering types which mature in June and July. Or plant the more recently developed *autumn* sets, which normally reach a usable size by June. (For cultivation of both see Autumn sown crop below.)

Spring-sown crop
Raising from seeds For an early start sow indoors in January or February, at a temperature of 10 – 16 C (50 – 60 F). Either sow in seedtrays and prick out, or sow into small pots or modules. Onions can be multi-sown, with at least six seeds per module. (See Sowing indoors, p 35.) Harden off very carefully before planting out in March (in mild areas) or April, at the stage when the seedlings have two true leaves.

Onions can also be raised by fluid sowing. (See Sowing outdoors, p 32.) Both fluid sowing and the use of transplants raised indoors lead to increased yields.

Outdoor sowings can be made as soon as the soil conditions are reasonable, from February to early April. In cold, wet soils the seeds germinate slowly and are susceptible to damping off and other diseases, so where possible warm the soil with cloches before sowing. Treated seeds can be used to give protection against fungus diseases. Prepare a fairly firmly consolidated seedbed with a fine tilth. Sow seeds very thinly in drills 13 – 20 mm (½ – ¾ in) deep, in rows 30 cm (12 in) apart.

Once the onions have germinated thin if necessary until they are 4 cm (1½ in) apart. This spacing will give the maximum yield of medium-sized onions. If large and extra large onions are required thin to 7.5 – 10 cm (3 – 4 in) apart. The larger thinnings can be used as green salad onions.

Multi-sown blocks can be planted 25 – 30 cm (10 – 12 in) apart each way.

Raising from sets Sets have several advantages over seeds. They are easier to grow, less prone to disease, can give reasonable crops in poor soil conditions, and often escape onion fly attacks. Being more substantial than seeds, they mature earlier than seed-raised plants. Their disadvantages are that they are more expensive, that only certain cultivars are available as sets, and that they are more likely to bolt, that is run to seed, resulting in poor onions which will not store. The risk of bolting is lessened by selecting small, rather than large sets, and by using 'heat-treated' sets, where available. These have been prepared by storing at high temperatures for 20 weeks to destroy the flower embryo.

Plant sets as soon as soil conditions allow from February to early April, except for 'heat-treated' sets which should not be planted until late March or early April. Plant in shallow drills or push gently into the soil without firming so that just the tips are protruding. If planted more shallowly birds are liable to uproot them. For high yields of medium-sized bulbs plant the sets 5 cm (2 in) apart in rows 25 cm (10 in) apart, or at equidistant spacing 15 cm (6 in) apart each way. For larger bulbs, space them up to 10 cm (4 in) apart in rows 25 cm (10 in) apart.

Cultivation
Onions are particularly susceptible to weed competition in the first six weeks after sowing or planting. So keep them well-weeded in the early stages, both within and between the rows. Watering is generally unnecessary after the plants have become established, except in very dry weather. If bulb onions are watered after mid-July maturity may be delayed and keeping qualities impaired.

Harvesting and storage
Bulbs can be pulled for use fresh at any stage. They are ready to harvest for storage once the foliage starts to die back and the tops bend over naturally. The traditional practice of bending the leaves over 'to assist ripening' is not recommended: it can have an adverse effect on storability. Always handle storage bulbs very carefully to avoid bruising. The bulbs should be lifted and dried until all the green parts and the papery skins are rustling dry. Do not try to store thick-necked onions. They should be used first. Onions rarely store beyond April. (See Storage, p 52.)

Recommended cultivars
Brown skinned (for use fresh and storage, in order of maturity) F₁ 'Caribo', 'Rijnsburger–Balstora', F₁ 'Hygro', 'Rijnsburger–Robusta'.
Red-skinned 'Red Baron', 'Mammoth Red Onion' (storage), 'Southport Red Globe' (storage).
Sets 'Giant Fen Globe', 'Sturon', 'Sturon Autumn Gold', 'Stuttgarter Giant'.

Autumn-sown crop
These sowings are made with the hardy Japanese overwintering cultivars, or similar European-bred types. The sowing dates for different parts of the country are critical. If sown too early the seedlings become too large and may bolt in spring; if sown too late – they may be too small to survive winter. Sow in

Plant onion sets in shallow drills.

Bulb onion thinnings can be used in salads.

Use an onion hoe carefully to control weeds.

Bulb onions as the tops start to bend over.

well-drained soil. Autumn sowings are sometimes made in a 'stale' seedbed (p 56), to deter attacks from the onion fly.

Recommended sowing dates in August are:

- second week in the north;
- third week in the midlands and east;
- fourth week in the south.

Ideally aim to establish 10 plants per 30-cm (12-in) row, assuming that a number of seedlings will inevitably be lost during the winter. This can be done by sowing seeds 2.5 cm (1 in) apart, in rows 30 cm (12 in) apart. In very hot weather the seeds may not germinate well.

Watering several times after sowing, or covering the bed with white reflective material, helps to lower the temperature and encourage germination. In spring thin the remaining seedlings to about 5 cm (2 in) apart. The onions will be ready for use from early June until August, but cannot be stored for the winter period.

These overwintered onions have somewhat higher nitrogen requirements than spring-sown bulb onions. A moderate dressing of a nitrogenous fertilizer can be worked into the seedbed before sowing (see Fertilizers, p 18), and a topdressing can be applied in early January to stimulate growth. A dressing of Nitro-chalk at the rate of 70–100 g / sq m (2–3 oz / sq yd), is recommended. Organic gardeners can apply a foliar feed in early spring.

Several old onion cultivars were traditionally sown in August in mild parts of the country, thinning to about 2.5 cm (1 in) apart in autumn, and thinning or transplanting in spring. These are less hardy, later maturing, and less reliable than the newer cultivars now available.

Recommended cultivars
(New Japanese-type cultivars in order of maturity.)
'Express Yellow O-X', F_1 'Buffalo', F_1 'Keepwell', 'Imai Early Yellow', 'Senshyu Semi-globe Yellow'.

Dry onions off the ground until they rustle.

(Traditional overwintering cultivars.)
'Reliance' ('Autumn Queen'/'Oakey'), 'Southport Red Globe'.

Autumn-planted sets
These sets have been selected for their hardiness and have proved highly successful in recent years. They must be grown in a well-drained soil; waterlogging and prolonged wet weather have proved more damaging than low temperatures.

The sets can be planted any time from September until the end of November. Recommended spacing is 10–15 cm (4–6 in) apart in rows 30–40 cm (12–16 in) apart. Currently the principal cultivar available is 'Unwins First Early' which matures in July but reaches a usable size in June. It can be lifted for storage, but will not normally keep beyond Christmas.

PICKLING ONIONS

While pickling onions will tolerate poorer and drier soils than bulb or spring onions, they will yield better when grown on fertile soil. Sow *in situ* in March or April. Aim for a population of 30 plants per 30 cm^2 (12in^2). So if sowing in rows 30 cm (12 in) apart, sow seeds 6 mm (¼ in) apart. Allowing for non-germination this should give the right plant numbers. Pickling onions can also be sown thinly in bands about 23 cm (9 in) wide. There is no need to thin them out, as competition keeps the bulbs small: they are used about thumb nail size. Pickling onions are normally ready in August. After the foliage has died down they can be lifted as bulb onions, and stored until required for pickling.

Recommended cultivars
'Barletta', 'Paris Silver Skin'.

BUNCHING OR SPRING ONIONS

These are grown primarily for use of the small white shank and green leaves in salads. The thinnings from maincrop onions can be used in the same way.

The soil and seedbed are prepared as for bulb onions. Acid soils must be limed as spring onions are very sensitive to acidity. Sow from February (in mild areas) to June at two- to three-week intervals for continuous supplies in summer and autumn. Sow the extra hardy cultivars in July (in the north), and August to early September (in the south), for an overwintering crop which will be ready for use the following March to May.

The highest yields are obtained by sowing in rows 10 cm (4in) apart, aiming for 30 plants per 30 cm^2 (12 in^2). Alternatively, spring onions can be grown in bands 7.5 cm (3 in) wide, with 15 cm (6 in) between the bands. Sow thinly so that there is no need to thin further; the onions can be pulled as required.

They can be watered at any stage if the soil gets dry, at the rate of 1 litre / 1.3 m of row (1 gal / 20 ft row). The winter crop can be given cloche protection in cold areas.

Recommended cultivars
'White Lisbon', 'White Lisbon–Winter Hardy' (hardiest).

Pests and diseases
The most common pest is onion fly, which is especially serious on dry soils. Stem and bulb eelworm can also be serious on infected soils.

The most common diseases are downy mildew, white rot, and neck rot in stored onions. Losses from *Botrytis* in overwintered crops can be serious. For symptoms and control, see p58ff.

PERENNIAL GREEN ONIONS

Welsh onion (*Allium fistulosum*)
The Welsh onion or ciboule is a relatively hardy, hollow-leaved onion, growing in clumps about 60 cm (2 ft) tall. The base of the stem is thickened but does not form a true bulb. As the leaves normally remain green all year, Welsh onions are especially useful in winter for seasoning or salads.

Sow Welsh onions in spring or August, in rows 23 cm (9 in) apart, thinning to 20 cm (8 in) apart. Spring-sown onions will be a usable size by the autumn; August-sown onions by the following spring.

Either cut single leaves, or lift single plants or lift a whole clump for use.

If left in the ground the clumps become thicker every year. To keep them growing vigorously lift them every two or three years in spring or autumn, divide up the clumps, and replant the younger parts about 20 cm (8 in) apart.

In areas with very severe winters the Welsh onion is treated as an annual or biennial and sown annually. Seed-raised plants tend to be hardier than plants raised by division.

Japanese bunching onions (*Allium fistulosum*)
These are improved forms of Welsh onions, being more vigorous and more substantial in size. They are loosely divided into two main types: the multistemmed, which are more like the traditional Welsh onion, dividing into a mass of stems, and the single-stemmed, in which the lower part of the stem can develop into a leek-like shaft about 2.5 cm (1 in) in diameter. Japanese onions can be used at all stages from 'spring onion' to the thick-stem stage. There is a wide range of cultivars, some being multi-purpose, some more suited to particular purposes than others. Japanese bunching onions are notable for tolerating both very high and very low temperatures.

Although perennial, Japanese bunching onions are usually grown as annuals or biennials to keep the plants healthy. The types currently available in Europe are mainly grown for use as reasonably large leafy onions, harvested in the autumn and winter months. If several sowings are made they can be used for much of the year.

Sow outdoors *in situ* in spring and early summer, making the first sowings as soon as the soil is workable. Seeds can be sown in rows 30 cm (12 in) apart, and plants can be thinned in stages to 7.5 cm (3 in) apart. The thinnings can be pulled for use as spring onions about three months after sowing. Earlier sowings can be made indoors (see Bulb onions) for transplanting outside. Two or three seedlings can be planted together in one clump. (See also Further reading, 'oriental vegetables' p 158.)

Everlasting Onion (*Allium perutile*)
Also known as the 'ever-ready' onion, this is another evergreen perennial onion, similar to the Welsh onion in habit, but with finer, flatter leaves and a somewhat milder flavour. It does not set seed, so has to be propagated by division of existing clumps. Space the clumps about 20 cm (8 in) apart. Divide them up and replant from time to time (see Welsh onions) if they seem to be weakening.

EGYPTIAN OR TREE ONION
(*Allium cepa* Proliferum Group)

This curious onion produces clusters of very small aerial bulbs instead of flowers. These can sprout while attached to the mother plant, developing shoots and further clusters of bulbs, to form a multi-tiered plant. Eventually the stems flop over on to the ground, where bulbs in contact with the soil will take root to form new plants.

The Egyptian onion is extremely hardy: the aerial bulbs can be picked in mid winter if necessary. Yields however, are very low. It grows best in a sunny situation in fertile, well-drained soil. Plant single bulbs or clusters about 25 cm (10 in) apart in spring or autumn. The plants will often perpetuate themselves, but may need to be thinned out periodically. A few bulbs can be saved for further planting if necessary.

SHALLOTS
(*Allium escalonicum=A. cepa* Aggregatum Group)

This member of the onion family is notable for its distinct flavour. It is used raw, in cooking and for pickling. In the British Isles the types with firm, onion-shaped bulbs are most popular: there are yellow- and red-skinned forms. A pear-shaped cultivar ('Hâtive de Niort') is slower growing and is mainly grown for showing. On the Continent there are many forms, some crescent-shaped, some purple-skinned. Some types of shallot, notably the yellow-skinned, have exceptional keeping qualities and can be stored through into June which is considerably longer than any of the onions. Shallots are an easily grown crop.

Site / soil
See onions. Compacted soils should be avoided as the growing roots often force the shallots out of the ground.

Cultivation
Shallots are usually raised from sets (single shallots), each of which multiplies into a clump. Wherever possible buy stocks that are guaranteed virus-free, as many stocks have deteriorated with virus infection in recent years. Only save your own shallots if they are very healthy. The ideal size for planting is about 2 cm (¾ in) diameter, and about 10 g (⅓ oz) in weight. Small sets are less likely to bolt than large ones, and will produce a clump of reasonably-sized shallots. Larger sets tend to produce a larger clump, but smaller individual shallots.

Shallots need as long a growing season as possible. In very mild areas, and on well-drained soils, they can be planted in December and January. Otherwise plant in February and March, as soon as the soil can be worked. Remove any loose scales and plant in a drill so that only the tips protrude. In very light soils sets can be pushed in: otherwise plant with a trowel. If they are planted very shallowly they are sometimes tweaked out by birds, or pushed out by worms or by the developing roots. If they *are* pushed out, dig them up and replant, rather than pushing them back into the soil, which will break the roots.

To get maximum yields of good-sized shallots plant sets 15 cm (6 in) apart in rows 20 cm (8 in) apart or 18 cm (7 in), apart each way. Large sets can be planted at 15 cm (6 in) apart in rows 30 cm (12 in) apart, or 20 cm (8 in) apart each way. Small sets can also be planted 2.5 cm (1 in) apart each way to give early crops of salad onions. If planted in seed boxes in a greenhouse they can be harvested very early.

Water shallots after planting if the soil is dry, at the rate of about 70 ml (⅛ pint) per day. They rarely require watering once established. No attention is required other than keeping the crop weeded.

Note Shallots raised from seed are currently being introduced. Sow early, as for spring sown bulb onions (see p 121), spacing seedlings 5 cm (2 in) apart each way.

Harvesting
During the summer a few shoots can be used as green onions if required. Bulbs are mature and

Pickling onions need to be closely spaced to keep them small (see p 122).

Plant shallots so that just the tips of the sets are showing.

In summer a few shoots of shallots can be cut and used as green onions.

ready for harvesting in July or August, after the tops have died down. Dry them in the same way as onions, and store them on trays or in bags in a frost-free place. (See Storage, p 52.) Provided they are healthy, reserve a few of the optimum size (see above) for planting the following season.

Pests and diseases

Shallots are normally a trouble-free crop, though they can be subject to any of the pests and diseases which attack onions. The most likely pests are onion fly and stem and bulb eelworm. For symptoms and control, see p 58ff.

GARLIC
(Allium sativum)

In Europe garlic is grown for its strongly flavoured cloves, which play a distinctive role in cooking many dishes. In the east it is also cultivated for its young leafy shoots and for its flowering stem. (For the cultivation of these see Further reading, 'oriental vegetables', p 158.)

Garlic is very hardy, and far more easily grown than is generally realized. There are pink and white forms, some with better storage qualities than others. Garlic is unusual in that bolted plants can still produce reasonable bulbs for use.

Soil / site

Garlic requires an open, sunny situation, and does best on light, well-drained soil. On heavy soils it is sometimes grown on ridges to improve drainage; otherwise a little sand, ashes, or potting compost can be worked into the drill before planting to improve drainage. It does not have high nutrient requirements so it is usually sufficient to manure the soil for the previous crop. It should not be grown on freshly manured soil. Acid soils should be limed.

Cultivation

Garlic is normally raised by planting individual cloves, split off from the bulb. Wherever possible, use garlic that is guaranteed virus- and nematode-free, and never plant diseased or unhealthy looking cloves. Cloves used for planting should be at least 13 mm (½ in) in diameter, or about 10 g (⅓ oz) in weight. Where smaller cloves are used, plant them relatively far apart to compensate for their small size. As a general rule, the larger the clove, and the further apart cloves are planted, the larger the garlic bulb will be.

Most selections of garlic require a cold period of one to two months at temperatures of 0–10 C (32–50 F). This is why garlic should be planted in late autumn, between late October and November, wherever possible. Short-storage types should always be planted in the autumn. Garlic also benefits from a long growing period. Where autumn planting is impossible, and on very heavy soils, planting can be delayed until February or March. In poor summers spring-planted garlic may not mature and dry satisfactorily.

Where soil is heavy garlic cloves can be planted in modules (see Sowing indoors, p 35) any time during the winter. Put the modules in a sheltered place outdoors to get the required low temperatures. As soon as the soil is workable in spring plant out any cloves which have sprouted. This method usually ensures a good crop.

Plant garlic cloves straight, and the right way up. It is not always obvious which *is* the right way up: look for the flattish base 'plate'. Garlic can be planted fairly deeply, as cloves are apt to work their way up. The traditional rule of thumb was to plant at about twice the depth of the clove, with at least 2.5 cm (1 in) of soil above the clove. Planting up to 10 cm (4 in) deep (except on heavy, wet soils), appears to increase the yield.

For high yields space garlic cloves 18 cm (7 in) apart each way. Or grow in rows 25–30 cm (10–12 in) apart, with the cloves 7.5–10 cm (3–4 in) apart in the rows. Keep the plants weed free. Otherwise they require little attention.

Harvesting

Unlike onions, garlic should be lifted for drying when the leaves start to fade and turn yellow. If harvesting is delayed there is a risk that the bulbs will start to resprout, and an increased chance of rots developing in store. Harvesting methods and storage are the same as for bulb onions, and garlic bulbs should similarly be handled very carefully to avoid bruising. Garlic should be stored in the driest conditions possible, at temperatures between 5–10 C (41–50 F). Well-stored garlic can keep up to 10 months, depending on the selection.

Pests and diseases
See onions.

Recommended cultivars
Although there are numerous selections of garlic, there is normally little choice in the British Isles, and few selections have been made specifically for our conditions. This situation may change as garlic becomes more widely grown.

Parsley

(Petroselinum crispum)

Parsley is a biennial herb, running to seed in its second year. It is the most commonly used herb in English cooking, and besides its decorative and seasoning qualities, it is very rich in vitamins. Both the leaves and the stems can be used. Parsley is difficult to dry satisfactorily, but can be frozen well.

Parsley is relatively hardy (hardiness depends on the cultivar), but the quality of the foliage deteriorates in winter. Unless protected, the plants tend to die back or die off completely in severe weather.

There are two main forms, the curled and the French, plain or broadleaved. The curled is more popular, but the broadleaved is said to be better flavoured and is easier to grow.

Hamburg or turnip-rooted parsley is a dual-purpose form: the smooth parsnip-like roots make an excellent winter vegetable (cooked like parsnip), while the plain leaves remain green throughout winter, withstanding more severe weather than ordinary parsley and forming a useful substitute. For cultivation, see Parsnips, p 128.

Site / soil

Parsley can be grown in sunny or partially shaded positions. It requires reasonably fertile, moisture-retentive soil, and does not generally do well on poor or very light soils.

Types of parsley: **1** *French, plain or broadleaved;* **2** *Hamburg or turnip-rooted;* **3** *curled.*

Common curled parsley is both a decorative and vitamin-rich crop. Both the leaves and stems can be used.

Cultivation

To ensure continuous supplies of good-quality parsley it is advisable to make two sowings a year. Sow in March for the main summer supply, and again in June or July, to give a fresh crop for autumn and early winter.

Parsley is well known for its slow germination, sometimes taking as long as four to six weeks to germinate. Never sow in cold, wet soils, but make sure the ground remains moist until the seedlings are through. Traditional methods for aiding germination were to water the drills beforehand with boiling water, or, in heavy soils, to line the drills with moist peat or potting compost. (See also Sowing in dry conditions, Sowing outdoors, p 32.)

For the spring sowing the most satisfactory method is to sow indoors in gentle heat in March, either in seedtrays followed by pricking out, or in modules. (See Sowing indoors, p 35). Once the seeds have germinated keep seedlings somewhere cool, and plant out in May. Unless raised in modules, seedlings must be planted out young before the tap-root starts to develop. Parsley is also a good subject for fluid sowing. (See Sowing outdoors, p 32.) Otherwise wait until the soil has warmed up and sow *in situ* in drills about 15 mm (⅝ in) deep. Plants can be thinned in stages to about 15 cm (6 in) apart each way, or grown closer and cut more frequently. Parsley tends to be slow growing, taking about four months to reach a reasonable size.

The second sowing, in summer, is best made *in situ*, as this seems to produce stronger plants with longer tap-roots, which overwinter better.

During the growing season the plants need to be kept weed free. They should be watered if conditions are very dry.

Harvesting

Parsley is cut as required, cutting either single leaves, or the whole plant. Plants can be cut back to ground level once or twice during the year. At the onset of cold weather cover plants with cloches or bracken, to conserve the quality as long as possible. Protected plants normally supply some leaf through to the following spring.

Alternatively, a few plants from the second sowing can be potted up in September, and brought indoors or planted in a cool greenhouse for use during winter.

Parsley which has overwintered runs to seed in its second season. If the flowering stems are cut back the plants will continue to produce some leaf for another month or so, though the quality will deteriorate. If the stem is left the plants will often self-seed. Young seedlings can be transplanted carefully to where they are wanted.

Pests and diseases

The most likely pests are carrot fly and aphids. (For symptoms and control, see p 58ff.) In dry seasons in particular, parsley may start to yellow, sometimes even becoming bluish, with growth being stunted. This is probably caused by a combination of viruses, frequently including the carrot motley dwarf virus, which is probably aphid-borne. There is no remedy other than pulling up and burning diseased plants. If the crop is looking poorly, make a second sowing right away: this will normally escape attack.

Recommended cultivars

'Bravour' (curly, good hardiness), 'Curlina' (curly), 'Plain-leaved' (broad), 'Giant Italian' (broad).

Parsnip

(Pastinaca sativa)

Parsnips are a valuable winter root vegetable, combining hardiness with a distinct flavour. Roots vary in length from about 13 – 20 cm (5 – 8 in) long. They also vary in shape: bulbous types are squat with rounded shoulders, wedge types have broad shoulders and a wedge-shaped root, while the bayonet types tend to be narrow and longer. Hamburg parsley (see p 126), is very similar in appearance and taste to parsnips, and is grown in the same way.

Site / soil

Parsnips require an open site. Although they grow best on light, deeply cultivated, stone-free soils, they will grow satisfactorily on most soils. The optimum pH is 6.5. Acid soils should be limed. On very shallow soils use the shorter cultivars such as 'Avonresister'. It was always said that parsnips grown on freshly manured soil were more likely to be fanged, but recent research has found no evidence of this. They do not have high nutrient requirements, but should be rotated.

Parsnip roots: **1** *long narrow bayonet type;* **2** *squat rounded bulbous type;* **3** *broad-shouldered wedge type.*

As germination of parsnip seed can be poor, station sow at two to four seeds per station and thin out later.

Cultivation

Parsnip seeds do not remain viable for very long, so never use seeds that are more than two years' old. Seeds germinate slowly and erratically in cold soil, so although standard advice was always to sow in February or March (to get a long growing season), in most parts of the country outdoor sowings are much more successful if delayed until April or May. There is also less risk of canker infection – which causes the shoulder and crown to rot – with later sowings. Canker tends to be common in peaty soils and gardens where parsnips have been grown for many years. Parsnips are normally sown *in situ* as they do not transplant well. However, they can be sown indoors in gentle heat in modules (see Sowing indoors, p 35.) from late February to early April, planting out before the tap-roots have started to develop. Fluid sowing is also successful with parsnips. (See p 32.)

Parsnip seeds are light and fragile-looking, so the seedbed should be worked into a reasonably fine tilth before sowing. Sow seeds in drills about 15 mm (⅝ in) deep. As germination is lower than with most vegetable seeds it is advisable to 'station-sow' (see Sowing outdoors, p 31), sowing two to four seeds per station, and thinning to one after germination. For large roots – with crowns over 5 cm (2 in) diameter – aim to grow plants 15 cm (6 in) apart in rows 30 cm (12 in) apart. For smaller roots, with crowns 4-5 cm (1½ – 2 in) diameter, sow 7.5 cm (3 in) apart in rows 20 cm (8 in) apart. Parsnips can also be grown at equidistant spacing.

As parsnip seeds are slow to germinate, they are often intersown in the row with radish or small lettuce. These germinate faster than the parsnip seeds, so marking the rows for weeding. The radishes or lettuces can often be harvested before the space is required by the parsnips; but take care the parsnip seedlings are not overshadowed by them.

Other than weeding parsnips require little attention. Watering is only necessary in very dry weather, when steady growth can be maintained by watering every two or three weeks at the rate of about 11 litres / sq m (2 gal / sq yd). This will improve the quality and size of the roots. Roots are likely to split if water is applied suddenly, either by rainfall or watering after a dry spell.

Harvesting

Roots are normally ready for lifting from October onwards. They can be left in the soil all winter, lifting as required. As the foliage dies down completely it is advisable to mark the rows with canes so the roots can be found if it snows. Covering the tops with a layer of straw or bracken will make lifting easier in frosty weather. Any roots remaining in March can be lifted and heeled in, or temporarily stored in sand, to prevent them resprouting and so becoming soft.

Pests and diseases

The most common pests are celery fly and carrot fly. The most serious disease is canker, for which there is no remedy. Fortunately, several cultivars now have good resistance to canker. Lettuce root aphis is sometimes a problem. For symptoms, control and preventive measures, see p 58ff.

Recommended cultivars

(*All have good resistance to canker*)
'Avonresister', 'Cobham Improved Marrow', F₁ 'Gladiator', 'White Gem'.

Peas

(Pisum sativum)

Ordinary garden peas are grown for the peas inside the pod. They are either wrinkle- or round-seeded, the former being the sweeter, but the latter hardier, and therefore normally used for the very late and very early sowings. Most peas have green pods, though there are some purple-podded cultivars which look very attractive while growing. Petit Pois is a distinct type of very small pea, with an excellent flavour.

Mangetout or Sugar peas are types in which the entire pod is eaten when the peas are immature. There are many kinds, one of the more recently introduced being the 'Sugar Snap' type. This has exceptionally succulent pods and is very sweet-flavoured. Some of the mangetout peas are dual purpose, in that the pods can be eaten when young, but can be shelled for peas at a more mature stage. On the whole the mangetout types are notable for their flavour, and seem to be easier to grow, and higher yielding, than ordinary garden peas.

In older pea cultivars peas grow on leafy stems or vines, with a number of tendrils which cling to supports. A modern development has been the semi-leafless pea, in which some of the leaves have been modified into tendrils. Originally developed for mechanical harvesting of the commercial pea crop, these cultivars can be useful to amateur gardeners. The numerous tendrils twine around neighbouring plants, making them almost self-supporting; the plants tend to be healthy as the crop is less leafy and better ventilated; and they seem to be less frequently attacked by birds.

Both ordinary peas and mangetout peas can be frozen. Garden peas can also be allowed to dry and

Types of peas: **1** *purple-podded;* **2** *mangetout or sugar;* **3** *garden peas;* **4** *petit pois;* **5** *semi-leafless.*

shelled for use as dried peas. Some cultivars have been specially bred for this purpose. In Asia the young tendrils and the tips of pea shoots, that is the youngest pair of leaves at the tip of the stem, are eaten raw or lightly steamed as a delicacy. A few can be picked off without harming the plant.

Garden peas vary in height from 45 cm (18 in) to 1.5m (5 ft) tall. They are grouped by season into earlies, second earlies (or early maincrop), and maincrop. Depending on day temperature earlies mature on average in 11 to 12 weeks, second earlies in 12 to 13 weeks and maincrop in 13 to 14 weeks, progressing from shorter, lower-yielding cultivars which require less space, to taller, higher-yielding ones which require considerable space. Earlies and early maincrop cultivars are more suited to small gardens

Peas sown traditionally in a V-shaped drill, 5cm (2in) deep.

Sow peas widely spaced in three-row bands to extend cropping.

Yields are increased if peas are supported from an early stage.

Wide mesh wire netting is an effective method of support.

The many tendrils of semi-leafless peas make them self-supporting.

Some purple-poldded cultivars have attractive purple flowers.

and light soils, and can be sown in succession throughout the summer to give a continuous crop.

Site / soil

Peas require an open but not exposed position. They are by nature a cool-weather crop, growing best in spring and cool summers, and disliking intense heat, drought, and poorly drained soils. Provided it has ample moisture, the summer crop can be grown in light shade. The soil needs to be fertile and deeply cultivated, preferably working in manure or compost the autumn before sowing to make the soil as moisture retentive as possible. A trench can be dug as for beans, incorporating manure or compost into the lower spit (see p 26). No extra nitrogen is required during growth, as nodules on the pea roots 'fix' atmospheric nitrogen in the soil. Peas should be rotated to avoid any build-up of soil-borne diseases.

Cultivation

Peas germinate poorly in cold soils, and where germination is slow, losses are liable to be high due to mice damage and fungus and bacterial diseases attacking the seeds. Little is gained by sowing early in a cold spring.

In warm areas the earliest outdoor sowings, which will be ready at the end of May or early June, can be made in a sheltered position from late February onwards. Where possible, sow under cloches. Alternatively, warm the soil in advance with cloches, or take out the drill on a sunny morning, and leave it for a few hours before sowing. Early outdoor sowings can be protected with crop covers (see Protected cropping, p 49) until the peas require support. Seeds treated against fungus diseases can be used for early sowings.

For the main summer crop, maturing from mid-June onwards, sow seeds of early or second early cultivars at intervals of about three to four weeks from April to early July, or sow cultivars from different seasonal groups on the same date in April or May, to give staggered maturity.

In July sow an early dwarf cultivar, which will crop in autumn if the weather remains fine.

In mild parts of the country hardy overwintering early peas can be sown outdoors in October or November for an early crop in the following year. The success of this crop depends on the winter weather, so cloche protection is advisable. Measures must be taken against mice, who tend to assume this sowing has been made for their benefit.

Sow seeds 2.5 – 5 cm (1 – 2 in) deep. There are various methods of sowing. The traditional way is to sow peas about 5 cm (2 in) apart, either in a 23 cm (9 in) wide, flat-bottomed drill, or in a single row in a V-shaped drill. The distance between the rows or drills should be about that of the height of the peas at maturity. A more recent recommendation, to encourage cropping over a fairly long period, is to grow peas less densely in bands of three rows, each row 11 cm (4½ in) apart, with the seeds 11 cm (4½ in) apart within the rows, and 45 cm (18 in) between the bands.

Peas can also be grown successfully on the bed system in patches 90 – 120 cm (3 – 4 ft) wide, spacing the peas at equidistant spacing 5 – 7.5 cm (2 – 3 in) each way. Use the closer spacing for the semi-leafless cultivars. With all peas early sowings can be thicker to allow for losses.

Whatever method is used, yields are increased if peas are given support from an early stage, as soon as the tendrils appear, using pea sticks, wide-mesh wire netting or nylon net. The support for a single row can be on one side of the row; for wide drills or bands it can run down the centre or be on either side; where grown in a patch wire netting can be staked around the edge of the patch, as the peas in the centre more or less support each other.

The commonest causes of failure with peas are mice eating the seed, and birds attacking both the seedlings and the pods. When making the early and overwintered sowings it is advisable to set mouse traps alongside the rows, putting them under tiles to keep the bait dry and to prevent birds getting caught.

All sowings need to be protected from birds in the early stages (until supports are erected), with black cotton strung over the rows, (see Pests and Diseases, p 54) or by using wire or net pea-guards.

Young plants need to be hoed carefully or hand weeded. The stems of the overwintered and early spring sowings can be earthed up a little to give them extra support.

Unless conditions are very dry in the early stages of growth, watering is unnecessary until the peas start to flower. Watering at the rate of 22 litres / sq m (4 gal / sq yd) per week, from the start of flowering and throughout the pod-forming and picking period will increase both the yields and quality of the crop.

Peas benefit from being mulched, to conserve the moisture in the soil and keep the roots cool.

Harvesting

Pick peas regularly to encourage further cropping, and to enjoy them in their prime. Most mangetout peas should be picked when the tiny pea is just visible as a swelling inside the pod.

Where peas are to be dried leave them on the plant as long as possible, and then hang the bundles of uprooted vines in an airy, sheltered place until the pods are dry enough to split open.

Pests and diseases

Apart from birds and mice, the most serious pest is pea moth. In hot seasons, pea thrips can be damaging. Seedlings are at risk from damping off and various rotting diseases when sown in cold, wet conditions. Pod-spotting can also be severe in wet conditions. The disease pea wilt (*Fusarium*) has been on the increase in recent years; several cultivars have resistance. Rotation helps to prevent both these diseases. (For Symptoms and control measures, see p 58ff.)

Recommended cultivars

Garden peas 'Hurst Beagle' (early, second early, suitable for overwintering), 'Hurst Green Shaft' (main), 'Tristar' (main), 'Twiggy' (leafless, main).
Mangetout 'Sugar Rae' (main), 'Sugar Snap' (main). (All the above except 'Tristar' have resistance to wilt.)
Drying peas 'Maro'.

Peppers
Sweet pepper; chilli pepper

(*Capsicum annuum* Grossum Group; *C. annuum* Longum Group)

The chances of growing peppers successfully in this country are much higher than they used to be, with the robust, more cold-tolerant cultivars now available. There are two main types: the sweet or green pepper (often listed as capsicum) and the hot-flavoured chilli pepper. Shape and colour are no guide as in to which category a particular pepper falls: both types can be almost any shape and a range of colours. Peppers are closely related to tomatoes and generally grown in much the same way. Many interesting cultivars are becoming available to amateurs, and the choice is likely to be extended in future.

The sweet peppers are mainly greenish or yellow when young. In warm conditions they mature to red, yellow, orange or purplish black, depending on the cultivar. The thin-walled types, which are usually bell-shaped, are generally earlier maturing and more suitable for cold climates. The thick-walled types, more often rather square-shaped, are excellent for stuffing, but tend to be later maturing. Fruits can also be tapering, roundish, and a flat tomato or bonnet shape.

Chilli or cayenne peppers are generally narrow and tapering, but vary considerably in size; there are

A range of red, yellow and green fleshed sweet peppers and the small fruited chilli type (top centre).

also round 'cherry' cultivars. The degree of piquancy in flavour ranges from mild to extremely piquant. Cultivars tend to be green or yellowish when young, maturing to red. Contrary to popular belief, the chillies are in practice no harder to grow than sweet peppers.

Pepper plants are 45 cm (18 in) high on average, and have a 38 cm (15 in) spread when mature. Recently some very compact cultivars have been bred, which are excellent for pots or confined spaces.

Site / soil
Peppers need high light intensity and warm conditions. As a rough guide, they need slightly warmer conditions than tomatoes, but slightly cooler conditions than aubergines. They can be grown successfully without any protection outdoors only in the milder parts of the country. In most areas they crop far more reliably if grown in frames, unheated polytunnels or greenhouses, or, in the early stages at least, under cloches. They can also be grown in 'growing bags' and in pots at least 20 cm (8 in) wide and deep. The outdoor crop should be grown in a warm, sheltered position.

The soil needs to be slightly acid, preferably pH 6 – 6.5, fertile and moisture-retentive with plenty of humus worked into it. It should not be freshly manured, or growth is liable to be too lush, resulting in leafy growth rather than fruit. A base-dressing can be applied before planting (see Fertilizers, p 17), but peppers are less demanding in this respect than tomatoes.

Cultivation
On the whole the early fruiting F_1 hybrid cultivars are the most suitable for cultivation in this country.

Sow early indoors in mid-March for growing under cover and early April for growing outside, at a minimum temperature of 21 C (70 F). Sow seeds shallowly, about 6 mm (¼ in) deep, in seedtrays or modules. (See Sowing indoors p 35.) Alternatively, sow two to three seeds in small pots, thinning to one after germination. If sown in seedtrays prick out into 5 – 7.5 cm (2 – 3 in) pots or modules at the three-leaf stage.

As the seedlings grow the temperature should be lowered. Plant them in their permanent positions, either in the ground or in pots, when the first flowers are showing, usually when the plants are about 10-13 cm (4 – 5 in) high. Plant out under cover in early May in the south of the British Isles, late May in the north. Harden off very well before planting outside two to three weeks later. *Never* plant into cold soil, or if there is still a danger of frost.

Space plants 38 – 45 cm (15 – 18 in) apart each way; dwarf cultivars can be spaced 30 cm (12 in)

Plant peppers into their permanent positions when the first flowers are showing.

apart. The plants normally grow first on a single stem, which then branches naturally, when 3 cm (5 in) or so high, into two, producing a 'crown' or fruit bud at the joint. If the plant is growing vigorously this can be left to develop into a fruit; its development will help to balance excessive vegetative growth. If the plant is growing slowly, remove the crown bud to encourage the development of more sideshoots, and to make a sturdy plant. The aim with peppers is to develop strong plants which can sustain the development and weight of the fruits. If plants seem very weak and spindly, nip out the growing points of the main shoot or shoots when the plants are about 30 – 38 cm (12 – 15 in) high.

Peppers do not normally require staking, but if it seems necessary they can be tied to canes. The 'branches' of pepper plants are sometimes rather brittle. Peppers grow poorly if the soil either becomes waterlogged or dries out. If necessary, water little and often to prevent plants drying out. Plants benefit from being kept mulched.

In hot weather peppers grown indoors benefit from relatively high humidity, which helps fruit to set and prevents buds dropping off. Spray plants gently with water in the morning and at midday, and/or place buckets of water among the plants. These measures also discourage infestations of red spider mite.

Once the fruits start to swell the plants can be given a liquid feed every two weeks or so, though this is often unnecessary. A tomato feed, which is high in potassium, is often recommended, but in fact peppers have lower potash requirements than tomatoes.

Harvesting

The first peppers can usually be picked in July under cover, and in August outdoors, when still green. Fruits are ready for picking when smooth and glossy: immature fruits tend to be slightly crinkly and have a matt surface. Start picking sweet peppers when fruits are tennis-ball size to encourage the development of more fruits.

Alternatively, fruits can be left on the plant to turn red, or whatever colour they eventually become, towards the end of the season. They are sweeter flavoured and richer in vitamins when their full colour develops, but whether it will do so depends on the cultivar and the season. Where fruits are left on the plant to redden, the total yield will be lower. Chillies can be similarly picked for use at any stage from green to red. 'Hotness' tends to increase with maturity.

When frost seems imminent pull up the plants by their roots and hang them in a sunny porch, or frost-free shed. Sweet peppers often keep in reasonable condition on the plant for several months, even continuing to change colour. They also freeze well. Chillies can be treated similarly and will eventually shrivel up and dry on the plant. They will keep up to two years this way. Alternatively, they can be picked off and stored in jars.

The most piquant parts of chillies are the seeds and surrounding pith, which can be scraped away carefully if the peppers are too hot. Take care not to rub the eyes after touching the seeds.

Pests and diseases

The outdoor crop is relatively trouble free. When grown under cover aphids, whitefly and red spider mite can be problems. For symptoms and control measures, see p 58ff.

Recommended cultivars

Sweet peppers F$_1$ 'Canape', F$_1$ 'New Ace', F$_1$ 'Early Prolific' (thin-walled types), F$_1$ 'Redskin' (dwarf), F$_1$ 'Bellboy' (thick-walled), 'Luteus' (thick-walled; yellow fully ripe).

Chilli peppers 'Red Chili', 'Hungarian Wax' (sweet and hot), F$_1$ 'Apache' (dwarf).

Potatoes

(*Solanum tuberosum*)

Potato cultivars are grouped according to the season of lifting as earlies, second earlies and maincrop. Early potatoes mature in 100 to 110 days, second earlies in 110 to 120 days, and maincrop in 125 to 140 days depending on the weather. Generally speaking the early groups are lower yielding, require less space, escape some of the diseases which affect the maincrop potatoes, and are ready for use in June or early July when potato prices in shops are still high.

Maincrop potatoes are normally ready from late July onwards, and are either lifted for immediate use or, when fully mature, stored for winter supplies. As they take up considerable space for much of the growing season, in a small garden it is probably only worth growing early potatoes, where the difference in quality between home-grown and shop-bought potatoes is most marked.

Site / soil

Potatoes require an open site; frost pockets should be avoided for early potatoes, as there is a danger that the young shoots may be damaged by a late frost. Acid soils (pH 5 to 6) are preferred, but potatoes will grow on a wide range of soils, doing best on deep, fertile, well-drained but moisture-retentive soil. Early potatoes should be grown on a three-year rotation and maincrop potatoes on a five-year rotation, to avoid build-up of eelworm and other soil pests.

Chitting seed potatoes: tubers ready for planting showing most of the shoots at the rose end.

Prepare the soil by digging in plenty of farmyard manure or compost in the autumn before planting. Maincrop potatoes have very high nitrogen requirements; the early crop slightly lower nitrogen requirements. (See Fertilizers, p 18.) Potatoes are often the first crop to be planted in new gardens on 'new' soils. Although their yields may not be high, they help to improve the soil structure with their extensive root system.

Cultivation

Potatoes are almost always raised by planting seed potatoes. These are small potatoes, grown in areas where the risk of virus infection is lowest. It is essential to start with good quality, healthy, certified seed potatoes. It is unwise to save your own seed.

Provided the soil is fertile and disease-free, the key to a high yield of potatoes is plenty of moisture throughout growth, and a long growing season. As potatoes are susceptible to frost, the growing season is extended by starting potatoes into growth indoors, a process known as 'sprouting' or 'chitting'. This is most valuable for early cultivars.

Chitting The normal method is to buy certified seed potatoes in February, and to place the tubers in shallow trays, in the light but not in direct sunlight, in a frost-free shed or cool room. Stand them upright side by side, with the 'rose' end uppermost; this is the end in which most of the dormant sprouts (potato eyes) are concentrated. Chitting takes about six weeks, during which time several shoots develop. The potatoes are ready for planting when the shoots are 2–2.5cm (¾–1in) long; if the shoots are longer, they will need to be handled very carefully so that they are not broken in planting.

If large-sized, early potatoes are wanted surplus sprouts can be rubbed off at planting, leaving only two or three on a plant; this will not result in as high a yield. With maincrop potatoes the aim is to have as many eyes and sprouts as possible.

Planting Planting can start in mid-March or early April, starting with the earliest cultivars. Avoid planting in cold soils: theoretically the soil at a depth of 10 cm (4 in) should have reached a temperature of 6 C (43 F) for three consecutive days before planting. Don't plant where the risk of heavy frost is still high. Early plantings can also be protected with cloches or films (see below). Planting with later cultivars can continue in April and May. Close planting of small tubers in June and July will give 'new potatoes' late in the year.

A general fertilizer can be worked into the soil just before planting, followed by a nitrogenous topdressing during growth. (See Fertilizers, p 17.)

The highest yields of large potatoes are obtained

Plant potato tubers rose end uppermost.

Earth up tubers to prevent them greening.

Early potatoes are lifted when required.

Maincrop potatoes being dried before storage.

by planting fairly small seed potatoes, about the size of a hen's egg. The old practice of cutting large potatoes in half is not recommended as it encourages disease. Reject any diseased potatoes.

A drill 7.5–15 cm (3–6 in) deep is made with a draw hoe or spade, or individual holes are made with a trowel. Plant the rose end uppermost, so that the seed is covered by about 2.5 cm (1 in) of soil. If the tubers have been sprouted, take care not to break the sprouts in planting and when raking the soil back into the drill or hole.

Early potatoes are planted 30–38 cm (12–15 in) apart in rows 38–50 cm (15–20 in) apart. Maincrop potatoes are normally grown 38 cm (15 in) apart in rows 76 cm (2½ ft) apart. However, optimum yields are obtained by varying the spacing according to the size of the tuber and the growth characteristics of the cultivar. In practice there is much latitude over spacing.

Protecting the early crop The early potato crop can be brought on up to two weeks earlier by covering with a crop covers (see Protected cropping, p 49), or simply with ordinary clear polythene film over hoops. Anchor the films into the soil after planting. With a perforated film, allow the potatoes to grow under it for about four weeks after emerging through the soil, then slit the film in stages down the centre. (See Protected cropping, p 49.) Fleecy films can be left in place until all risk of frost is past.

The young growths of early potatoes can be protected from late frost by drawing up a little soil over them, or by covering them with up to 5 cm (2 in) of straw or bracken, or even with a couple of layers of newspaper, if frost is forecast in late spring. Plants affected with frost suffer a setback, but normally recover, though there may be a reduction in yield.

Earthing up

Potatoes are 'earthed up' during growth, to prevent the greening of tubers which are pushed to the surface. Green potatoes are poisonous and should never be eaten. Earthing up is best done in one operation when the plants are about 23 cm (9 in) high, drawing earth 10 – 13 cm (4 – 5 in) high around the stems. It can also be done in several stages.

Several methods can be adopted to avoid earthing up. One is to plant very small tubers, each about 10–20 g (⅓–⅔ oz) in weight, about 10 cm (4 in) deep and 25 cm (10 in) apart. With this moderately close spacing of small tubers none is forced to the surface and the crop can be grown flat. It will give reasonable yields.

Early potatoes can also be grown under black polythene sheeting to exclude light. Plant the potatoes, then cover the ground with the film, anchoring the edges in slits made in the soil with a trowel. When the potato shoots push up against the film, cut slits in it and pull the plants through. Alternatively, lay the film flat on the ground, make holes in it, and plant the potatoes through the holes. When ready the potatoes are harvested simply by pulling back the film. They will be found on the soil surface.

Watering

The yield, quality and earliness of potatoes is influenced by the water supply. With early potatoes, *highest yields* are obtained by watering every 10 to 14 days in dry weather during the growing period, at the rate of 16–22 litres / sq m (3–4 gal / sq yd). To get high yields the potatoes should not be lifted until the foliage starts to die back. However, if very early potatoes are wanted, the plants should be watered when the tubers are just starting to form and are the size of marbles. This usually coincides with flowering. Water at similar rates as above.

With maincrop potatoes, watering is generally unnecessary until the marble stage. A single heavy watering of about 22–27 litres / sq m (4–5 gal / sq yd) at this stage increases both the total yield and tuber size. Watering can start about 10 days earlier with small-tubered cultivars. There is some evidence that watering reduces the number of potatoes with common scab.

Raising potatoes from seed and plantlets

An innovation which may become established practice in future is to raise potatoes from true seeds, as opposed to seed potato tubers. The advantages lie in the seeds being very healthy, and far less bulky to handle than tubers. Seeds are sown indoors in potting compost, the seedlings eventually being potted up in 5 cm (2 in) pots, and hardened off well before planting out. Once established the plants are earthed up and grown as normal potatoes.

Potato 'plantlets' are a parallel development in which disease-free, very small plants are initially raised by tissue culture. The plants are similarly potted up, hardened off and planted out. At present not many cultivars suited to English conditions are available in either of these forms, but they are widely used in other parts of the world and may become popular here in future.

Potatoes in containers

Early, and even maincrop potatoes, are sometimes grown in pots or tubs. The minimum size of container would be 30 cm (12 in) width and depth. Use potting compost or good garden soil into which plenty of compost has been worked. Plant two chitted potatoes in a 30 cm (12 in) pot, resting on 10–13 cm (4–5 in) of soil or compost. Add another 10 cm (4 in) of soil or compost to cover them. When the stems are about 15 cm (6 in) high add another 10 cm (4 in) of soil or compost, and repeat if necessary until

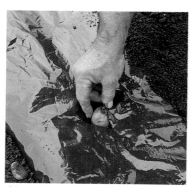

Plant potatoes through black film to avoid earthing up.

The shoots grow through the film while tubers develop below.

Pull back the film to harvest surface-growing tubers.

the plants are within 5 cm (2 in) of the rim of the container.

Harvesting

Early potatoes are lifted as required, as early in the season as possible. Opening of the flowers is often an indicator that the tubers have reached an edible size.

If the maincrop potatoes are healthy, and the growing conditions good, they can be left in the soil to bulk up until September. The later they are left, however, the greater the slug damage is likely to be in gardens where slugs are a problem.

The haulm can be cut back in September, leaving the plants another two weeks before lifting. Choose a good drying day, and lift them carefully to minimize damage. Leave the tubers on the ground to dry for two or three hours before storing them. Take care to dig up any tiny tubers, which can carry over disease in the soil for another year. Potatoes can be stored in frost-free sheds. (See Storage, p 51.) They must be always kept in the dark, or they will turn green. Never store diseased or damaged tubers. Stored potatoes normally keep in good condition until the following May or June.

Pests and diseases

The most common pests are wireworm, cutworm, slugs and various species of potato cyst eelworm. Some cultivars have resistance to some species or strains of eelworm (such as the RO_1 strain), but it is a very complex situation. The best course in infected soils is to avoid growing potatoes or tomatoes for at least six years. The most serious diseases are potato blight, common scab, potato mosaic virus and potato leaf roll virus. Some potatoes have a degree of resistance to potato blight. For symptoms and other control measures, see p 58ff.

Measures against potato blight One of the commonest problems with potatoes, the disease potato blight, is first seen as brown patches on the leaves. (See also Pests and diseases, p 62.) It is most likely to be serious in warm, wet weather in late June, July and August. Crops can be sprayed preventively and in the early stages of infection to try and limit incidence. (Organic gardeners can spray with a copper fungicide.) Some modern potato cultivars have some resistance to blight, but this applies to few of the early cultivars. Early potatoes should therefore be lifted as early as possible, in June or July, to avoid infection and prevent blight spreading.

Where potatoes are starting to be badly affected cut back the haulm – the stems and leaves – to about 5 cm (2in) above ground level, in late August. Leave the crop another two weeks for the tuber skins to harden before lifting. Burn the infected leaves. This measure will help to prevent the spread of blight.

Recommended cultivars

Early 'Arran Pilot', 'Epicure', 'Foremost', 'Maris Bard', 'Pentland Javelin' (resistant to RO_1 eelworm).
Second early 'Estima' (blight-resistant), 'Marfona', 'Wilja'.
Maincrop 'Cara' (resistant to RO_1 eelworm), 'Desiree', 'Maris Piper' (resistant to RO_1 eelworm), 'Pentland Squire' (some slug resistance), 'Romano'.

(Cultivars vary considerably in their cooking qualities and in resistance and susceptibility to a wide range of pests, including slugs, diseases, and conditions such as drought.)

Potatoes can be grown in containers.

New potatoes harvested from a container-grown plant.

Cut back and burn blighted potato haulm.

Radishes
(Raphanus sativus)

In this country radishes are grown almost entirely for their roots, which can be available from the garden all year round. There are two main types. The small radishes are grown mainly in the summer months for use raw. They are round or long in shape, with white, red, pink or bicoloured skin. Most cultivars have to be used soon after maturing or the plants start to run to seed and the roots become woody or hollow.

Less well-known are the various types of large radishes. These include the long white Japanese 'mooli' types, used in summer, and the hardy Chinese and Spanish winter radishes, which can be either lifted and stored, or left in the soil, for use in winter. The average mooli is about 20 cm (8 in) long and 5 cm (2 in) diameter, while the winter radishes, which can be red-, white-, black- or violet-skinned and round or long, often weigh 500 g (over 1 lb). All the large radishes can be used raw or cooked like turnips. They may need to be peeled. (For the many colourful types of oriental radish see Further reading, 'Oriental Vegetables', p 158.)

Radishes can be cultivated also for the young seed pods, which can be very crisp and tasty, and for the seedling leaves, grown as a cut-and-come-again salad crop. This crop is sometimes known as 'leaf radish'. (For cultivation of leaf radish see Salad plants, p 152.)

Soil / site
Radishes normally require an open site, though mid-summer sowings can be made in light shade, or intersown between other crops. Soil should be light, well-drained and fertile: rich, sandy soils are ideal. The soil should have been manured for a previous crop. Rotate radishes in the brassica group, as they are subject to the same pests and diseases. This is more important for winter radishes, which are in the soil for several months, than for the summer radishes which may be ready within a month of sowing.

Cultivation
Provided radish seeds are stored properly (see Seeds p 29), they will retain viability up to 10 years. Seeds will germinate in a wide range of soil temperatures, and can be sown for much of the year. Some cultivars are more suited to sowing at some seasons than others. The principal sowing times are given below.

Sow *in situ* 13 mm (½ in) deep, as thinly as possibly, ideally about 2.5 cm (1 in) apart in rows about 15 cm (6 in) apart. If seeds are sown more thickly seedlings will need to be thinned to 2.5 cm (1 in)

Winter radish 'Black Spanish Round' is white fleshed beneath its dark skin.

apart. Alternatively, the seeds can be broadcast.

As radishes mature rapidly they are often used for catch crops and intersowing. (See Planning for continuity, p 25.) The seeds can also be mixed before sowing with the seeds of a slow-germinating crop, such as parsnip or parsley, or can be 'station sown' with them (see p 31). The radishes germinate first and so mark the rows for weeding. They can be pulled for use while the other seedlings are still small.

Radishes never develop well if at any stage they become overcrowded and lanky. The quality of all types is best where they are grown fast. In dry soil conditions water the bottom of the drills before sowing to encourage rapid germination. (See Sowing outdoors, p 31). Radishes must also have adequate water throughout growth to prevent them becoming woody or running to seed, but they should not be overwatered or leaves develop at the expense of roots. In dry weather water at the rate of 11 litres / sq m (2 gal / sq yd) per week. Radishes should not require any feeding during growth. (For Fertilizers, see p 17.)

The season can be extended by sowing under cover in cloches or frames. (See Protected cropping, p 46.) Make early sowings from February to April, and late sowings in September and October.

Small radishes For a continuous crop throughout the summer months make small successional sowings outdoors at about 10-day intervals from late February (in warm situations and light soil), until September.

A range of small summer radishes showing the various shapes available.

Summer radish ready for harvest. If any run to seed, the young crisp seed pods can be used.

Sow *in situ* 13 mm (½ in) deep, as thinly as possibly, ideally about 2.5 cm (1 in) apart in rows about 15 cm (6 in) apart. If seeds are sown more thickly seedlings will need to be thinned to 2.5 cm (1 in) apart. Alternatively, the seeds can be broadcast.

Small radishes can be sown also in unheated (or slightly heated) greenhouses and tunnels, roughly from mid-October to February. *Use special cultivars bred for the purpose;* these have less leaf than summer cultivars and take longer to develop. Thin to about 5 cm (2 in) apart each way. Take care not to overwater them, but very dark-looking leaves are a sign that watering is necessary. This winter crop may not always succeed but is worth trying.

Mooli radish With most types it is advisable to delay sowing until June, as mooli radishes have a tendency to bolt if sown early in the year. A few cultivars are bolt-resistant, and can be sown a month or so earlier. Thin standard mooli to 7.5–10 cm (3–4 in) apart. On average they take seven to eight weeks to mature.

Large types of winter radish Sow in July and August a little deeper and more thinly than small radishes (see above). Seedlings can be thinned in stages to about 15-23 cm (6–9 in) apart each way, depending on the cultivar, or grown in rows 20–25 cm (8–10 in) apart.

Harvesting
Small radishes are pulled as required. Winter radishes can be left in the ground during the winter. Cover them with straw to make lifting easier in severe weather. Alternatively, in very cold areas or very heavy soils where slug damage is likely to be serious lift winter radishes in autumn, trim the tops, and store the radishes in boxes in a cool shed or outdoors in clamps. (See Storage, p 51.)

Radish seed pods Immature, green, radish seed pods can be used raw in salads, or cooked or pickled. On the whole the bigger the radish the larger the seed pod, though there is enormous variation in flavour from mild to piquant. Some cultivars, such as 'Munchen Bier' are especially grown for the seed pod. Otherwise use ordinary radishes which have run to seed, or leave a few winter radishes in the soil to run to seed in spring. Radish seed pods *must* be picked when they are still crisp and green and can be snapped in half.

Pests
The most serious pest is flea beetle, which attacks seedlings. Slugs and cabbage root fly can both attack roots. Damage is most serious on large types of radish. For symptoms and control, see p 58ff.

Recommended cultivars
Small radishes 'Crystal Ball', 'French Breakfast', 'Long White Icicle', 'Pink Beauty', 'Pontvil', 'Red Prince' ('Prinz Rotin'), 'Sparkler'.
Small radishes for winter crops under cover 'Helro', 'Robino', 'Saxa'.
Mooli radish F_1 'April Cross' (slow-bolting), 'Mino Early', F_1 'Minowase Summer Cross' (slow-bolting).
Winter Radish 'Black Spanish Round' (round and long), 'Cherokee', 'China Rose'.

Rhubarb

(Rheum × cultorum)

Although used as a fruit, rhubarb is always considered a part of the vegetable garden. It is a perennial plant with very large leaves, grown for its pink or greenish leaf stalks. The stalks are ready from late spring into summer, but can be forced in darkness for an earlier crop. In good conditions rhubarb can grow into large plants up to 1.8 m (6 ft) across.

Site / soil

Rhubarb is deep rooting, and will grow on almost any soil, including peat, sand or clay, provided it is well drained and fertile. It tolerates acid soils. Rhubarb needs an open site and will not grow well in the shade. With its large, broad leaves it can make a good weed-smothering boundary to a vegetable plot.

Prepare the soil beforehand by digging in plenty of farmyard manure or compost, and removing perennial weeds. This is most important, as a healthy crop can remain in the ground for 10 or more years. On very heavy soil or in waterlogged situations rhubarb is sometimes planted on ridges.

Cultivation

Rhubarb can be raised from seeds (see below), but is normally raised by planting 'sets' obtained by dividing up established plants. A set consists of a piece of chunky rhubarb root or rootstock with some fibrous root attached, plus at least one bud.

Rhubarb plants are liable to suffer from virus diseases (which gradually weaken them), so to start growing rhubarb either buy sets of a good cultivar which is guaranteed virus-free or dig up a vigorous, healthy plant for division. This must be done during the dormant season when the leaves have died back, usually between late October and March. If possible choose a two- or three-year-old plant; if an older plant is used select the buds from the outside edges which are more vigorous. Use a spade to divide the root into several wedge-shaped pieces about 10 cm (4 in) across the top.

The best time to plant rhubarb is November or December, though it can be planted up to March. Later plantings, however, may suffer from the desiccating effects of spring winds. Plant sets 76 – 90 cm (2½ – 3ft) apart. Commercial growers plant rhubarb so that the buds are covered by 2.5 cm (1 in) of soil; traditionally, cultivars with large buds were planted with buds just sticking out of the ground to prevent them rotting.

Cultivars of rhubarb can also be raised from seeds. Sow seeds in March or April in a seedbed, in drills about 2.5 cm (1 in) deep and 30 cm (12 in) apart. Thin seedlings to 15 cm (6 in) apart. There is bound to be a lot of variation in quality, so try and select the strongest looking plants for planting out in autumn or the following spring. In subsequent years divide the most productive plants to increase your stock. Seed-raised plants should not normally be pulled for use until the second season after planting.

Seeds can also be sown indoors, and seedlings pricked out into small pots for planting out in early summer. This results in good plants and light pulling may be possible in the following season.

The secret of good rhubarb is to keep it moist in summer and dry in winter. It will respond to watering in summer, and apply a mulch to retain moisture in the soil. (See Mulching, p 44.) Every year spread a thick layer of well-rotted manure or compost around the plants in autumn or spring. A nitrogenous fertilizer can also be applied in spring (see Fertilizers, p 18), but where heavy dressings of manure are used this is unnecessary.

Provided the ground is relatively free of perennial weeds initially, little further weeding is required as the rhubarb leaves blanket the ground. Remove any flowering stems which appear. If plants are allowed

Divide established, dormant plants to get sets for planting.

Rhubarb sets are best planted in November and December.

Forcing rhubarb with a traditional lidded clay pot.

to flower the stems tend to become paler, and rots may set in when the hollow flower stems die back. Some cultivars are more likely to flower than others. Flowering is also more common in wet seasons and where too much nitrogen has been applied.

Plants normally remain productive for at least five seasons, sometimes longer. If they show signs of decline, by producing masses of thin stalks, lift and divide the crowns (the whole root). It is sound practice to divide up and replant a few crowns each year.

Harvesting

The first rhubarb is ready in February or March, and harvesting can continue into summer, depending on the cultivar. Rhubarb should be pulled rather than cut. Hold the stem near the base and pull outwards. With plants raised from sets don't pull any stems until the second growing season, and then pull sparingly. In the following years plants can be harvested as long as the stems are firm: there is little risk of weakening a well-established plant.

Forcing

The purpose of forcing is to bring the plant into production a little sooner, and to produce exceptionally tender shoots. The simplest method of forcing is to cover the dormant crowns in December or January with a layer of straw, dead leaves or bracken about 10 cm (4 in) thick, and then to exclude light completely by putting an upturned bucket, or a traditional, lidded, clay rhubarb blanching pot over the plant. This stimulates growth, producing very tender pinkish stalks two to three weeks earlier than otherwise.

For an even earlier crop lift a root or two in November. Unless there has been cold weather already, leave the roots on the ground for a few days to expose them to low temperatures. This helps to break their natural dormancy. They can then be forced indoors in a cool room, or in a greenhouse. For forcing indoors pack the roots close together in a large box or bin, with soil around them to prevent them drying out. Otherwise plant them in the soil under the staging in a greenhouse. In either case exclude light by covering them with an upturned box, bucket, or any small frame covered with black polythene. The covering will need to be about 38–45 cm (15–18 in) high to allow for the growth of the stems. Forcing is sometimes done in black plastic sacks. Keep the plants watered so they do not dry out. High temperatures are unnecessary: growth starts at temperatures between 7.5 and 16 C (45 and 60 F). The stems can normally be pulled within about five weeks. In most cases the roots are exhausted by being forced and should be thrown out. Sets can be taken from them for replanting *before* forcing.

Diseases

Rhubarb plants may become diseased-looking and weakened through attacks by honey fungus, crown rot or virus diseases. There is no remedy, so plants must be dug up and burnt, and new stock planted on a fresh site.

Recommended cultivars

Early: 'Champagne', 'Timperley Early'.
Late: 'Victoria'.

Salsify flower buds and flowering shoots are tender and delicious if cooked like asparagus.

Salsify (left) has light brown roots in contrast to the black skinned scorzonera (right).

Salsify and scorzonera
(Tragopogon porrifolius, Scorzonera hispanica)

Salsify is a hardy biennial grown for its roots, which are creamy white and are used in winter. The young shoots (chards) of overwintered plants, and the mauve flower buds and flowering shoots are edible.

Soil / situation / cultivation
Salsify needs a relatively open situation. The roots develop best on deep, light, stone-free soil. The soil should have been manured for the previous crop.

Sow from March to May, 10 mm (⅜ in) deep, in rows 15 cm (6 in) apart. Thin to 10 cm (4 in) apart. Use fresh seeds as the viability of the seeds falls off rapidly. Keep the plants weeded and watered during the summer. The roots are ready for use from October onwards. For convenience or in very cold areas they can be lifted and stored in boxes (see Storage, p 51), otherwise they can be left in the soil during the winter.

If chards are required, cut off the old leaves about 2.5 cm (1 in) above ground level in autumn, and earth up the roots with about 13 cm (5 in) of soil. Well-blanched chards will push their way through and be ready in spring. Alternatively, cover the tops of the plants with at least 13 cm (5 in) of straw, bracken or dry leaves when growth starts in spring.

If flower buds and flowering shoots are required leave a few plants in the soil to flower the following spring. Pick the buds just before they open with about 10 cm (4 in) of stem. Buds and stems are tender and delicious. Cook them like asparagus.

SCORZONERA

Scorzonera is very similar to salsify, although it is a hardy perennial, with broader leaves, black-skinned roots and yellow flowers.

Soil / situation / cultivation
See salsify. Scorzonera is generally grown and used like salsify. However, being a perennial it can be left in the ground for a second season. Lift a few roots in the autumn, and if they are only pencil thick, leave the remainder in the ground until the following autumn. They will thicken up without toughening. Scorzonera can also be sown in August for use the following autumn. The flower buds are thick and succulent.

Seakale
(Crambe maritima)

Seakale is an exceptionally handsome, very hardy, perennial plant. It is native to the British Isles and is often found growing on sandy and shingle beaches, cliffs and rocks. A well-established plant can easily be 1m (3 ft 6 in) in diameter, with stems up to 60 cm (2 ft) high. Seakale is grown mainly for the unique flavoured stems, which are eaten raw after blanching in spring. The young flower heads and very young leaves can also be eaten raw, and the leaf midribs can be cooked.

Site / soil
Seakale should be grown in deep, rich, sandy soil. A pH of 7 is ideal: acid soils should be limed. Good drainage is essential, and heavy soils should be lightened with sand or grit. In very heavy soils it is difficult to lift the roots for forcing without damaging them. Work in plenty of well-rotted manure or compost before planting. Seakale must be in an open, sunny position, where it can be left undisturbed. It is closely related to brassicas, so should not be planted on soil infected with clubroot. It is a deep-rooting plant, and established plants survive drought well.

Cultivation
Seakale is normally raised from root cuttings, known as 'thongs', though it can also be raised from seeds. Seed-raised plants may be more vigorous. Plants often last eight or ten years, but they generally start

*Blanched shoots of seakale after being forced **in situ** using a traditional clay forcing pot.*

to deteriorate after about seven years, so it is advisable to replace a few plants each year.

Raising from thongs Thongs can be purchased or obtained from established plants. To take a thong from an established plant, select a healthy plant that is at least three years old, with no sign of rotting on the crown, and lift it carefully after the leaves have died back in November or December. Select side roots that are about pencil thickness, and cut them into pieces 7.5–15 cm (3–6 in) long. To avoid planting them upside down, make a straight cut across the top and a slanting cut across the bottom. Tie the cuttings into bundles, and stand them in a box of sand in a cool shed until March. By then buds will have appeared on the shoots.

Rub out all but the strongest central bud in preparation for planting out. Make a hole with a dibber, and plant the cuttings 2.5 cm (1 in) below soil level, 38 cm (15 in) apart each way. It is sometimes possible to buy young plants: they can be planted in spring or autumn.

Although thong-raised plants can be forced in the January following planting, it is best to allow the plants to build up for a complete year, and to start forcing the following winter or very early spring.

Raising from seed Seakale has very corky seeds, which enable them to float at sea for several years. For this reason germination can be very slow and erratic: it *can* take two to three years! The corky outer case can be removed carefully to speed up germination. Sow the seeds about 2.5 cm (1 in) deep in moist soil in spring, either in seedtrays, following by pricking out, or in a seedbed for transplanting, or *in situ*. If sowing *in situ*, start thinning the seedlings when they have three or four leaves. Results from seeds will be variable, so select and plant out only the strongest looking plants. They should not be forced until they are in their third season.

After planting little further attention is required. Remove any flowering shoots so the plant's energy goes into building up a good root system. The plants can be given a dressing of well-rotted manure in spring, or a general fertilizer or liquid feed. A seaweed-based fertilizer is suitable.

Forcing and harvesting
Plants can be either gently forced and blanched *in situ*, in which case the same plants can be grown for several years, or they can be lifted and forced in warmer conditions indoors. In this case they normally have to be discarded after forcing as the plants are exhausted.

Forcing in situ Any time after the crowns have died right back, from autumn until January, clear away the debris of rotting leaves, and cover the crowns with about 7.5 cm (3 in) of dry leaves. This helps raise the temperature. Then exclude light by covering them with a large 25–30 cm (10–12 in) bucket or flower pot with the drainage hole blocked, or black polythene attached to a wooden frame. Alternatively, use a traditional clay seakale pot. Whatever covering is used should be at least 38 cm (15in) high. Stems are ready for cutting within about three months. They can be cut when anything from 10–20 cm (4–8 in) long, using a sharp knife to cut them low down with a little piece of root attached. Stop cutting in May, and allow the plants to re-grow. They can be then blanched again the following year.

Forcing indoors Dig up the roots after the first frosts – or lift the roots earlier, but leave them on the ground to expose them to frost. Pack them into boxes or large pots, trimming off any awkward side roots; exclude light and force them in exactly the same way as rhubarb (*qv*) in a temperature of 16–21 C (60–70 F). Water sufficiently to keep the plants moist. They will be ready within a few weeks.

Pests and disease
Flea beetle may attack seedlings; clubroot can be a problem in infected soils. For control measures, see p 58ff.

Spinaches: **1** *'Ruby Chard';* **2** *Swiss chard;* **3** *perpetual spinach;* **4** *summer spinach;* **5** *New Zealand spinach.*

Spinach, leaf beets, New Zealand spinach

(*Spinacia oleracea, Beta vulgaris* subsp. *cicla, Tetragonia expansa*)

Several different vegetables are known or used as spinach.

The true spinaches are annuals, which will seed in their first season. They are relatively small leaved, though the leaves can be round or pointed, and thin, thick, smooth or crinkled in texture. Spinach is reasonably hardy.

The leaf beets belong to the beetroot family, but in this case the leaves, rather than the roots, are developed. They are hardy biennials, so do not normally run to seed in their first season. They are less susceptible to drought than true spinach, larger leaved, more prolific and robust, though perhaps less delicately flavoured.

The leaf beet group includes spinach beet or perpetual spinach, which looks like a dark, large-leaved spinach, and the Swiss chards, also known as seakale beet or silver chard. In the chards the leaf midrib and the leaf stalks are very swollen, and can be cut and used as a separate vegetable from the green parts of the leaf. The chards are robust, prolific and very handsome. Many forms have beautiful rose, red and silver coloured tints to the leaves, veins and stems. The best known of these is the red-stemmed 'Ruby Chard', which is, unfortunately, prone to bolting.

Yet another type of spinach is the half-hardy perennial, New Zealand spinach, a somewhat spiky-leaved, succulent plant, which spreads over the ground. It grows well in dry soils and in hot conditions which are unsuitable for the other spinaches and most leaf beets.

Site / soil

True spinach and leaf beets tolerate light shade. To grow well they need very fertile soil, rich in organic matter, well drained but moisture-retentive. Poor soils which dry out should be generally avoided as they encourage premature bolting. However, established Swiss chard plants in fertile soil can prove drought-tolerant. The pH should be neutral to slightly alkaline: acid soils should be limed. True spinach and leaf beets have high nitrogen requirements and respond to topdressings of general fertilizer or organic liquid feeds during growth. (See Fertilizers, p 17.)

The large dark leaves of perpetual spinach are ready for picking 10-12 weeks after sowing.

The pointed leaves of true or summer spinach.

New Zealand spinach needs frequent picking.

Both midrib and leaf of Swiss chard are edible.

'Ruby Chard' has red midribs and leaf veins.

New Zealand spinach requires an open position. Although it grows well in moist, fertile soils, it is also very drought-resistant and can grow in poorer dry soils without bolting.

Cultivation

Spinach Spinach grows best in the cooler, moist conditions of spring and autumn, when it grows rapidly. It is apt to run to seed in dry weather, especially if grown on dry soils. It matures rapidly, and can be used for catch-cropping and intercropping, especially where grown as a cut-and-come-again seedling crop. (See Sowing outdoors, p 33.) Young seedling spinach can be either cooked or used raw as a salad. Traditionally, 'round-seeded' types of spinach, which were considered better adapted to high temperatures, were used for the summer crop, and the 'prickly-seeded' types, which were reputedly hardier, for the winter crop. However the improved modern cultivars are often dual purpose, and the demarcation between the two types is becoming blurred.

For summer spinach sow *in situ* outdoors from late February (in mild areas, provided the soil is workable), until May. Early outdoor sowings can be protected with cloches or with crop covers (see Protected cropping, p 46), which in most cases should be removed by the end of April.

For a continuous supply make small successional sowings at three-week intervals. They will provide pickings from May to November, unless they bolt prematurely in hot weather. The crop can be covered with cloches in autumn to improve its quality.

Sow seeds about 2 cm (¾ in) deep, in rows about 30 cm (12 in) apart, thinning to 15 cm (6 in) between plants. Spinach and leaf beet should be sown thinly, and thinned early where necessary, to avoid overcrowding which encourages mildew.

For the cut-and-come-again crop sow thinly, spacing seeds about 5 cm (2 in) apart in rows 10 cm (4 in) apart, or broadcast seeds thinning out to about 7.5 cm (3 in) apart each way. The young leaves can be cut when 5-10 cm (2 – 4 in) high. Provided the soil is moist and fertile, often several cuttings can be made.

For winter spinach sow in August and September; thin plants to 23 cm (9 in) apart. These crops should give supplies from November until the following spring. The quality will be improved if they are sown under cloches, or with some form of protection. A late sowing in an unheated greenhouse or polytunnel can give excellent winter pickings. Cut-and-come-again sowings in August outdoors and September under cover are very productive.

Leaf beet The main sowings are made *in situ* in March and April for crops during summer and winter; these plants frequently continue cropping until the following May or June before running to seed. Sow as for spinach in rows 38-45 cm (15-18in) apart, thinning to 30 cm (12 in) apart.

A second sowing can be made in July and August. This will give lower yields, but will crop throughout winter and well into the following summer. Again, the overwintered crop will be of better quality if protected in some way. It is worth making an extra sowing in July or early August in seedtrays or modules for transplanting into an unheated polytunnel, greenhouse or frame in late summer or early autumn after the summer crops are lifted. This can often provide pickings in early spring when good quality fresh vegetables are scarce.

The perpetual spinach types are also very suited to growing as cut-and-come-again seedling crops; the larger leaved chards less so. (See spinach above.)

New Zealand spinach Seeds can be sown indoors in April, hardened off, and planted out after risk of frost at the end of May, or sown directly outdoors in mid-May. Sow or transplant about 45 cm (18in) apart each way; the plants can easily cover a square metre (square yard) of ground when mature. Seeds are sometimes slow to germinate, and can be soaked in water overnight before sowing to hasten germination.

Harvesting

Spinach may be ready for use 10 to 12 weeks after sowing. With true spinach and leaf beets either pick individual leaves, or cut the whole plant about 2.5 cm (1 in) above ground level, leaving it to resprout. With New Zealand spinach keep picking the young leaves and the tips of the shoots. The stem is discarded. Pick regularly or the leaves become tough.

Pests and diseases

The most common diseases of true spinach and leaf beet are downy mildew and leaf spots, usually due to poor drainage and lack of thinning. For symptoms and control, see p 63ff. Birds are also a serious problem, sparrows in particular attacking spinach and leaf beet, both at the young-seedling stage and when plants are mature. Preventive measures should be taken when the seed is sown. (See p 54.)

Some recommended cultivars

Spinach (Dual purpose) 'Norvak', 'Sigmaleaf'.
Swiss chard 'Fordhook Giant', 'Lucullus'.

Cultivars of perpetual spinach and New Zealand spinach are rarely listed.

Sweet corn

(Zea mays)

Sweet corn is a tender crop which needs a long growing season to do well. Currently, if grown north or west of a region roughly delineated by a line drawn from the Isle of Wight to the Wash, it will be successful outdoors only if fast-maturing, early cultivars are grown. This situation may change as improved cultivars are developed. Generally speaking, the later cultivars tend to be of better quality than the early cultivars.

The 'supersweet' sweet corn cultivars are about twice as sweet at the older cultivars, retain their sweetness longer after picking, and freeze well. However, they are less vigorous than other cultivars, and sowing must be delayed until conditions are warmer. They must also be grown in isolation from normal sweet corn cultivars or they will be cross-pollinated and lose their sweetness. In theory this should be a distance of about 540 m (1770 ft), so in small gardens it is advisable to grow either one type or the other.

'Mini-corn' cobs harvested when very tiny and immature are normally obtained by planting early cultivars about 15 cm (6 in) apart, and harvesting the cobs when about 7.5 cm (3 in) long. However very prolific cultivars are now being developed especially for harvest as 'mini-corn'.

Site / soil

Choose a warm, sheltered site, avoiding an exposed position. Sweet corn grows best on deep, well-drained, reasonably fertile, slightly acid soils. Avoid very dry soils and heavy, clay soils. The soil is best when it has been manured for a previous crop. Otherwise apply a base-dressing before sowing or planting. (See Fertilizers, p 17.)

Sweet corn leaves do not form a dense canopy, so sweet corn can be easily undercropped with crops such as marrows, courgettes, French beans, slow-bolting oriental greens, such as mizuna greens, and salad plants.

Cultivation

Sweet corn will not germinate at soil temperatures below 10 C (50 F). On average, this temperature is reached in early to mid-May in the south of the British Isles, and a couple of weeks later in the north. Plants are checked by transplanting and cannot be planted out until risk of frost is passed. So the most satisfactory way of starting sweet corn is to sow seeds in small pots or modules indoors. (See Sowing indoors, p 35.) This method is especially recommended for the supersweet cultivars.

Sow indoors in gentle heat in April. Sow two to three seeds per pot or module, 2.5–4 cm (1–1½ in) deep. Thin to one seedling after germination. Harden off well before planting out in late May or early June. If possible plant out under cloches, or use crop covers in the early stages. (See Protective cropping, p 46.)

Sweet corn can be sown *in situ* outdoors in May or early June, provided the soil is warm. These crops will be later than those sown indoors. Sow under cloches, or under individual jam jars, both of which must be removed when outgrown. Sweet corn can also be sown under clear plastic film, which will warm up the soil. After sowing the seeds cover them with the film. When the seeds germinate cut holes in the film and pull the seedlings through. (See also Mulching, p 44.) Sweet corn can also be covered with fine or fleecy net films after sowing or planting (see Protected cropping, p 49). Remove the film at the five-leaf stage. This will protect vulnerable seeds and seedlings against birds and the frit fly.

For outdoor sowings sow two to three seeds per station, thinning to one seedling after germination. Dressed seeds can be used to combat fungus diseases and frit fly. (See also pests below). Sweet corn is also a good subject for fluid sowing. (See Sowing outdoors, p 32.)

Sweet corn is wind-pollinated. Each of the 'silks' on the female flower has to be pollinated to get a well-filled cob. To help pollination sweet corn should be planted in a block formation rather than in long rows. Either plant 35 cm (14 in) apart each way,

Sow sweetcorn in blocks to aid pollination.

Thin the seedlings after germination.

Earth up stems to keep the plants stable.

Sow sweetcorn outdoors under jam jars.

Sweetcorn is ripe and ready for harvest when the tassle at the end of the cob turns brown.

or 25–30 cm (10–12 in) apart in rows about 60 cm (2 ft) apart. Short cultivars such as 'Butter Imp' can be planted a little closer. Pollination may be poor in wet summers, resulting in 'gappy' cobs.

Sweet corn seems to yield more highly if mulched with black plastic film. This is best done by raising plants indoors, and planting them through the film. (See Mulching, p 44.) Mulching with plastic film or organic material will help control weeds and conserve moisture.

When plants are between 30–45 cm (12–18 in) high, the stems can be earthed up to make the plants more stable. This cannot be done where they are mulched with plastic film. In very windy areas they can be tied to canes. If necessary hoe them in the early stages, but only hoe shallowly, or the roots will be damaged.

Little watering is necessary until flowering begins, and later when the grains are swelling. At these stages give a heavy watering of 22 litres / sq m (4 gal / sq yd) to improve the size and quality of the cobs.

Harvesting

A sweet corn plant normally produces only one or two cobs. These are ready from July to October, depending on the cultivar. There is a tendency in this country to harvest cobs when over-mature. They are more tender and digestible if picked earlier. An indication of ripeness is the tassel turning brown, and the cobs leaning at about a 45-degree angle to the stem. Another clue is obtained by pressing a thumb nail into one of the grains. If the juice

exuded is milky, the cob is ready: if it is watery it is under-ripe; if doughy over-ripe. Snap off the cobs just before they are required, as in most cultivars the sugar is rapidly converted to starch after picking, so the flavour is lost. This may be delayed in some new cultivars, while the supersweet cultivars may retain their sweetness for up to a week after picking.

Pests

Frit fly is the most common pest. (For symptoms and control, see p 62.) Mice can steal the seeds; slugs feed on young seedlings and birds sometimes uproot seedlings. Take measures against slugs, set mouse traps, and protect seedlings from birds with strong black cotton over the rows.

Recommended cultivars

(*Hybrids, in approximate order of maturity.*)
Earlies 'Earliking', 'Sunrise', 'Earlibelle', 'Candle' (supersweet), 'Sweet Nugget' (supersweet).
Late 'Reward', 'Sundance', 'Sweet 77' (supersweet).

Different types of tomatoes: **1** *large yellow fruited;* **2** *beefsteak fruited;* **3** *cherry fruited;* **4** *small red and yellow pear-shaped;* **5** *standard fruited;* **6** *currant fruited.*

films, either as a low tunnel laid over hoops, or laid flat over the plants as a 'floating film'. (See Protected cropping, p 49.)

After planting cover the plants with the film, using either method. Leave the film in place until the flowers can be seen pressing against it, usually some time in mid-June. At this stage start to 'wean' the plants by making intermittent cuts about 1 m (3 ft 6 in) long in the film, down the centre. A week later cut the remaining gaps, but leave the film in place on either side of the plants to give additional shelter. Tomatoes grown under these systems can be raised by fluid sowing, and be planted through plastic film mulches. (For both see above.)

Tall tomato cultivars need to be tied to 1.2 m (4 ft) canes or stakes, put in when planting, or to two or three parallel wires run between stakes. In greenhouses the stems can be twisted as they grow around strings suspended from above.

With tall cultivars the sideshoots which develop in the axils of the leaves must be removed as they appear. To ensure that a reasonable crop matures and ripens before the end of the growing season plants have to be 'stopped' by removing the growing point. This is generally done in late July or early August: in the north this is usually after three trusses have set; in the south after four or five have set. Cut or nip out the growing point a couple of leaves above the top truss.

Once outdoor tomatoes are established watering is not usually required until flowering starts. From this stage onwards, especially in dry weather, plants benefit from fairly heavy watering at the rate of at least 11 litres / sq m (2 gal / sq yd) per week. This will result in higher yields of larger fruit, but may jeopardize the flavour. Tomatoes grown in pots or growing bags need regular watering throughout growth. Irregular watering often results in blossom end rot, a disorder in which sunken patches appear on the top of fruit. (See p 65.)

The outdoor crop normally requires no supplementary feeding, unless grown in a container. In this case use a tomato liquid feed according to the manufacturer's instructions, or an organic liquid feed. Bush tomatoes should never be given too much nitrogen, or they tend to make leafy growth at the expense of fruit.

During the growing season remove and burn withered and diseased leaves.

Harvesting

Unless given protection, outdoor tomatoes are normally ready from about mid-August. Pick fruit as ripe as possible to get the best flavour. In late September cordon plants can be mulched with straw, then cut down from their supports (leaving the roots

Mulch with straw to keep bush fruits clean.   *Ripen bush type* in situ *under cloches.*

in the soil) and laid on the straw. Cover them with cloches to enable the fruit to ripen. Bush cultivars can be cloched *in situ*.

Tomato fruits are damaged by exposure to frost or very low temperatures, so if frost threatens uproot the plants, and hang them by their roots in a greenhouse or indoors; the fruit will continue ripening slowly. Fruits can also be cut with about 10 cm (4 in) of stem, like a bunch of grapes, and hung between two horizontal canes to ripen outdoors or in a greenhouse. Or they can be picked individually, wrapped loosely in paper, and put in a drawer or cupboard to ripen.

Pests, diseases and disorders

Outdoor tomatoes suffer from few pests, other than potato cyst eelworm. The most serious diseases are damping off in the seedling stage, and grey mould (*Botrytis*), stem rot, potato blight and potato mosaic virus. Tomatoes are also very susceptible to hormone weedkiller damage and magnesium deficiency, which causes the leaves to yellow. (For symptoms and control measures, see p 58ff.) Indoor tomatoes suffer in addition from leaf mould (*Cladosporium*), various wilting diseases caused by diseased roots, greenback, blotchy ripening, sunscorch and oedema. (See Further reading, p 158.) Tomatoes in unheated greenhouses suffer from whitefly.

Recommended cultivars

Tall cultivars 'Britain's Breakfast', 'Dombito' (beefsteak), 'Gardener's Delight' (cherry), 'Golden Sunrise' (yellow), F_1 'Super Marmande' (semi-tall 'Marmande' type), F_1 'Sweet 100' (cherry).
Tall cultivars for unheated greenhouses (all hybrids) 'Danny', 'Shirley'.
Bush cultivars (all hybrids) 'Alfresco', 'Red Alert', 'Sleaford Abundance', 'Tumbler'.
Dwarf F_1 'Totem'.

Salad plants

The following are brief notes on the cultivation of some traditional, low-growing plants often described as 'salad herbs' as their main use is in salads. Most are winter-hardy and particularly useful in autumn, winter and early spring, when lettuces are hard to grow. Many respond well to cut-and-come-again treatment. (See Sowing outdoors, p 33.)

Those marked * can be left in the open in winter. However, if protected with cloches, or planted under cover, say in an unheated greenhouse or polytunnel, their quality and yield will be improved greatly, and they will start into renewed growth earlier in spring.

Claytonia / winter purslane
(*Montia perfoliata*)*
This is a mild-flavoured, normally hardy annual with very pretty, succulent, heart-shaped leaves. It grows best on light, sandy soils and tolerates low fertility, but can be grown also on heavier soils. It tolerates shade. It is most useful in spring when growth is very rapid.

Sow seeds in April and May for summer crops, and in July and August for winter use. A late sowing can be made at the end of August or early September to transplant under cover for a very early spring crop. Claytonia can be grown either as individual plants, or as a cut-and-come-again seedling crop. It is normally sown *in situ*, though seeds can be sown in seedtrays and seedlings transplanted.

For individual plants sow very thinly in rows about 23 cm (9in) apart, thinning to 13–15 cm (5–6 in) apart. For a seedling crop sow in wide drills or broadcast.

The leaves, stems, and flower stalks are all edible. The plant re-sprouts several times after cutting. If a few plants are allowed to run to seed they will seed themselves. The seedlings can be transplanted to a selected site. Be warned, however, that claytonia can become a highly invasive weed.

Corn salad / lamb's lettuce
(*Valerianella locusta*)*
Corn salad is a very hardy annual, with small, mild-flavoured leaves. The most productive English or Dutch type has rather floppy leaves. A smaller, rosette-shaped French type has deep green, smaller, more erect leaves and is exceptionally hardy.

Corn salad will grow in most soils and situations. Being small and undemanding it is suited to intercropping and undercropping. Make the main sowings for winter use in July and August, sowing seeds on a firm seedbed either broadcast, or in rows about 15 cm (6 in) apart. Keep the seeds moist until they have germinated. (See sowing in dry conditions, p 32.) Thin plants to about 10 cm (4 in) apart. A second sowing can be made in March and April for summer use. Seeds can also be sown in wide drills or broadcast, and the seedlings left unthinned, as a cut-and-come-again seedling crop, though corn salad does not regrow as rapidly as some salad plants. Harvest corn salad either by picking off a few leaves at a time, or by cutting the whole plant 2.5 cm (1 in) above ground level, or by uprooting it. A few plants left to run to seed will seed themselves; seedlings are easily transplanted.

Dandelion (*Taraxacum officinale*)*
A comon garden weed, dandelion is a hardy perennial plant, though the leaves normally die back in midwinter. It is used as a salad plant, mainly in autumn and spring. The leaves are sharp-flavoured, but the plant can be blanched in darkness to make the leaves paler and sweeter. Young leaves can be used unblanched. The top of the root is distinctly flavoured and is also eaten in salads. The flowers are used to make wine. Ordinary wild dandelions are

Leaves, stems and flowers of claytonia are edible.

Corn salad is a hardy annual with a mild flavour.

The pale, sweet leaves of blanched dandelion.

edible, but the selected cultivars offered in seed catalogues are more productive.

Dandelion tolerates a wide range of soils, though it does not grow well in waterlogged conditions. Sow seeds in spring and early summer, either *in situ* or in seedtrays for transplanting. Thin or plant so plants are spaced 35 cm (14 in) apart. Seedlings are sometimes thinned to only 5 cm (2 in) apart, so one flower pot can be used to blanch a group of seedlings. From late summer onwards blanch a few plants at a time by covering them with a darkened upturned pot. (See Endive, p 110.) It is not necessary to cut back the leaves. In very cold areas dandelion roots can be lifted, the leaves trimmed, and the roots forced as for Witloof chicory. (See p 104.)

Iceplant (*Mesembryanthemum crystallinum*)

This is a tender plant. It is a perennial in warm climates, but is grown as an annual in cool climates. It has very thick, succulent leaves and fleshy stems, both covered in tiny bladders which give it a sparkling appearance. It has a refreshing, slightly salty flavour, and is good in salads: it will keep without wilting for a couple of days after picking. It grows best in a sunny, sheltered situation, on fertile soil but tolerates poor soil.

Sow seeds indoors in late spring, and transplant seedlings outside after all danger of frost is past. Space plants about 30 cm (12 in) apart. During the summer stem cuttings can be taken to obtain a follow-on crop. In poor summers iceplant will do best under cloches or with some form of protection. Keep picking the young leaves and shoot tips, and remove any flowers which appear. Cover with cloches in autumn to prolong the season. Slugs can be a problem in wet and cold weather.

Land cress / American land cress
(*Barbarea verna*)*

This is a hardy biennial with shiny green, deeply indented leaves with a very strong watercress flavour. It is used both sparingly in salads and as a watercress substitute. It does best in fairly rich soils, and tolerates moist soils and shady situations. The summer crop is best sown in light shade.

Sow in July and August for supplies from autumn to spring, and in March to June for a summer supply. Sow seeds *in situ*, in rows about 20 cm (8 in) apart, thinning plants to about 15 cm (6 in) apart each way. Or grow them at equidistant spacing about 18 cm (7 in) apart each way. Transplant a few August-sown seedlings under cover for a more tender winter crop.

SALAD PLANNING CHART

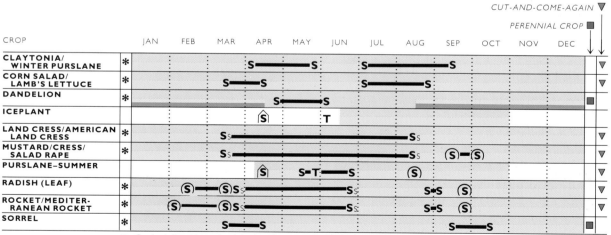

CUT-AND-COME-AGAIN ▼

PERENNIAL CROP ■

CROP		JAN	FEB	MAR	APR	MAY	JUN	JUL	AUG	SEP	OCT	NOV	DEC		
CLAYTONIA/ WINTER PURSLANE	*				S——S		S————S							▼
CORN SALAD/ LAMB'S LETTUCE	*			S——S			S————S							▼
DANDELION	*				S——S						■			
ICEPLANT					(S)		T							
LAND CRESS/AMERICAN LAND CRESS	*			Ss———————————Ss									▼
MUSTARD/CRESS/ SALAD RAPE	*			Ss———————————Ss			(S)—(S)					▼
PURSLANE–SUMMER					(S)	S–T——S		(S)					▼
RADISH (LEAF)	*		(S)——(S)Ss———————Ss			S–S	(S)					▼
ROCKET/MEDITER-RANEAN ROCKET	*		(S)——(S)Ss———————Ss			S–S	(S)					▼
SORREL	*		S———S					S———S		■			

*   Can be left outdoors in winter but if protected with cloches or planted in unheated polytunnel/greenhouse earlier growth with improved quality and yield will result.

KEY TO CHART SYMBOLS AND COLOURS

S Sow outdoors.

T Transplant to cropping position.

    Fresh harvest period.

    Forcing/Blanching period.

Ss Successional sowing/cropping outdoors.

(S) Sow outdoors under protection.

    Actual period of growth in the cropping situation.

    Cropping area *not* occupied.

(S) Sow in heat under protection.

▬▬▬▬ Duration of sowing period.

A few plants left to run to seed in spring will seed themselves; seedlings are easily transplanted. Land cress is often attacked by flea beetle at the seedling stage.

Mustard (*Sinapsis alba*)*
Cress / garden cress (*Lepidium sativum*)*
Salad rape (*Brassica napus* var. *napus*)*

These salad plants can be grown either without soil in dishes indoors, or in shallow seedtrays filled with soil or potting compost, or in garden soil. In seedtrays or garden soil they can be grown as a cut-and-come-again crop. In seedtrays they could be harvested over several weeks; in garden soil over several months depending on the conditions. Cress is the hottest-flavoured, mustard is milder, rape is very mild-flavoured.

For sowing indoors, line a dish with blotting paper or flannel to retain moisture, and sow the seeds evenly over it. To encourage growth seeds can be started in the dark and moved into the light after germination, when the seedlings are about 2.5 cm (1 in) high. Mustard and rape germinate slightly faster than cress, so if all three are wanted together, sow the cress a day or two sooner. Cut for use when 4–5 cm (1½–2 in) high. For a continuous supply sow at seven- to ten-day intervals.

If sowing in a seedtray simply sprinkle seeds evenly over the surface. For a cut-and-come-again seedling crop outdoors sow broadcast or in drills. The most successful sowings are in spring and late summer or autumn, as crops tend to run to seed in hot summer weather. Useful late sowings can be made in September and early October under cover of some kind, or in unheated greenhouses after tomatoes and summer crops are lifted. Often the results of these sowings can be cut a couple of times in autumn, and again in spring when temperatures warm up. Of the three plants, mustard tends to run to seed most rapidly, followed by cress and then rape. Rape can even be allowed to grow to about 20 cm (8 in) tall and used as greens for cooking.

Summer purslane (*Portulaca oleracea*)

This is a half-hardy annual, with succulent green or golden leaves and stems; both leaves and stems are edible. It has a mild, refreshing flavour. Purslane only grows well in warm conditions: grow it in a sunny, sheltered spot outdoors, or under some kind of protection. It does best on light, well-drained soils.

Sow in seedtrays indoors in April, or *in situ* outdoors in May or June, after all risk of frost is past. Purslane seedlings are very prone to damping off diseases (see p 63) if sown in cold soil or at low temperatures. Purslane is normally grown as single plants, which can be spaced about 15 cm (6 in) apart each way. It can also be grown very successfully as a cut-and-come-again seedling crop, when seeds are sown in wide drills or broadcast. Useful early and late crops can be obtained by sowing this way in an unheated greenhouse or frame. Sow in April for an early crop, and August for a late crop.

Keep picking the leaves and shoot tips, always leaving two leaves at the base of the stem to encourage further growth. Pick off any flowers which appear, or the leaves start to toughen. Any seed heads which develop are knobbly and unpleasant to eat. Take precautions against slugs when the plants are young.

Leaf radish (*Raphanus sativus*)*

Young radish leaves are tender and tasty and can be used in salads. Although most radish cultivars probably can be sown closely for use of the leaves, some have been selected especially for the purpose, notably the Japanese cultivar 'Bisai'. This cultivar is both heat- and cold-tolerant, is very vigorous, and is a useful cut-and-come-again seedling crop, best sown broadcast or in wide drills.

For a very early crop sow seeds under cover, in unheated greenhouses, frames, or polytunnels, in February or March. Follow this with outdoor sowings as soon as the ground is workable, and continue sowing in May and June. Sow again outdoors in late August or September, or under cover in late September or October for a winter crop. Midsummer sowings are likely to bolt prematurely. The plants can be cut at 5–7.5 cm (2–3 in) high as a seedling crop for salads, or left to grow to about 20 cm (8 in) high and cooked as greens. If they are thinned out a few 'mooli' type radishes will develop. Flea beetle can be a problem in the early stages. (See p 60.)

Rocket / Mediterranean rocket / Italian cress / rucola (*Eruca sativa*)*

This fairly hardy annual survives most winters in the open. Young leaves have an attractive, slightly spicy flavour, which can become very hot in mature leaves, or when plants are running to seed, or in hot, dry conditions. Rocket is used raw and cooked. It can be grown as individual plants, or as a cut-and-come-again seedling crop. It germinates at fairly low temperatures, but is apt to run to seed rapidly in hot weather.

Sow as for 'Biasai' radish above. If growing as single plants, thin seedlings to 15 cm (6 in) apart each way. Either pick single leaves for use, or cut the whole plant, or seedlings, about 2.5 cm (1 in) above ground level. In both cases plants will normally re-sprout. Flea beetle can be a problem at the seedling stage. (See p 60.)

Iceplant (see p 151) has succulent leaves and stems.

Landcress (see p 151) can be used like watercress.

A cut-and-come-again crop of cress outdoors.

A golden leaved form of summer purslane.

Mediterranean rocket is a spicy salad herb.

The large upright leaves of 'French' sorrel.

Sorrel (*Rumex* spp.)*

Sorrel is a very hardy perennial plant, native to the British Isles. The leaves have a sharp, lemony flavour, and are used sparingly in salads or to make soup. Sorrel is tolerant of a wide range of soil types, but grows best in fertile, moist conditions. It tolerates light shade, and is a useful city-garden plant. It can be grown as a semi-permanent edging to vegetable beds.

The large-leaved 'French' sorrel grows about 30 cm (12 in) tall, but 'buckler-leaved' sorrel, which has small, arrow-shaped leaves, is a somewhat sprawling ground-cover plant, about 20 cm (8 in) tall. In mild areas, and if grown under cover or protected with cloches, sorrel normally remains green all winter.

Either sow seeds *in situ* in spring or autumn, thinning seedlings to 25 – 30 cm (10 – 12 in) apart, or sow in seedtrays and transplant. Use the outer leaves of the plant first, leaving the central leaves to continue growing. Remove any seed heads which appear. It is advisable to renew plants every three or four years, as they may decline in vigour if constantly picked. If grown in moist soil a few plants can be left to run to seed and the seedlings can be transplanted to where they are required.

See also Texsel greens, p 96, and Oriental greens (pak choi, komatsuna and mizuna greens, p 93), all of which can be used as salad plants.

Culinary Herbs

As there are many specialist books on herbs, only brief notes on some of the most useful culinary herbs are included here. (For Parsley see p 126.) Most herbs can now be bought as young plants.

Basil (*Ocimum basilicum*)
Basil is a tender Mediterranean herb with a clove-like flavour. It grows best under cloches, or in a frame or greenhouse. Sow in seedtrays indoors in March or April, planting out under cover in May or outside when there is no longer any risk of frost, about 13 cm (5 in) apart. A second sowing can be made in June and July and the plants potted up to bring indoors for use during the winter. They normally last till about Christmas.

Besides the ordinary bush basil, the many interesting types now available include purple-leaved basil, lettuce-leaved basil (which has very large leaves), lemon-scented basil, and the tiny-leaved, very fragrant and compact Greek and dwarf basils.

Chervil (*Anthriscus cerefolium*)
Chervil is a rapidly growing hardy annual, rather like parsley in appearance, with an aniseed flavour. It can be available all year round, remaining green in winter. The summer crop should be grown in a shady position in fertile, moisture-retentive soil. The winter crop is best in a sunny position or under cover. Sow *in situ* in February to April for summer use. Sow in August for the autumn to spring crop, either *in situ* or in modules for transplanting under cover. (See Sowing indoors, p 33.) Thin or plant to about 10 cm (4 in) apart. Seedlings can be transplanted into a cold greenhouse or frame in September or October to give fresh supplies during the winter. A few plants left to run to seed in spring will often seed themselves and reappear later in the year.

Chives (*Allium schoenoprasum*)
Among the most commonly grown herbs, chives are often used as a substitute for spring onions, though they have a distinct flavour of their own. They need reasonably fertile, moisture-retentive soil to grow well. They are best sown in seedtrays indoors in spring, and planted out in groups of three or four seedlings with 23 cm (9 in) between clumps. Once established the clumps can be divided every few years in spring or autumn, and small clumps of a few plants replanted.

Chives should be cut back to ground level several times during the season to encourage vigorous growth. The flowering heads should be cut back

also, unless required for their decorative or culinary value. (The tiny individual flowers are colourful and tasty in salads and cooked dishes.) The foliage dies down in winter, but if a few plants are cloched they will start growing early in the year.

Chinese or garlic chives (*Allium tuberosum*) form

Sweet basil needs protection.

Chervil is a fast growing annual.

Chives have edible flowers and foliage.

Marjoram needs a summer trim.

Spearmint spreads rapidly.

Rosemary needs to be kept in shape.

Green-leaved common sage.

Summer savory is an annual.

an attractive, slow-growing plant with garlic-flavoured leaves and beautiful white flowers, both of which are edible and used for flavouring. Sow as ordinary chives above. (See also Further reading, 'oriental vegetables', p 158.)

Marjoram (*Origanum* spp.)

The marjorams have a very pleasant characteristic flavour. They grow best in good soil in a sunny position. Sweet or knotted marjoram (*O. marjorana*), is treated as an annual. Sow seeds indoors in March, or outdoors in April, eventually thinning or planting seedlings about 20 cm (8 in) apart. Pot marjoram (*O. vulgare*), is hardier and grown as a perennial. It can be similarly raised from seeds, or from softwood cuttings taken in early summer, or by dividing plants in autumn. Space plants 25–30 cm (10–12 in) apart. Trim back foliage in summer.

Mint (*Mentha* spp.)

Very many types of mint are cultivated, the commonest culinary mints being ordinary spearmint (*M. × spicata*) and the two soft, round-leaved mints: apple mint (*M. suaveolens*) and Bowles' mint (*M. villosa alopecuroides*).

Mints require rich, moist, weed-free soil. The site needs to be well prepared beforehand, by working in well-rotted manure or compost. Plant either young shoots with roots, or pieces of root, preferably in March or early April. Lay the roots horizontally about 5 cm (2 in) deep and about 23 cm (9 in) apart. After three or four years mint tends to exhaust the soil, so plants should be lifted in autumn, divided up, and replanted in a fresh site. Some mints can also be raised from seeds.

Mint normally dies back in winter, but a few roots can be lifted in autumn and planted in a box for overwintering in a greenhouse. They will come into growth very early in spring.

Rosemary (*Rosmarinus officinalis*)

An evergreen, perennial, Mediterranean shrub, rosemary is only hardy in the warmest parts of the country. Elsewhere it should be protected in winter, or grown in pots and brought under cover in winter. Grow it in a sheltered, sunny site in well-drained soil.

Rosemary is normally propagated from softwood cuttings taken in spring, or from semi-hardwood cuttings taken after flowering, or by layering. It can also be raised from seeds sown indoors in spring, though germination is apt to be erratic. (Cultivars must be raised from cuttings.) Plants can be trimmed back after flowering in late spring to keep them compact.

Sage (*Salvia officianlis*)

Sage is a perennial bushy plant which does best on light, well-drained soil. The green-leaved common sage is much hardier than the red, gold, and variegated forms. It can be raised from seeds sown in spring, or by taking heel or tip cuttings in May. Plant young plants or rooted cuttings in spring about 45–60 cm (18 in–2 ft) apart. If the lower parts of the bush are earthed up in spring, the covered shoots will produce roots which can be separated off and planted out. Cut the young growths back lightly in July after flowering to keep the bushes compact. Sage bushes tend to become 'leggy' and are best replaced every four or five years.

Savory (*Satureja* spp.)

The savories are strongly flavoured herbs. Summer savory (*S. hortensis*) is a tender annual, and likes rich soil and a sunny position. Sow outdoors in April, thinning to about 15 cm (6 in) apart. Winter savory (*S. montana*) is perennial, and can be grown on poor soil, provided it is well drained. Seeds can also be sown outdoors in spring, or in a frame in August or September, and planted out the following spring 15– 20 cm (6–8 in) apart. It can be raised more quickly from heel cuttings taken in spring, or by the division of old plants in March. Winter savory can be potted up in late summer for use indoors in winter.

Thyme (*Thymus* spp.)

There are many different thymes, common (*T. vulgaris*), lemon-scented (*T. × citriodorus*) and broad leaf (*T. pulegoides*) being the most frequently used for culinary purposes. They are hardy, low-growing bushy perennials and like dry, well-drained, sunny positions. They can be propagated either by sowing seeds in spring, planting out the seedlings 15 – 30 cm (6 – 12 in) apart, depending on cultivar, or by taking cuttings in April or May, or by dividing old plants. The last two methods give usable plants sooner than the first method. Thyme tends to become straggly and woody after three or four years, and should then be replaced.

Winter savory, a sprawling perennial. *Thyme is easy to propagate.*

MONTH-BY-MONTH IN THE VEGETABLE GARDEN

This, a reminder of the principal jobs in season, is based on average conditions in the southern half of England. Allowance must always be made for weather and locality: in mild districts spring sowings and plantings can often be done earlier, and autumn sowings and planting later, than those given. In the north and in colder areas the reverse is the case.

The main text should be consulted for appropriate cultivars for each sowing. The symbols used are the same as those in the vegetable and salad planning charts (see pp 68 and 151), and should be read in conjunction with the key at the bottom of the page.

JANUARY

s bulb onions **s** sugar-loaf chicory, radish **P** rhubarb

Clear, dig and manure land if not too wet.
Order seeds, seed potatoes, onion sets.
Check stored vegetables for signs of rotting.
Force rhubarb, Witloof chicory, seakale.
Harvest fresh Chinese and Jerusalem artichokes, Brussels sprouts, winter cabbage, winter heading cauliflower, oriental greens, celeriac, chicories, endive, leeks, protected winter lettuce, parsley, parsnip, winter radish, salsify, scorzonera, winter spinach, Swiss chard, salad plants.
Use from store Jerusalem artichokes, beetroot, carrots, garlic, onions, maincrop potatoes, marrows, shallots, swedes, turnips, winter radish, salsify, scorzonera.

FEBRUARY

s celeriac, lettuce, bulb onion
s broad beans, beetroot, texsel greens, carrots, sugar-loaf chicory, bulb onions, early peas, summer radish, spinach, turnip, salad plants.
s kohl rabi, spring onion, summer radish.
P globe artichoke, Jerusalem artichoke, garlic, onion sets, shallots.

Force Witloof chicory, rhubarb, seakale.
Chit seed potatoes.
Top dress overwintered Japanese onions.
Dig and manure light ground when suitable, prepare early seed beds.
Harvest fresh Chinese and Jerusalem artichokes, sprouting broccoli, Brussels sprouts, winter cabbage, calabrese, winter heading cauliflower, kale, oriental greens, celeriac, chicories, endive, leeks, protected winter lettuce, parsley, parsnip, radish, rhubarb, salsify, scorzonera, seakale, winter spinach, Swiss chard, salad plants.
Use from store Jerusalem artichoke, beetroot, carrots, garlic, bulb onions, potatoes (maincrop), shallots, swedes, turnips, winter radish, salsify, scorzonera.

MARCH

s aubergine, celeriac, celery, lettuce, parsley, peppers, outdoor tomatoes.
s beetroot, summer cauliflower, carrots, salad plants.
s broad beans, beetroot, Brussels sprouts, summer and autumn cabbage, calabrese, texsel greens, carrots, sugar-loaf chicory, kohl rabi, leeks, summer lettuce, bulb onions, spring onions, early peas, summer radish, salsify, scorzonera, summer spinach, Swiss chard, turnips, salad plants.
P globe and Jerusalem artichokes, asparagus, garlic, onion sets, early potatoes, rhubarb, shallots.
P lettuce.
T early summer cauliflower.

Force Witloof chicory, seakale.
Harvest fresh Chinese and Jerusalem artichokes, sprouting broccoli, Brussels sprouts, winter cabbage, calabrese, winter and spring heading cauliflower, kale, oriental greens, texsel greens, celeriac, chicories, endive, leeks, protected winter lettuce, spring onions, parsley, parsnip, radish, rhubarb, salsify, scorzonera, seakale, winter spinach, Swiss chard, salad plants.
Use from store beetroot, carrots, garlic, bulb onions, maincrop potatoes, shallots, swedes, turnips, winter radish, salsify, scorzonera.

APRIL

s aubergine, celery, endive, peppers, sweetcorn, French and runner beans, outdoor cucumbers, marrows, courgettes, squashes, pumpkins, New Zealand spinach, outdoor tomatoes.
s French beans, early autumn cauliflower.
s asparagus pea, broad beans, sprouting broccoli, Brussels sprouts, summer, autumn and winter cabbage, calabrese, oriental greens (seedling crops and bolt-resistant types), kale, carrots, red chicory, kohl rabi, leeks, lettuce, bulb and spring onions, parsnip, maincrop peas, summer radish, salsify, scorzonera, spinach, Swiss chard, turnip, salad plants.
P Chinese, globe and Jerusalem artichokes, asparagus, bulb onions (pot raised), onion sets, early and maincrop potatoes.
P lettuce.

Force Witloof chicory, seakale.
Hoe and weed all crops.
Uproot and burn old brassica stumps.
Earth up early potatoes.
Harvest fresh Jerusalem artichoke, asparagus, sprouting broccoli, spring cabbage, spring heading cauliflower, texsel greens, celeriac, chicories, endive, leeks, spring onion, parsley, summer radish, winter radish, rhubarb, salsify, scorzonera, seakale, winter spinach, Swiss chard, salad plants, oriental greens (seedling crops).
Use from store garlic, bulb onions, maincrop potatoes, shallots.

MAY

s outdoor cucumber, marrows, courgettes, squashes, pumpkins, sweetcorn, French and runner beans, New Zealand spinach.

(S) outdoor tomato, French beans.
S asparagus pea, broad, French and runner beans, beetroot, sprouting broccoli, summer, autumn and winter cabbage, calabrese, autumn, winter and spring heading cauliflower, Chinese broccoli, kale, texsel greens, carrots, Witloof chicory, endive, Florence fennel, kohl rabi, leeks, lettuce, marrow, courgettes, squashes, pumpkins, spring onions, parsnips, maincrop peas, radish, salsify, scorzonera, seakale, ordinary and New Zealand spinach, swedes, turnips, salad plants.
P Jerusalem artichoke, aubergine, celeriac, celery, endive, lettuce, parsley, peppers, early and maincrop potatoes, seakale, outdoor tomatoes.
(P) outdoor cucumber, peppers, aubergine, sweetcorn, outdoor tomatoes.
T Brussels sprouts, summer and autumn cabbage, summer cauliflower.

Hoe and weed all crops.
Earth up potatoes.
Stake peas.
Watch out for pest and disease attack on all crops.
Harvest fresh asparagus, broad beans, sprouting broccoli, spring cabbage, spring heading cauliflower, texsel greens, carrots, celeriac, sugar-loaf chicory, endive, kohl rabi, lettuce, spring onions, early peas, radish, rhubarb, salsify, scorzonera, summer and winter spinach, Swiss chard, turnips, salad plants.
Use from store garlic, maincrop potatoes, shallots.

JUNE

(S) sweetcorn.
S French and runner beans, beetroot, calabrese, Chinese broccoli, Chinese cabbage, oriental greens, texsel greens, chicories, endive, Florence fennel, kohl rabi, lettuce, marrow, courgette, squash, pumpkin, spring onions, parsley, maincrop peas, summer radish, swedes, turnips, salad plants.
P celery, outdoor tomatoes.
(P) sweetcorn.
T sprouting broccoli, Brussels sprouts, summer, autumn and winter cabbage, early autumn and autumn cauliflower, leeks.

Hoe, weed, water and mulch all crops.
Watch out for pest and disease attacks on all crops.
Harvest fresh asparagus, asparagus pea, broad and French beans, beetroot, spring and summer

cabbage, calabrese, spring heading and early summer cauliflower, texsel greens, carrots, sugar-loaf chicory, endive, kohl rabi, lettuce, bulb onions (autumn sown), spring onions, parsley, early and maincrop peas, early potatoes, radish, rhubarb, summer spinach, Swiss chard, turnip, salad plants.
Use from store garlic, shallots.

JULY

S beetroot, spring cabbage, calabrese, oriental greens, texsel greens, sugar-loaf and red chicory, endive, Florence fennel, kohl rabi, lettuce, parsley, maincrop peas, summer and winter radish, Swiss chard, turnips, salad plants.
T sprouting broccoli, winter cabbage, winter and spring heading cauliflower, kale, leeks.

Hoe, weed and mulch all crops.
Tie in and remove side shoots and tops of outdoor tomatoes after four or five trusses have formed.
Earth up and stake brassicas on exposed sites.
Water and mulch where necessary.
Watch out for pest and disease attacks on all crops.
Spray maincrop potatoes for blight.
Harvest fresh globe artichokes, asparagus peas, broad, French and runner beans, beetroot, summer cabbage, calabrese, early summer cauliflower, texsel greens, carrots, self-blanching celery, sugar-loaf chicory, outdoor cucumber, endive, Florence fennel, kohl rabi, lettuce, marrows, courgettes, squashes and pumpkins, bulb onions, spring onions, parsley, peas, early potatoes, summer radish, rhubarb, summer and New Zealand spinach, shallots, Swiss chard, sweetcorn, turnips, salad plants.
Use from store garlic

AUGUST

S spring cabbage, Chinese cabbage, oriental greens, texsel greens, sugar-loaf and red chicory, endive, Florence fennel, kohl rabi, lettuce (protected and outdoor winter), bulb onions (autumn sown), spring onions (winter hardy), summer and winter radish, scorzonera, Swiss chard, turnip, salad plants.
T leeks.
TuP Florence fennel.

Hoe, weed, mulch and water where necessary.
Stop staked outdoor tomatoes after four or five trusses have set and

spray against blight.
Earth up and stake brassicas.
Lift and dry onions.
Cut off and burn potato haulms if infected by blight.
Harvest fresh globe artichokes, asparagus peas, aubergine, broad, French and runner beans, beetroot, summer and autumn cabbage, calabrese, summer and early autumn cauliflower, Chinese cabbage, oriental greens, texsel greens, carrots, self-blanching celery, sugar-loaf and red chicory, outdoor cucumber, endive, Florence fennel, garlic, kohl rabi, lettuce, leeks, marrows, courgettes, squashes and pumpkins, bulb and spring onions, parsley, maincrop peas, peppers, early and maincrop potatoes, summer radish, summer and New Zealand spinach, shallots, Swiss chard, sweetcorn, outdoor tomatoes, turnips, salad plants.
Use from store garlic.

SEPTEMBER

S texsel greens, lettuce (protected and outdoor winter), summer radish, winter spinach, calabrese, salad plants.
(S) pak choi, sugar-loaf chicory, summer radish, salad plants.
P onion sets (autumn planted)
T spring cabbage.
TuP oriental greens – Chinese cabbage, calabrese, komatsuna*, mizuna greens*, mustard greens* – sugar-loaf and red chicory, endive, Swiss chard. (* also survive outdoors in winter)

Earth up winter brassicas.
Cut down outdoor tomatoes, continue ripening fruits indoors or under cloches.
Cut off and burn potato haulms if infected by blight.
Cut marrows and store before frost.
Cut and ripen pumpkins
Harvest fresh globe artichoke, aubergine, French and runner beans, beetroot, Brussels sprouts, autumn cabbage, calabrese, summer, early autumn, and autumn cauliflower, oriental greens, texsel greens, carrots, self-blanching celery, sugar-loaf and red chicory, outdoor cucumber, endive, Florence fennel, garlic, kohl rabi, leeks, lettuce, marrows, courgettes, squashes, pumpkins, bulb and spring onions, parsley, parsnip, maincrop peas, peppers, maincrop potatoes, summer radish, summer and New Zealand spinach, Swiss chard, sweetcorn, outdoor tomatoes, turnips, salad plants.

OCTOBER

s broad beans, summer and winter spinach.

(s) early summer cauliflower, texsel greens, carrots, winter lettuce, early peas, indoor radish, salads for seedling crops.

P garlic, onion sets (autumn planted).

T spring cabbage.

Tu**P** Chinese broccoli, lettuce (protected winter), Swiss chard.

Lift and store beetroot, carrots, garlic, bulb onions, maincrop potatoes, shallots, Witloof chicory (for forcing), winter cabbages, turnips.

Earth up leeks.

Cut down asparagus fern and Jerusalem artichoke stems.

Protect late cauliflowers from frost by covering curds, and parsley, herbs and salad plants with cloches or low polythene tunnels.

Clear away pea sticks, bean supports, general debris.

Start digging and manuring. Apply lime if necessary.

Harvest fresh Chinese artichokes, French and runner beans, beetroot, Brussels sprouts, autumn cabbage and cauliflower, oriental greens, texsel greens, carrots, celeriac, self-blanching celery, sugar-loaf and red chicory, endive, Florence fennel, garlic, kohl rabi, leeks, lettuce, bulb and spring onions, parsley, parsnips, maincrop peas, peppers, maincrop potatoes, summer radish, salsify, scorzonera, summer spinach, swedes, Swiss chard, sweetcorn, outdoor tomatoes, turnip, salad plants.

Use from store garlic, maincrop potatoes, shallots.

NOVEMBER

s broad beans.

(s) early peas.

P garlic, onion sets (autumn planted), rhubarb.

Lift and store beetroot, carrots, turnips, swedes.

Force seakale.

Protect celeriac and globe artichokes with bracken.

Cover with straw root crops overwintered in the ground.

Continue clearing debris, digging and manuring.

Check stored vegetables for signs of rotting.

Harvest fresh Chinese and Jerusalem artichokes, Brussels sprouts, winter cabbage, autumn cauliflower, oriental greens, carrots, celeriac, sugar-loaf and red chicory, endive, kohl rabi, leeks, lettuce (protected winter), parsley, parsnips, summer and winter radish, salsify, scorzonera, summer and winter spinach, swedes, Swiss chard, turnips, salad plants.

Use from store beetroot, carrots, garlic, bulb onions, maincrop potatoes, shallots.

DECEMBER

s broad beans.

P rhubarb, shallots.

Lift and store carrots and swedes.

Force Witloof chicory, rhubarb, seakale.

Continue clearing debris, digging and manuring.

Check stored vegetables for signs of rotting.

Harvest fresh Chinese and Jerusalem artichokes, Brussels sprouts, winter cabbage, winter-heading cauliflower, oriental greens, carrots, celeriac, chicories, endive, kohl rabi, leeks, lettuce (protected winter) parsley, parsnips, radishes, salsify, scorzonera, winter spinach, swedes, Swiss chard, turnip, salad plants.

Use from store beetroot, carrots, garlic, bulb onions, maincrop potatoes, shallots, marrows.

Further reading

CULTIVARS
Vegetable varieties for the garden (Wisley Handbook) J R Chowings and M J Day (Cassell/RHS 1992)

CLOCHE GARDENING
Cloche gardening J L H Chase (Faber and Faber, 1948)
Early garden crops (Wisley Handbook) F W Shepherd (RHS, 1977)
Gardening with cloches Louis Flawn (John Gifford, 1957)

CONTAINERS
The contained garden Kenneth Beckett, David Carr and David Stephens (Frances Lincoln, 1982)

DECORATIVE VEGETABLE GARDENING
The ornamental kitchen garden Geoff Hamilton (BBC Books, 1990)
The integrated garden A M Cleveley (Barrie and Jenkins, 1988)

DEEP BEDS
Gardening on a bed system Pauline Pears (Search Press/ Henry Doubleday Research Association, 1992)

FLUID SOWING
The complete know and grow vegetables J K A Bleasdale, P J Salter and others (Oxford University Press, 1991)

GREENHOUSE GARDENING
The complete book of the greenhouse Ian G Walls (3rd ed) (Ward Lock, 1983)
Making the most of your greenhouse Ian G Walls (Ward Lock, 1975)

GREEN MANURES
Green manures Elm Farm Research Centre (available by post from Elm Farm Research Centre, Hamstead Marshall, nr Newbury Berks RG15 OHR)

GROWING FOR SHOW
Vegetables for garden and exhibition S M Gault (W H and L Collingridge, 1966)

HERBS
Herb gardening Clare Loewenfeld (Faber and Faber, 1970)
The complete new herbal Richard Mabey (ed) (Elm Tree Books, 1988)
The complete book of herbs Lesley Bremness (Dorling Kindersley, 1988)

ORGANIC GARDENING
Month by month organic gardening Lawrence Hills (Henry Doubleday Research Association, 1989)
Successful organic gardening Geoff Hamilton (Dorling Kindersley, 1987)
Organic gardening Roy Lacey (David and Charles, 1988)
Henry Doubleday Research Association publications (catalogue available from the address given below)

ORIENTAL VEGETABLES
Oriental vegetables: the complete guide for garden and kitchen Joy Larkcom (John Murray (Publishers) Ltd, 1991)

PEST AND DISEASE CONTROL
Be your own garden doctor D G Hessayon (Pan Britannica, 1978)
Collins' guide to the pests, diseases and disorders of garden plants Stefan Buczacki and Keith Harris (Collins, 1981)
Plant protection in the garden G W Ivens and J Stubbs (eds) (available from The British Crop Protection Council, Bear Farm, Binfield, Berks RH12 5QE)

SALAD VEGETABLES
The salad garden Joy Larkcom (Frances Lincoln, 1984)

Useful organizations

THE ROYAL HORTICULTURAL SOCIETY (see p 4)

FOR THE DISABLED
Gardens for the Disabled Trust, Church Cottage, Headcorn, Kent TN27 9NP: runs the Garden Club; offers gardening advice and support to disabled gardeners.
Horticultural Therapy (HT), Goulds Ground, Vallis Way, Frome, Somerset BA11 3DW: provides advice, information and support to elderly and disabled gardeners and to those who work with them.

ORGANIC GARDENING
Henry Doubleday Research Association (HDRA), Ryton-on-Dunsmore Coventry CV8 3LG: promotes organic gardening; Ryton Gardens open to the public; mail order catalogue on request.

INDEX

Page numbers in **bold** indicate main references.